SILVERTOWN

SILVERTOWN

The Lost Story of a Strike that Shook London and
Helped Launch the Modern Labor Movement

John Tully

MONTHLY REVIEW PRESS

New York

Library of Congress Cataloging-in-Publication Data
available from the publisher.

The right of John Tully to be identified as the author of this book has been asserted
by him in accordance with the Copyright Designs and Patents Act, 1988.

U.S. ISBN: 978-1-58367-434-5 (cloth)

Published in North America by:
Monthly Review Press
146 West 29th Street, Suite 6W
New York, New York 10001
www.monthlyreview.org

UK ISBN: 978-1-907-103-99-5 (cloth)

Published in the UK by:
Lawrence & Wishart
99a Wallis Road
London E9 5LN
www.lwbooks.co.uk

5 4 3 2 1

Contents

For Eleanor Marx

If this is the best that civilisation can do for the human, then give us howling and naked savagery. Far better to be people of the wilderness and desert, of the cave and the squatting-place, than to be a people of the machine and the Abyss.[1]
—JACK LONDON

Think of the darkness and the bitter weather
The cries of pain which echo round this world.[2]
—BERTOLT BRECHT

There never was any silver in Silvertown. Smoketown, Sulphurtown, Sugartown—the place could have been called any of those things and no one would have blinked.[3]
—MELANIE MCGRATH

Very sordid and hard is the life of the people of Silvertown.[4]
—*PENNY ILLUSTRATED PAPER*, 14 December 1889

Acknowledgements

WRITING IS A SOLITARY pursuit, yet paradoxically the writing of history is also a collective effort. Not only does the historian rely on the accumulated work of other writers, but s/he must also depend on friends, family, librarians, archivists, fellow historians, editors, political and cultural activists, and members of the general public for information, assistance, and interpretation of material. I am indebted to many people who helped in various ways with this book.

Thanks firstly to my family in Melbourne for putting up with my absences while I was in London throughout late autumn of 2011 and part of the winter of 2012 to carry out the primary research for this book. My wife, Dorothy Bruck, has always been supportive of my writing projects, many of which have involved my being away from home for extended periods, and this time was no different. Her involvement also included making shrewd suggestions about the content of the manuscript. Nor can I omit to voice my gratitude to my employer, Victoria University in Melbourne, for granting me sabbatical leave on full pay in late 2011 to carry out research in Britain. My university research funds also allowed me to return to London to complete my "digging" in December 2012. Mention must also be made of Michael Yates, Martin Paddio, Scott Borchert, Erin Clermont and others at Monthly Review Press in New York City. They have always been supportive of my work, and I owe them great gratitude. Nor can I omit my thanks to Sally Davison of Lawrence & Wishart in London for agreeing to co-publish this book.

I must also thank Peter Gurney, the editor of *Labour History Review*, and the two referees who read drafts of my 10,000-word article about Silvertown that appeared in the journal.[5] One of these was Sam Davies, of Liverpool John Moore's University; the other remains unknown to me.

Their astute criticisms sharpened my understanding of the dynamics of the class struggle in Britain in the 1880s and 1890s and enhanced both the article and this book. In particular, they drew my attention to an insightful essay on the New Unions and the employers' counteroffensive by the esteemed British Marxist historian, the late John Saville.[6] The essay enabled me to appreciate fully the historical significance of the workers' defeat at Silvertown for the broader labor movement and in particular for the development of today's General, Municipal and Boilermakers' Union, the GMB.

The GMB, as the successor to Will Thorne's National Union of Gasworkers & General Labourers (NUG&GL), was quick to see the value of this book in restoring an important part of their heritage. Thanks in particular to the union's General Secretary, Paul Kenny, for his interest in the project, and to John Callow, the union's Head of Research, for his eloquent Foreword to this book. A historian himself, John has written histories of the GMB and Unite the Union along with other books, and doubles as custodian of the archives of the Marx Memorial Library in London. Rose Conroy of the GMB responded quickly to my request for information and forwarded details of my project to the affiliates of the Greater London Association of Trade Union Councils. This did not turn up anything, but at least I could eliminate this from my list of possible sources.

My great hope is that my book will be useful for the GMB and trade union councils in the East End in providing an account of a largely forgotten struggle that deserves to be remembered as part of their heritage—and their future. I am also obliged to Andrew Murray, Chief of Staff of Unite the Union, for providing me with the full names of some officials of London maritime unions in 1889 and for his interest in the project.

Writing and research for the book also brought me into contact with academic staff from the University of East London, whose Docklands Campus is within sight of Silvertown across the Victoria and Albert docks. In particular, Alvaro De Miranda of UEL's London East Research Centre was unfailingly kind and helpful during my stay. Other current and former staff members who have helped include Catherine Harper, Andrew Calcutt, and Kate Hodgkin. Most of all, I must thank John Marriott, Emeritus Professor of History at UEL and author of the fine East End history, *London Beyond the Tower*, for his thoughtful introductory comment to this book.

The staff of many British libraries and archives went out of their way to assist. Among these were the staff of the Bishopsgate Institute in the inner East End; in particular, thanks to Elizabeth Webster for her speedy dispatch to Australia of photographs of 1880s Silvertown. James Goddard at the TUC Library at the London Metropolitan University in Islington was friendly and attentive to my needs and made valuable suggestions about secondary sources. Thanks also to Richard Durack and Jenni Munro-Collins of the Newham Library and Archives at Stratford, East London, for their assistance.

Thanks, too, to Darren Treadwell of the Labour History Archive and Study Centre at the People's History Museum/University of Central Lancashire in Manchester for making helpful suggestions on the location of information in Britain. I must also mention the staff at the following: the British Library at St. Pancras and at the library's newspaper annex at Colindale; the National Archives at Kew; the Marx Memorial Library in Clerkenwell; the University of Kent at Canterbury; the Cambridge University Library; the Essex Record Office at Chelmsford; and the London Metropolitan Archives in Clerkenwell.

Thanks also to Virginia Malone of the University of Greenwich Library for her help in providing access to Elisabeth Banks-Conney's PhD thesis on the labor movement in East London after my initial access had been denied by a fierce gatekeeper! Although I was unable to meet Elisabeth, I am grateful for her kind offer to meet with me to discuss her excellent but unpublished thesis. Thanks also to Helen Ford and other staff at the wonderful Modern Records Office at the University of Warwick at Coventry, with whose help I was able to dig out a considerable amount of useful material from their impressive collections. I am also grateful to Nick Buck for speedily granting me permission to quote from his fascinating 1980 PhD thesis on West Ham, and again to John Marriott for allowing me to cite his Cambridge PhD thesis on the East End.

Thanks also are due to Joan Self, the Archive Information Officer at the National Meteorological Archive at Sowton, Exeter, for providing me with detailed records of the daily weather at Kew and Greenwich during the period of the Silvertown strike. The onset of winter intensified the privations of the strikers, so knowledge of the weather conditions added to the "human" dimension of the narrative. Closer to my home, I am indebted to my colleague Mark Armstrong-Roper, the Arts librarian at the Victoria University Library in Melbourne. Mark was as usual courteous and efficient in locating materials for this study.

Thanks also to the numerous East Enders with whom I corresponded, and who helped me in various ways. These include Vera Bangs, Stephen Fisk, Stan Dyson, and Danny Budzak, who made useful suggestions about where to find material for this book, and to the fine local writers

Melanie McGrath and Nuala Calvi for their interest and useful suggestions. Another local man, Colin Grainger, deserves special mention. The former editor of the *Newham Gazette*, which circulates widely in the West Ham district, Colin is always interested in assisting with historical research. He readily published an article in the paper describing my research and asking people to contact me with information.

Gratitude is also due to Judith Garfield and the staff of Eastside Cultural Heritage (ECH) at Ilford, whose kindness one snowy day I shall always remember. Judith has been instrumental in a campaign for a West Ham people's museum, and I hope that this work will be of use to her in that excellent project. ECH is also to be commended for its valuable oral history projects on Silvertown and North Woolwich.

I must also express my thanks to Lawrence H. Officer and Samuel H. Williamson, of the MeasuringWorth.com website, which proved invaluable in calculating the relative worth of wages, profits, and commodities in today's terms. Thanks also to Martin Fido and Keith Skinner, co-authors of *The Official Encyclopaedia of Scotland Yard*, for alerting me to where the diary of Commissioner James Monro ought to have been in the London police archives at Fulham. Alas, the diary has been mislaid somewhere in a warehouse and my visit was in vain. It would make fascinating reading, and I suggest that it be rescued and re-housed in the National Archives at Kew.

On a personal note, I should not forget my former students, Gabrielle Thomson and Megan Bridger-Darling, for their friendship during the grey winter days in London. Nor can I forget my eldest son Sean, his wife Vicky, and my young granddaughters Mia and Eliza for making me welcome on my visits to their home in Twickenham, West London. Mention might also be made of my long-deceased "granda," George, a merchant seafarer who understood the industrial facts of life, and whose copy of Jack London's *The People of the Abyss* I first read at the age of twelve. Finally, it goes without saying that the responsibility for any factual errors in the book lies with me alone and that nothing above suggests that the interpretation of events is anything but my own.

A Note on the Old Currency

Foreigners and British people born since the abolition of the splendid but irrational Norman currency of pounds, shillings, and pence (pennies) (£ s d) might like some clarification of its mysteries. There were twelve pence in a shilling and twenty shillings in a pound. The penny was further divided into four farthings and two halfpennies, or ha'pence. Twenty-one shillings was known as a guinea; 2/6d as half a crown; and twopence and threepence were known colloquially as tuppence and thruppence. The famous "dockers' tanner"—the hourly rate won after the 1889 strike—was sixpence, or 6d. A shilling, often written as 1/-, was also known as a bob, and the ten-shilling note was called a ten-bob note. A five-pound note in popular parlance was a fiver and ten pounds a tenner—not that the Silvertown workers would ever have seen many of these (for the times) large-denomination banknotes. Decimalization has meant that we are in danger of losing some marvelous popular expressions such as "tuppenny ha'penny" for something commonplace as well as a small sum of money. Calculating how much sums of money from the time are worth today is not straightforward. However, according to the wonderful online MeasuringWorth.com calculator, the tanner of 1889 was worth £2.16 in 2010 using the retail price index as a guide.[7] The working day at the Silvertown Works was twelve hours, and pay rates varied from 1d to $5\frac{1}{2}$d an hour for the unskilled and semiskilled workers. In the light of this, the reader can do some simple sums to work out how much they earned each week. We should bear in mind that long hours of overtime were also the norm both through necessity on the part of the operatives and insistence on that of the employer. It is difficult to know what these sterling sums translate into in United States currency, given that exchange rates fluctuate, sometimes wildly, and that the events described in this book took place over a century ago. Even more problematic is the matter of the differing purchasing power of the two currencies. Therefore, dollar equivalents used in the text are very rough indications of value. However, in late 2013 1d was worth 2 cents and £1, $1.90. Shillings and half crowns are no longer used in Britain's decimalized currency, but if they were, the exchange rates for them would be approximately 19 cents and 47.5 cents respectively.[8] One writer estimates that the average daily wage of an unskilled male industrial worker in the United States in 1889 was $1.39, which works out at around 13 cents an hour on the basis of a ten-hour working day.[9]

Foreword

by John Callow, Political Education and Research Officer, GMB

⧫

HISTORY, LIKE POLITICS or any other industry, is a fiercely contested ideological space. With evidence marshalled like pieces on the chess board, the framing and interpretation of the game can radically alter our perceptions of the past and serve to either extend or to inhibit our horizons and goals in the present. History defines our sense of community and shared cultural values; it shapes our common vocabulary and even serves to forge our ideas about—and our responses to—the nature of contemporary political and industrial struggles.

History is, therefore, very much worth fighting for, and engaging with. John Tully's book is all about that battle and the sense of original archival discovery that permits the voices, actions, and ideals of long-forgotten working men and women to speak directly to us, in their own way and on their own terms. It is a considerable achievement; not least on account of the difficulties inherent in trying to reconstruct the lives and motivations of the silenced majority of Victorian Britain: the wealth creators, who were actively prohibited from sharing in their gains, and who, more often than not, had neither the leisure nor the opportunity to record their own thoughts and feelings.

In the case of the strikers at Silvertown, in the autumn and winter of 1889, this book demonstrates their utter refusal to be broken by poverty; to be ground down by cynicism; or to be cowed by the forces arrayed against them by both their employers and the state. Moreover, this determined stance led, swiftly and surely, to the realisation that rights and freedoms— to education, to health care, to meaningful and well-paid work, to social and economic justice, and to dignity in old age—were never going to be freely conceded by the privileged few. Rather, they would have to be won through concerted, collective action and shared principle, on the part of the many whose industry and life-blood drove the machines and fed the furnaces of the world's first industrial nation, the shock-centre of modern capitalism. Furthermore, as John Tully appreciates but many of our politicians, including some of those of the Left, would rather forget: those early socialist pioneers knew that these liberties, once won, would have to be jealously guarded and forcefully defended, each and every day, against those who would seize them back again or else seek to give them away without a struggle, a backwards glance, or second thought.

For these reasons, history is important to today's General, Municipal and Boilermakers' Union, the GMB. The union which was at the center of the storm at Silvertown welcomes this new book wholeheartedly, as it restores to prominence an important early chapter in its development. The union, like the solidarity of its members who fought so valiantly on the streets of London's East End, was founded upon a big idea. It sought to represent the underdog, the unskilled worker, and to unequivocally and unapologetically represent class as opposed to sectional interests. It was serious about redistributing power and wealth from the "haves" to the "have-nots"; appreciative of the risks it ran and of the destruction of earlier general unions; and driven by a clearly articulated Marxist vision that found its expression in the guiding objective of the union's first rule book. Thus, members were called upon to "remember that the interests of all Workers are one, and a wrong done to any kind of Labour is a wrong done to the whole of the Working Class, and that victory or defeat of any portion of the Army of Labour is a gain or a loss to the whole of that Army, which by its organisation and union is marching steadily and irresistibly forward to its ultimate goal—the Emancipation of the Working Class. That Emancipation can only be brought about by the strenuous and united efforts of the Working Class itself."

The prescience of this injunction would seem to be borne out in the pages of *Silvertown: The Lost Story of a Strike that Shook London and Helped Launch the Modern Labor Movement*, where two main factors are highlighted in the account of the defeat of the strikers. The first emphasises the sense of unity and ruthless purpose that characterised the board of management at the rubber works, which scorned any form of negotiation or compromise with their workforce. It understood, with absolute clarity, what was at stake for the capitalist system if concessions began to undermine the ability to amass private profit by any means at its disposal. Thus the ideology of the board members was more absolute, more explicitly adhered to, and more attuned to the single-minded practice and preservation of power than anything advanced by the Fabians in the Labour Movement, or by the vast majority of unions within the Trades Union Congress. The resilience, youth, and radicalism of Will Thorne, Eleanor Marx, Pete Curran, and Frederick Ling—whose leading role in the dispute is highlighted here, for the first time—were as new, as challenging and as controversial as the form of trade unionism that they collectively espoused and inspired. As a consequence, the second reason for the collapse of the strike lay in the antipathy felt by the older, skilled craft unions towards the new general union that sought to represent and to promote unskilled labor. On this occasion, the company directors and shareholders knew better than either the executive of the ASE or the London Trades Council that unity really was strength.

In this light, it is not difficult to understand why, until now, the Silvertown strike has not featured strongly in GMB histories. Industrial armies, like their military counterparts, usually seek to celebrate their victories, rather than to commemorate their defeats; and this was especially true as the dispute signalled the first major check by the employers to the growth of New Unionism. In its wake, the union and its leaders—who, like Thorne, had displayed an overconfidence that bordered upon hubris at Silvertown—were forced to acknowledge that the campaign for a better world would now be long and protracted, measured in months and years, rather than being the matter of a sudden, once-and-for-all clash between the forces of labor and capital, that hinged upon tactics formulated from day-to-day and from week-to-week. This repositioning would have profound consequences for the union that were still being felt in the 1970s, but before we fall back upon the old cries of betrayal and longings for what might have been, we would do well to consider the positive developments that the strike set in train.

Silvertown brought Eleanor Marx firmly into contact with both the union and with the women and men of the East End. It provided her with a new purpose and sense of comradeship, and permitted her to combine her own remarkable skills as both office administrator and as street corner orator. She appears to have been everywhere, in constant motion and creative symbiosis with her constituency—advising, heartening and finding new ways to feed the strikers and their families. Furthermore, she acted as a catalyst for the union's decision to admit women to membership, and founded the first women's branch at Silvertown, on 10 October 1889, enabling feminist, alongside Marxist, currents to course through every fibre of the new union. For the next six years, she successfully combined the roles of activist and propagandist—collecting branch donations and dues door-to-door in Silvertown—with the duties of a national trade union official, and her position as one of the leading figures within the Second Socialist International. The union was, for its first decade, deeply influenced by her example and ideals, and it was Silvertown which provided the cornerstone for her engagement with it.

In a similar vein, the dispute also set the scene for the first meeting between Will Thorne and Pete Curran, and set the seal upon their lasting friendship. Though his contribution to the formation of the Labour Party is now largely forgotten, Curran drove the political strategy of the union for more than twenty years and was one of the first Labour MPs, serving the Jarrow constituency from 1907 to 1910. At the time of the Silvertown strike, he had only just arrived in the capital from his hometown of Glasgow, and was employed as a steam-hammer operator in the Woolwich Arsenal. Like many of the early figures in the union's development, such as J. R. Clynes, Jim Connell, and Jack Jones, he came from an Irish background and combined the themes of anti-imperialism, opposition to militarism, and to the Boer War with an overtly Marxist conception of socialism and societal development. Though neither he nor Eleanor would live to see it, the election of Jack Jones as the union-sponsored MP for Silvertown, in 1918, provided a fitting tribute to the sacrifices and dedication of those who had gone on strike a generation earlier and who had first raised the red flag outside the walls of Matthew Gray's factory.

The GMB that has reemerged, since 2005, similarly exists to make life better, to seek to change the rules of the game and to positively load the dice in favour of the many rather than the few. Perhaps at no time since August 1914 has the union been closer to the vision of its founders and consequently it takes enormous pride in the course it charted at Silvertown. John Tully's book is as committed, as passionate, and as clear-sighted as those pioneers who staked everything they had for the sake of our tomorrow. It recalls tragedies and injustices, but it also encourages us to remember the scope of the Labour Movement's advance and the simple, un-declarative heroism that saw unskilled women and men, old and the young—with no financial reserves or access to the media, and with starvation threatening—brave police truncheons, pauperisation, and the chill of the cold to wage a strike that lasted some 89 days. How many more possibilities could be achieved by the unions of today, with full-time officers, legal teams, campaign funds, and access to the Internet and the press? In this light, we hope that *Silvertown: The Lost Story of a Strike that Shook London and Helped Launch the Modern Labor Movement* gains the widest possible audience, both union and non-union, academic and popular, and would wish to applaud his work in recovering this account of our past. It is for today's GMB to lay its own claim to shaping the future.

Introductory Comment

by John Marriott,
Emeritus Professor of History, University of East London

---◆◆◆---

THE CONDITIONS FOR determined industrial struggle by an unskilled labor force were hardly propitious. In the 1880s, Silver's India-Rubber, Gutta-Percha & Telegraph Company had emerged as a large manufacturer located by the Thames in the southern reaches of West Ham. The site was of significance, for the firm was part of an extraordinary concentration of industrial activity in the most advanced field of cable telegraphy which was fast revolutionizing the means of communication—the Internet of its day. Within four kilometers were to be found also other leading firms including W.T. Henley and Siemens Brothers, making this small area the hub of world production. Not only that, Silver's was at the heart of a complex imperial network relying on raw materials from the corners of empire and exporting manufactured goods to all corners of the world. This was a firm, therefore, with considerable financial, imperial, and technological power. No wonder that its shareholders included so many influential politicians, financiers, and aristocrats.

Furthermore, the labor force of Silver's comprised skilled workers belonging to the Amalgamated Society of Engineers and the body of unskilled laborers which formed a large overall majority. Politically and culturally a deep divide separated these two constituencies. Heretofore, skilled workers had organized and led political and industrial struggles which had culminated in the formation of the trade union movement, while the unskilled had repeatedly proven resistant to organization, much to the frustration of socialist leaders who from time to time had attempted to mobilize them.

Although possessing a degree of regular employment and therefore income, Silver's unskilled laborers lived at subsistence levels. Most of them lived nearby in the small district created by the factory and appropriately named Silvertown. Like so many of the riverside settlements, it had few prepossessing features and even fewer facilities. The housing was for the most part small terraced properties which had fallen into disrepair, little different from the overcrowded slums of the older settlements of East London.

And yet late in 1889, Silver's was hit by a strike of these unskilled laborers determined to better their working conditions and rates of pay. This may have startled the chairman, Matthew Gray, but in historical hindsight it can be seen as part of a momentous shift in the working-class struggle that was taking place in East London in the latter stages of the 1880s. West Ham in particular played a vital role as events unfolded. From the 1860s the area had been transformed by an unprecedented industrial growth, from a parish with a few isolated settlements to a modern urban center. Indeed, by the 1880s the borough had emerged as the industrial heartland of the metropolis. This growth had fostered a unique political culture, giving rise to the birth of new unionism, the first Labour council and the first independent Labour MP, Keir Hardie, all of which was built on the foundations laid by a series of remarkable industrial struggles over 1888–89. Most notable here were the Dock Strike, the gasworkers' strike, and the matchgirls' strike at Bryant & May, all of which have entered into the annals of the labor history of East London.

It is therefore somewhat surprising that the strike at Silver's, which followed in the immediate aftermath of these struggles, has been largely ignored, and we are in debt to John Tully for rescuing the strike and the remarkable fortitude of the strikers from historical obscurity. A powerful empathy with the strikers and their supporters drives the narrative of events. We learn about the circumstances of the strike, the obstinacy of the company in refusing to contemplate mediation, and the human side of the suffering endured by strikers and their families. For in the months following the outbreak of the strike, strikers held fast despite the desperate conditions forced on them and their families, the bitter hostility of a company resolute on crushing them, and the failure of skilled workers to act in any form of meaningful solidarity. In part, this resolve was hardened by the small cohort of people who supported them and were prepared to take action. At such moments, local leaders tend to spring up as if conjured. The remarkable Fred Ling was one. He emerged from an obscure background to shine briefly, only to disappear again into obscurity once the strike was over. Will Thorne, the leader of the National Union of Gas-workers & General Labourers, was there; so too was Eleanor Marx who devoted her considerable energy and skills to the cause of the laboring poor of the East End.

But above all, this is a story of a brave struggle conducted by the casual poor who found themselves at the bottom of the labor market. Tragically, faced with an intransigent company, a hostile press and parliament, an apathetic artisan elite, and above all a cabal of the police and justice system which prevented effective picketing, thereby allowing the free passage of strikebreaking labor, the strikers slowly drifted back to work.

John Tully importantly reminds us of the lessons to be learnt from such strikes. But there is another, related matter which deserves our attention. Labor history no longer enjoys the attention it once had. Historical fashions change, and so the centrality of class has been somewhat displaced by questions of race and gender. This has generally been of great benefit to an understanding of popular political culture, but taken too far it can lead to a certain historical amnesia. This book is a salutary reminder to us of the power of class as a force of historical change. In his preface the author expresses the hope that he has been able to tell adequately the story of the Silvertown strikers. Few reading this passionate and lively account can doubt that he has succeeded.

Preface

——◆◆——

THIS BOOK TELLS the story of a great strike at the India-Rubber, Gutta-Percha & Telegraph Works in the East End of London in 1889, hereafter referred to as Silver's after the firm's founders, the Silver family, who also gave their name to the suburb in which the factory was located. When I first became aware of the Silvertown strike, I had a limited understanding of its importance. Gradually, it became clear that what I had unearthed would fill a significant lacuna in British labor historiography, and at the same time restore to London workers a forgotten part of their heritage.

That an Australian author came to write about events in Silvertown might seem strange, but the explanation is simple. Historical research is often rather like mining: the researcher finds a rich seam of "ore" and keeps digging until the lode is exhausted. So too it has been with my interest in rubber and rubber workers. The Silvertown project was a logical extension of work I began some years ago. Researching for a general history of the colonial period in Cambodia,[10] I came across large amounts of archival material about the country's French-owned rubber plantations and this formed the basis of a chapter of the book. Later, I wrote a book titled *The Devil's Milk* about the rubber industry on a world scale,[11] but could not do the Silvertown strike justice in so general a work. In the course of research in London during the northern autumn of 2011 and the winter of 2012, I was able to unearth so much material directly and indirectly relevant to the 1889 strike that what I originally envisaged as an article mutated into a much longer work. It also became clear that the book should contain some treatment of an even longer strike by members of the Amalgamated Society of Engineers (ASE) at Silver's in 1897–98. I have also included some material in the Epilogue on the flowering of the political wing of the labor movement in Silvertown and West Ham.

Conservatives have attacked some of my previous work as being partisan, and this book should upset them again. One right-wing reviewer complained that my book *The Devil's Milk* "tend[ed] to pit grasping and greedy planters and industrialists against a combative and heroic workforce." There was, he insisted, "little room here for cross-class unity emerging from loyalty to commodity and firm."[12] In fact, there has been precious little evidence of such "cross-class unity" in the rubber industry, regardless of that reviewer's pious hopes. He himself admits elsewhere that class struggle did not abate much in the U.S. rubber industry even during wartime, and it is stretching credulity to believe that there was any "unity" between white planters and the colored laborers on the plantations of Africa, Oceania, and Asia. This was also the case in the British rubber industry in Victorian times. The reviewer fails to grasp that conflict between the laborer and the capitalist is inevitable under capitalism, although it might vary in intensity. As the British socialist E. Belfort Bax explained just before the Silvertown strike:

> The capitalist, *as* capitalist, *must* seek to lengthen the working day and to keep down wages, in order thereby to increase his share in the product of labour—his profit. The labourer has to defend himself against the capitalist; and he soon finds out that the only way he can do this is by organization. Hence the trades unions.[13]

Historically, too, heavy industry such as Silver's has been the site of particularly intense class struggle. The Silvertown strike of 1889 was, as we shall see, a pivotal event in a period when relations between the classes were brutal and raw. Further, though conservatives might sneer at my solidarity with the working class as indicative of a "goodies and baddies" mindset, I have always believed that workers are only human, not Stakhanovite caricatures. Nevertheless, it is surely self-evident that the history of industrial society brims with examples of enormous courage and fortitude on the part of the working class. Again, though, it would be foolish to ignore Frederick Engels's observation that "the workers of the [Victorian] period were often ignorant, brutalized, and shortsighted."[14] Given the atrocious living and working conditions of the time, it could scarcely be otherwise. This was very true of what Jack London called the "Abyss" of the East End. As he wrote in 1904:

The London Abyss is a vast shambles. Year by year, and decade after decade, rural England pours in a flood of vigorous strong life, that not only does not renew itself, but perishes by the third generation.[15]

Though they sometimes acknowledged the horror, the ruling class justified appalling social conditions as inevitable, perhaps even necessary. In the words of the ineffable Victorian bourgeois housekeeper Mrs. Beeton, for example:

> It has justly been said . . . that the children of the poor are not brought up, but *dragged up*. However facetious this remark may seem, there is much truth in it; and that children, reared in the reeking dens of squalor and poverty, live at all, is an apparent anomaly in the course of things, that, at first sight, would seem to set the laws of sanitary provision at defiance, and make it appear a perfect waste of time to insist on pure air and exercise as indispensable necessaries of life, and especially so as regards infantine existence.[16]

As Bertolt Brecht once noted sardonically, "As you know, it's all right to treat barbarians barbarically." At Silvertown, the "barbarians" stood up and challenged the barbarians in frock coats who exploited them. They contributed to a vast social movement that was eventually to change the face of British society, winning important social, political, and industrial rights for the working class—but only after a period of savage class warfare. This begs the question of whether one can really be "nonpartisan" in the face of such events.

Historians must always be scrupulous with the facts, but we should be deeply suspicious of claims that studies of human society can be "value free." History has always been a discipline bristling with debates. Though we should never twist, omit, or invent facts, we should be frank about our biases. Historians have established that the Victorian era was a time of endless pain for the British working class. The Industrial Revolution had turned the world upside down. There was technological progress and wealth creation unparalleled in human history, but someone had to pay for it. Incredibly, there are some today who deny the undeniable, just as there were many at the time who ignored the conditions that created their wealth. In his masterful essay "History and the 'Dark Satanic Mills,'" the late Eric Hobsbawm demolished the attempts of historical revisionists such as W. H. Chaloner, W. O. Henderson, and W. Hutt to "whitewash" the Victorian period and who, as he puts it, seek to "defend the good name

of capitalism against the historians."[17] "Few serious scholars," Hobsbawm
argues, "could do more than discover a few silver linings to a very large
and very black cloud."[18] Hobsbawm also quotes a passage from Thomas
Peacock's novel *Crotchet Castle* in which an intelligent Tory says of the
rioting of a "Swing"[19] crowd of angry and hungry agricultural laborers:

> It is the natural result . . . of a system of state seamanship, which your
> service upholds. Putting the crew on short allowances, and doubling
> the rations of the officers, is the sure way to make a mutiny on board a
> ship in distress.[20]

If that was the way an intelligent Tory saw things in nineteenth-century England, Hobsbawm argues, then what can we say of those today
who seek to prettify the condition of the Victorian working class, who
argue that black is white or at least there isn't black "or possibly that if it
is, it is nobody's fault"?[21] Further, while Peacock's perspicacious Tory recognized the causes of revolt, and might even have sympathized with the
Swing rioters to some degree, he was just as anxious as his bullish Tory
and Whig brethren "to scatter the miserable labourers into the night."[22]
Likewise, in 1889 a correspondent of the pro-establishment London
Times admitted that while it was "impossible to deny some sympathy for
the Silvertown labourers" he could find "no cause for real regret" in their
defeat.[23] The Silvertown strikers had to be crushed just as the ruling class
had earlier seen off other disturbers of the social order, even if one granted
they had real grounds for grievance.

Silver's was an enormously powerful firm, backed by the government
and police against its ill-fed, ill-paid, ill-housed, ill-medicated, ill-used,
ill-educated, and overworked laborers, most of whom could not expect to
live long past their thirty-fifth birthdays. The largest rubber, telegraph,
and electrical manufacturer in the country, it consistently paid high dividends to shareholders throughout the economic doldrums of the 1870s
and '80s, and the depression of the following decade. It could easily have
paid the modest wage increases demanded by the laborers. Refusing all
offers of mediation, Silver's won by starving the strikers back to work—
and was applauded by the employing class and the political establishment
for doing so. In fact, the methods used by the firm became a blueprint for
other British union busters to follow.

I cannot apologize for having written these "miserable labourers"
back into history, and my only regret would be to fail to tell their story
adequately.

I.
Prologue: Wednesday, 11 September 1889

~◆~

> The grey-eyed morn smiles on the frowning night
> Checkering the eastern clouds with streaks of light . . .[24]
> —WILLIAM SHAKESPEARE

DAWN BROKE OVER Silvertown on Wednesday 11 September 1889 with the promise of yet another sweltering day. There could be a strange beauty in an East End dawn. As a newspaperman later wrote of sunrise over Victoria and Albert Docks on a similar morning: "First a silvery light in the air, a chilly greyness, then a flush in the east, and with startling suddenness every mast, every funnel, every leaning crane is silhouetted jet-black against the pearl-coloured sky . . . Unreal . . . still . . . silent."[25] This morning in 1889 was full of portent. The docks did not awaken as they had on so many mornings before, but remained silent. As the sun crept high into the sky, the mercury rose to just under 82° Fahrenheit—almost 28° Celsius—which for Londoners was a scorcher. The fashionable folk of the West End—many of them only up from their beds long after daybreak—could promenade under the trees in Hyde Park, sip cool drinks, or make an excursion to the seaside to revel in the heat of an Indian summer. The workers at Samuel Silver's factory, however, could not enjoy the sunshine. They were up before the sun rose and had made their way to Silver's as usual, where, cooped up in the giant factory's workshops, they worked a nominal twelve-hour day, from 6:00 a.m. to 6:00 p.m. By the time they had finished work, walked home, and eaten their frugal suppers, the shadows of evening would have lengthened. Indeed, many of them went home in the dark, for long hours of compulsory overtime were the norm and

Samuel Silver's factory was working flat-out to fill orders for a booming industry. The firm's ships were girdling the ocean beds with a network of telegraph cables and there was a burgeoning demand for the electrical equipment and rubber goods that were assuming ever-greater importance for Britain's economy. Silver's was dependent upon the labor of a disciplined army of some 3,000 laborers and artisans, with casual workers taken on during peak periods. Hitherto, Silver's workforce had been obedient and if individuals harbored resentment against their employer, they must have been resigned to their lot in life. Many perhaps believed that they deserved to stand humbly at the rich man's gate, thankful to be in relatively continuous employment, spared the terrible lot of the casual laborers who swarmed in the East End. Others may have reasoned that it had always been so and they had to endure what life served up to them.

Whiff of Revolt

Although it was business as usual at Silver's on that Indian summer's morning, the perceptive observer might have detected a change in the mood of the workers. After almost forty years of "industrial peace," there was a whiff of revolt in the air. The mood of the East End workers as a whole matched the weather: bright, confident perhaps that there was hope for a better future. All eyes were on the 16,000 striking dockers, whose pickets stood at the nearby Victoria and Albert dock gates, becalming hundreds of ships at the quays. Few at Silver's would have been unaware, either, of the startling victory recently won by Will Thorne's new union at the Beckton gasworks, a huge plant within sight and smell of Silvertown. A year earlier, the maltreated women at Bryant & May's match factory in Bow had walked off the job. Very soon, Silver's own enormous factory would also be strikebound, the rubber, telegraph, and electrical workers inspired by the dock struggle that was unfolding almost literally on their doorsteps.

Silver's great works lay sandwiched between the River Thames and Victoria Dock. Its river frontage was lined with a kilometer of wharves and jetties at which the company's fleet of four cable-laying steamships docked—the largest of their type afloat. The dock basins were plainly visible from the workers' houses scattered along the roads outside the works. Old photographs show the skyline bristling with the funnels, masts, and superstructures of hundreds, perhaps thousands of vessels, some of them towering like iron cliffs above the houses, others tiny salt-stained coasters whose decks bobbed below the level of the quays. The Victoria and Albert docks were "the largest artificial sheet of water in the world, being nearly three miles long, with a water space of 185 acres, and seven miles of quay," marveled a contemporary observer.[26] Abandoned in the 1970s and 80s for the vast new container port far downstream at Tilbury, the Royal Docks are still impressive, large enough to boast waves to topple windsurfers when a strong wind blows. They were an intimate part of the world of the Silver's workers, many of whom counted family, friends, neighbors, and acquaintances among the swarms of dock laborers. The names of the dock strike leaders—Ben Tillett, Tom Mann, John Burns, and others—were already household words. Walter Drummond of the Stevedores' Union told a meeting of Silver's workers that he was glad to see faces he knew from the crowds of supporters at the Dockers' meetings.[27]

Sun, Sun, and More Sun!

Five days before the Silvertown dispute began, huge crowds of dock laborers and their families and sympathizers had converged on Tower Hill in a demonstration of newfound power. "Sun, sun, and more sun!" enthused H. H. Champion's socialist paper, the *Labour Elector,* "Men, men, and more men!"[28] The week before, the *Elector* had reported that the dock strike "has now assumed such gigantic proportions as to totally eclipse any previous strike of the same class of men in our history."[29] By 11 September, the strike was in its fifth week and although distress was mounting in dockside communities, the strikers showed no sign of returning to work on the dock company's terms. Among those watching the progress of the strike was Frederick Engels, who rejoiced at this rebellion of

> the most miserable of all the *misérables* of the East End, the broken-down ones of all trades, the lowest stratum above the Lumpenproletariat. That these poor, famished, broken-down creatures who bodily fight amongst each other every morning for admission to work, should organise for resistance, turn out 40–50,000 strong . . . hold out for above a week and terrify the wealthy and powerful dock companies— that is a revival I am proud *erlebt zu haben* (to have lived to see).[30]

Tom Mann later recalled that "in the struggle against death by starvation, a larger percentage of work-out men (cast-offs from other occupations) made their way to compete for casual labour at the docks and wharves of London."[31] Subsequent studies confirm Engels's depiction of the wretched lives of the dockers. The labor historian John Lovell believes that the dock companies "deliberately spread the [available] work out amongst the greater number in order that they may keep as many men about as possible."[32] The social consequences of this hiring policy were deplorable. Many of those weakened or made chronically infirm by such a life simply gave up: at the very bottom of this human pile were the "loafers," men who had become so demoralized as to be unemployable.[33] Safety was a farce. Ben Tillett recalled that "every dock was a shambles," with "bodies flattened out to unrecognisable human wreckage." "Only too often," he wrote, "the poor, bloody tatters of a man were gathered up and thrown into the wings of a ship."[34] One such unfortunate was a man called Plumb, crushed to death at Victoria Dock shortly before the strike when a bale of greasy wool slipped from a sling.[35] There was no compensation for a family left destitute by their breadwinner's death.

A Vast Sponge for the Displaced

Life and labor was plentiful and cheap in the East End. The Industrial Revolution had turned traditional British society upside down, and East London had become a vast sponge soaking up men and women displaced from the British and Irish countryside. These internal migrants formed an industrial reserve army of labor: vast numbers of unemployed and precariously employed laborers desperate for any chance of any work. Casual dock work was stigmatized, but workless men were prepared to assemble at the dock gates each morning, sometimes fighting each other to get the foreman's nod for a few hours of work.

Such conditions cried out for redress, yet for many years the efforts of union organizers had been fruitless. Before 1889, the only successful industrial organizations at the docks, apart from those of the skilled artisans such as the engineers, were the stevedores' and lightermen's unions, their success a reflection of their members' highly prized niche skills.[36] Laborers were despised. Tillett recalls that "many of the skilled workers believed that the general labourer could not be a Trade Unionist," that he "was beyond the pale." "Revolutions," he added, "are not made as a result by hungry men" who "as a rule lack the courage, the divine anger, the necessary recklessness of consequences which produce revolutionary movements."[37] Spies and police swarmed on the quaysides, and it was a simple matter for the dock companies to send "drunken fools" equipped with brass knuckles to bash unionists.[38] Men like Tillett, however, were filled with "divine anger" against so cruel a system, and the result was the massive London Dock Strike of the hot late summer of 1889. The dockers threw up picket lines along the sixteen miles from the Pool of London to Tilbury Docks in weeks of hope and frenetic activity. By 28 August, noted William Morris's socialist paper *Commonweal*, the strike "threatened to become general," with coal heavers, brass finishers, printers' laborers, rope makers, and tailors downing tools.[39] Curiously, the police kept a low profile until early September, when they arrived in force at Canning Town[40] in response to frantic lobbying of Scotland Yard by the dock companies.[41]

The downside of the strike was the destitution suffered by the strikers and their families. A letter from a clergyman to the *East and West Ham Gazette* drew attention to the case of a woman with a baby at her breast who had subsisted on "nothing but dry bread for three weeks."[42] As Henry Mayers Hyndman, the founder of the Social Democratic Federation, later mused, "Can anything be imagined more foolish, more harmful, more, in the widest sense of the word, unsocial, than a strike?. . . It is a desperate method of fighting."[43] Yet what other course for redress was possible? Remarkably, too, the starvelings of the East End fought on to victory. Near the end, when strike leader John Burns addressed a mass meeting on Tower Hill, he pointed theatrically to a shining coin in his hand, and shouted "This, lads, is the Lucknow of Labour," an allusion to the relief of the British garrison in that city during the Indian Mutiny.[44] On 20 September, "The dock strike . . . ended with the complete victory of the men," trumpeted the *Labour Elector*.[45] They had won the famous "dockers' tanner"—sixpence an hour—and they were to inspire other East Enders to organize.

The Petition of Silver's Yardmen

Among those swept up in the euphoria were the yard laborers in the India-Rubber, Gutta-Percha & Telegraph Works at Silvertown. Working outside the factory buildings, they would have watched developments on the nearby docks and it is possible that some had been dockers themselves, or had dockers in their own kin and friendship networks. On that sunny morning of 11 September 1889, these yardmen, 280 strong, submitted a written petition for a pay rise to management. The names of the three delegates who wrote and presented it are not recorded in existing company records, union minutes, or newspaper accounts of the Great Strike. One of them, perhaps, was Harry Stone, a yardman domiciled at 33 Archer Street, Silvertown. Stone was both brave and literate enough to write and sign his name to a letter, published in the 8 November 1889 edition of the *India-Rubber Journal* (hereafter *IRJ*), in which he rebutted claims made by company secretary William Tyler about wages and conditions in the yard.[46] The yardmen's petition asked the Board of Directors to raise their wages, on average, from $4\frac{3}{4}$d to 6d an hour (very roughly 7.5 to 10 cents in today's U.S. currency).

Probably a slight majority of the skilled artisans in the factory were union members, but Silver's "unskilled" operatives, the yard laborers included, were unorganized, as was the case with most British workers at the time. None of the existing craft unions would admit them as members.[47] With those unions aloof and even hostile, the unskilled workers at Silver's had to take matters in their own hands. The division between the two categories of workers was to lead to an acrimonious interunion dispute that saw the engineers' union (ASE) executive lambasted as industrial villains and their Silvertown members pilloried as blacklegs (scabs) for undermining the laborers' strike. The stage was set for a bitter struggle that would end later that year in tragedy for the Silvertown workers and triumph for the employers. The yard laborers, however, could have foreseen none of this on that brilliant Indian summer's day. They were probably unaware, too, of an ominous change in the attitudes of the British middle classes to strikes and trade unionism.

II.
Introduction to a Forgotten Struggle

◆◆◆

> The spirit of the "New Unionism" was flaming across
> the country. . . . Workers were rising for improvements
> in their wages and conditions; often unorganised, down-
> trodden, they took action without planning ahead; sheer
> desperation drove them to striking revolt, and with their
> striking came organisation. In this way a big strike broke
> out at a gutta-percha and rubber works in Silvertown . . .
> their demand was for . . . "the dockers' tanner."[48]
> —WILL THORNE

THIS BOOK TELLS the story of the great strike at Silvertown in the
autumn and winter of 1889. The Epilogue includes some discussion of
another strike by members of the Amalgamated Society of Engineers in
the same factory in 1897, and sketches in the growth of industrial and
political labor in the district. The 1889 strike lasted three months, and
that of 1897 lasted three months longer, although it involved only the
skilled engineering workers in the plant. Today, both struggles have been
comprehensively forgotten. With the exception of Yvonne Kapp in volume
2 of her admirable biography of Eleanor Marx,[49] the 1889 strike has
received only passing mention by other authors, including participants
such as Will Thorne, the first General Secretary of the National Union of
Gasworkers & General Labourers (NUG&GL). The same is true of labor
historians. John Saville's masterful essay on the rise of the New Unions
and the employers' counter-offensive does not mention the Silver's strike,
although it was a pivot point in the class warfare he describes. Similarly,
nothing at all seems to have been written about the 1897 engineers' strike

at Silver's. Today in Silvertown, there is little memory of Silver's Works itself despite the district bearing the name of the firm's founder, Samuel Winkworth Silver. One local historian wrongly described Silver's as an explosives works,[50] perhaps conflating it with the Brunner Mond munitions plant that blew up spectacularly in 1917.[51] Many Londoners have never even heard of Silvertown let alone set foot in it. Such collective ignorance and amnesia belies the fact that Silver's was once Britain's leading rubber and electrical firm and that Silvertown's "Golden Mile" was once a key section of the greatest agglomeration of heavy industry in southern England. Local collective memory of the strikes also seems to be dead. When I spoke with some Silvertown locals in late 2011, I could not find anyone who knew anything about the strikes, although one very old person knew of the Great Explosion of 1917, and collective memory of the Blitz lingered. In 2012, Colin Grainger, the editor of the *Newham Gazette*, kindly ran an article about my research with an appeal for people to contact me, but it turned up very little. Later, however, I was delighted to learn that an old Silvertown Labour Party and union activist knew that Cundy's pub was "known to have hosted meetings organised by Eleanor Marx after the great Dock strike in 1889" and that "she supported the efforts of the workers at the India Rubber Factory in Silvertown to obtain an increase in pay."[52] This aside, the thread of collective memory in Silvertown has almost snapped. If the celebrated historian E. P. Thompson's mission in writing *The Making of the English Working Class* was "to rescue the poor stockinger, the Luddite cropper, the 'obsolete' handloom weaver, the 'utopian' artisan, even the deluded followers of Joanna Southcott, from the enormous condescension of posterity,"[53] then my task is even more basic. It is to alert posterity to the fact that the events presented in this book even happened.

Memories Too Frail a Thread

Why, then, has there been such forgetting? Part of the answer is that the great 1889 strike occurred over 120 years ago. A worker in his or her prime in 1889 would have been born in, say, 1849 or 1859. Children born around the time of the strike—had they survived the appalling infant and child mortality of the day—would have died in the 1950s or 1960s. We live in restless times. The old fabric of community has been torn apart forever. During the Blitz in the Second World War, Silver's factory sustained heavy bomb damage and never completely recovered. It limped on with obsolete technology until the 1960s, when the company razed the site and memories of it died.[54] The Nazi bombing, too, was so destructive that according to some accounts the close-knit local community virtually ceased to exist. When the painter Graham Sutherland visited Silvertown during the Blitz in 1941, he saw "the shells of long terraces of houses, great—surprisingly wide—perspectives of destruction seeming to recede into infinity. The windowless blocks were like sightless eyes." His painting of the scene, "Devastation 1941: An East End Street," hangs in London's Tate Gallery. An extant photograph shows a visibly shocked Winston Churchill surveying the bomb damage from the old Silvertown viaduct. So intense were the air raids that between 1939 and 1945 the number of people on the electoral roll in Central Silvertown ward fell from 1,155 to 64.[55] The writer Nuala Calvi also drew my attention to the effects of slum clearance in Silvertown, writing that "[t]he impression we got was that people whose houses weren't bombed would return after being evacuated, and those who were bombed out would be likely to find another house a few streets away. I think the slum clearances after the war had more of an effect because people were moved further away."[56] ("Further away" meant the vast public housing estates—"projects" in U.S. parlance—on the fringes of greater London.) Today, after the de-industrialization begun during the Thatcher years, a scant 11 percent of the British workforce remains in manufacturing industry. In Silvertown, only Tate & Lyle's sugar refinery survives to remind us of the time when the suburb sported a forest of factory chimneys and exported its multifarious wares to the world. By closing the docks and factories, one elderly local resident observes that "they achieved what Hitler started, wiped out the East End."[57]

The 1889 strikers lost, but after decades of dogged struggle West Ham and Silvertown were to become bastions of trade unionism, the Social Democratic Federation, the Independent Labour Party (ILP), and the Labour Party. The British labor movement has, alas, declined in recent decades, and neoliberal ideology, "Blairism," economic globalization, and structural "reforms" have gravely weakened working-class solidarity and collective memory. The labor movement, too, savors its victories and prefers to forget its defeats; the Silvertown strike was a tragic setback for organized labor, a story that workers' leaders such as Will Thorne may have felt were best forgotten. The 1897 strike, too, was a defeat for the militants who had replaced the conservative old guard in the engineers' union. If, as the writer John Still put it, the "memories of men are too frail a thread to hang history from,"[58] at Silvertown the thread was broken.

Any collective memory of the 1889 defeat has also been overshadowed by the memory of the great contemporaneous East End union victories at Beckton, Bow, and on the docks. This is a great pity, for despite the defeats, the Silvertown struggles were an important part of the battle to establish the militant New Unions.

In 1889, most British workers were unorganized. This was especially the case with the great mass of unskilled and semiskilled operatives created by the factory system. When it came, the great labor upsurge of 1889 was welcomed, supported, and led enthusiastically by the small socialist movement that had long awaited it. The strike leaders were, as Frederick Engels noted, "*our* people,"[59] that is, socialists such as John Burns, Tom Mann, and Ben Tillett. As Tillett notes in his autobiography, "I was a Socialist because I was a Trade Unionist, and I saw clearly that an alliance of Trade Unionism and Socialism was a necessary and legitimate consummation of the life-giving impulses of both."[60] In a pamphlet written shortly after the dock strike, Tillett joined with Mann to insist that the trade union struggle was inseparable from the fight for "a CO-OPERATIVE COMMONWEALTH."[61] This prediction was borne out in the new heavy-industry belt on the fringes of London, but was less true of the older districts of the East End during the period covered by this book.

In July 1888, the "match girls" strike at the Bryant & May factory in Bow brought some of the most downtrodden members of the East End working class into struggle. Triply oppressed as working-class women of Irish birth or extraction, they won a stunning victory against a cynical and callous employer. Shortly afterward, another struggle broke out at the huge Beckton Gasworks a few miles down the Thames from Silvertown and the stokers won a huge reduction of hours without loss of pay. On 31 March 1889, their leader, the socialist firebrand Will Thorne, launched the NUG&GL at a mass meeting in Canning Town,[62] a suburb adjacent to Silvertown. Eight hundred men joined by throwing their dues into a bucket.[63] Then came the great dock strike itself. These struggles laid the foundations for the "New Unionism" of the general labor unions—and later the "New Politics" of the mass Labour Party. This is not to say, however, that those were days of plain sailing for the unions. From Silvertown on, the employers threw everything they had into a desperate struggle to crush the new movement. If the London dock strike, as John Burns put it, had been "the Lucknow of labor," then Silvertown was perhaps its Alamo.

Historical Discontinuity

There is a tremendous historical discontinuity here. Until the late 1880s, the labor movement had organized only a small minority of British workers, and these were concentrated in the craft unions. In 1871, for example, the combined membership of four of the most well-established trade unions in the East End—the Engineers, Bricklayers, Carpenters, and Masons—amounted to a mere 1,001 individuals spread across thirteen branches.[64] According to Tillett and Mann, there were 700,000 unorganized workers in London in 1890.[65] From 1888, masses of previously unorganized workers came into struggle in a piecemeal fashion. Despite sharp fluctuations in membership and other severe setbacks during the Great Depression of the 1890s, the New Unions survived to grow exponentially after 1914.[66] This was the case in Silvertown.

With hindsight, though the rise of the New Unionism might appear to have been inevitable, it caught most people—workers and capitalists, socialists, trade unionists and non-unionists, Liberals, and Tories alike— by surprise. Many who were familiar with conditions in the East End had despaired of change. George Sims in his book *Horrible London*, published in 1889, concluded that the case of the London poor "seemed utterly hopeless."[67] Cynics and Social Darwinists sneered at the efforts of social reformers and put mass penury down to the alleged laziness, stupidity, or moral turpitude of the poor, and many believed them.[68] The East Enders' own reaction to oppression and poverty was as likely to manifest itself in criminal as in political terms. Or they might emigrate to the colonies in Australasia, the Cape, and Canada, or to the United States. The East End in the late nineteenth century discouraged working-class agitators. It was an appalling place in which to live and work, but as writers such as Gareth Stedman Jones,[69] Alex Windscheffel,[70] and Diana Banks-Conney[71] have shown, horrible conditions did not equate automatically with heightened class consciousness. Popular music hall songs scoffed at the puny efforts of the socialists, whom they lumped in with Christian evangelists and other "do-gooders." Working-class Toryism and political apathy were deeply entrenched, particularly in the older, inner parts of the district, buoyed up on a "wave of imperialism," for this was the zenith of the British Empire.[72] Enormous crowds from across the class spectrum celebrated the imperial victories and the births, deaths, marriages, and coronations of the royal family. In 1901, Jack London recorded his dismal impressions of the royal coronation:

Vivat Rex Edwardus! They crowned a king this day, and there has
been great rejoicing and tomfoolery, and I am perplexed and saddened.
I never saw anything to compare with the pageant, except Yankee cir-
cuses and Alhambra ballets; nor did I ever see anything so hopeless
and so tragic.[73]

Many of those lining the streets were desperately poor, yet they cheered
themselves hoarse at the spectacle of Britannia's bluebloods flaunting
their ill-gotten wealth and privilege. Those showing themselves, London
recorded, included the "five hundred hereditary peers [who] own one-
fifth of England; and [who with] ... the officers and servants under the
king, and those that compose the powers that be, yearly spend in wasteful
luxury $1,850,000,000 or £370,000,000, which is thirty-two percent of
the total wealth produced by all the toilers of the country."[74] One year earlier, Charles Masterman recorded the scenes of rejoicing after the relief of
the siege of Mafeking in South Africa in the Boer War, a hats-off carnival
with free beer, not just in the West End or the City, but in the East End
too.[75] Such a political and cultural landscape made the task of organizing
trade unions very difficult.

   Yet, under the crust of obsequious deferral to pelf and privilege, anger
was brewing. In 1886 and 1887, crowds of East Enders had erupted into
the West End, breaking windows and looting shops. The first riot, on 8
February 1886, broke out when a breakaway group from an unemployment
demonstration organized by the Social Democratic Federation (SDF)
looted clubs and shops. Historian Roy Porter considers that members
of the misnamed Reform Club provoked the riot when they "insolently
tossed nailbrushes at the demonstrators." SDF founder Henry Hyndman
insisted that "on all social questions they [the club's members] were out-
and-out reactionaries."[76] For days afterward, "shop windows were boarded
up, banks closed, troops stood by, while threatening meetings and clashes
were reported" from around the country. For their part, the unemployed
staged further marches and set up camp in the royal parks.[77] A second
riot exploded in the autumn of 1887 after demonstrators flouted a government ban on assemblies in Trafalgar Square. The police responded
"with unusual brutality," writes Porter, and a section of the crowd broke
through the cordon into the West End, where they overturned carriages
and smashed windows.[78] Although the riots conjured up the specter of an
uprising for the bourgeois, Porter's assessment that "the crowd had never
offered any real prospect of revolution" rings true.[79] They were more a
scream of feral rage rather than an expression of constructive revolt.[80]

Today, we might be tempted with some justification to see parallels with the 2011 British youth riots and the establishment's hysterical response to them. Although they were a barometer of despair and discontent, even the socialists doubted that anything "political" might come from them. Margaret Harkness and George Gissing, who wrote "social" novels about the East End, were two left-wing intellectuals who despaired.[81] Before 1889, attempts to organize the unskilled and semiskilled workers of the East End had largely failed, including at the massive Beckton gasworks.[82] Many observers felt it was not possible to organize the unskilled workers and many of the "respectable" leaders of the craft unions did not feel it was desirable to do so. As a result, the great bulk of the nation's workers endured abject poverty in the midst of what Jack London was to describe as "the greatest, wealthiest, and most powerful empire the world has ever seen."[83]

An Example to the World

Margaret Harkness, a good friend of Eleanor Marx and her guide to the East End, was not alone in her sense of powerlessness. In April 1888, Frederick Engels criticized Harkness's depiction in her novel *City Girl* of the East End workers as a "passive mass," yet he conceded that "nowhere in the civilized world are the working people less actively resistant, more passively submitting to fate, more *hébétés* [dulled, dazed, or bewildered] than in the East End of London."[84] Yet, delighted by the events of 1889, Engels reversed his opinion and expressed his profound admiration for the selfsame Cockney toilers. Things had begun to change in the East End. Though claims of historical "turning points" are often exaggerated, the claim does fit the Britain—and London specifically—of 1888–89. Likewise, the prediction of George Shipton, the old guard Secretary of the London Trades Council, that the New Unions would prove to be "'mushroom' societies likely to die an early death"[85] proved false, although some did perish and others came perilously close to doing so in the dog days of the 1890s.

Part of the reason for the New Union upsurge was the emergence of an extraordinary layer of militant working-class leaders. People such as Tom Mann, Will Thorne, Eleanor Marx, and Ben Tillett challenged the arid sectarianism of the Hyndman wing of the Social Democratic Federation, which scorned trade unions as at best weak social palliatives and at worst as barriers to socialism.[86] The new militants also had little time for the parlor-pink reformism of the Fabians, middle-class reformers who wished to ameliorate the lot of the workers by action from above rather than organize them from below to emancipate themselves. What Arthur Field wrote about Eleanor Marx in the *Social Democrat* applied to the rest of her comrades: "As the Revolutionary Socialist she was, she naturally had nothing but contempt for the 'Practical Socialism' which ends in the quagmire of Liberalism."[87] Marx and her comrades, however, had no truck with sectarians who lectured from the sidelines. On the contrary, they "heartily advocated the only immediate practicable effort of any socialistic value—to wit, political agitation for industrial reforms."[88] In 1930, Will Thorne's NUG&GL proclaimed proudly that "until the Gasworkers came along, no Union had Socialism as its objective, but this pioneer body emblazoned Socialism on its banner from the start." Moreover, the NUG&GL "was the first Union effectively to advocate the international bond between the workers of the world."[89]

We should be aware, in addition, that though jingoism, apathy, and working-class Toryism abounded in the East End, a significant minority of Cockney workers were socialists. One hundred and twenty years after the famous match girls strike at Bow in 1888, Louise Raw found that many of their direct descendants still shared the Irish socialist republican views of their feisty great grandmothers. Raw's iconoclastic book, *Striking a Light*,[90] also challenges the sexist stereotype of the "girls" as passive creatures unable to organize without the direction of middle-class intellectuals such as the sometime Fabian Annie Besant and her friends. As Raw demonstrates, the women themselves made the decision to strike, and Besant was not happy about it. A young woman explained that the strike began spontaneously: "'Well, it just went like tinder,' she said. 'One girl began, and the rest said yes, so out we all went.'"[91]

As Engels realized, 1888–89 marked "the *real* beginning of a movement,"[92] and though the movement did not achieve a workers' commonwealth, the mass party of labor created by the unions did blunt the worst excesses of capitalism, and the employers had to accept the reality of collective bargaining with the unions. From 1889, for the first time since the mass Chartist agitations of the 1830s, the working class took center stage and began to act as *a class for itself*, rather than as an appendage of the Liberal Party and the middle classes. To be fair, some radicals did provide invaluable assistance, including during the Silver's strike. Silvertown and West Ham as a whole were to become citadels of *independent* political and industrial labor. As Karl Marx had noted in 1844, ideas could become a material force when they had gripped the minds of the masses,[93] and this was the case with the rise of the New Unionism. Though early twenty-first-century Britain has relapsed into a kind of reserve for brutal, feral, and parasitic Capital, the new movement recast the face of British society and won major social gains for the working class in the form of the welfare state—the price the ruling class had to pay to avert revolutionary change. A century later, those gains are under concerted attack and most trade union struggles in Britain today are defensive in nature, fighting to preserve what was won by past generations of workers.

The Silvertown Formula

When not completely forgotten, the 1889 strike has never been fully appreciated. Yvonne Kapp believed that although the 1889 Silvertown strike "did not make history … in a particular sense, it is of historical interest."[94] In fact, it is of *considerable historical interest*, much more so than Kapp realized. It is a truism that history is often written—or ignored—by the victors, and Silvertown is a case in point. The defeat of the strike was of great significance for the employing class as a whole. This was illustrated by a letter sent to Silver's after the defeat of the strike by the famous Manchester rubber firm of Charles Macintosh & Co. The letter acknowledged "the service rendered to other manufacturers by this Company's refusal to pay higher wages."[95] Silver's had held the line against the New Unionism and for this the bourgeoisie was grateful. Higher wages paid to one employer might give other capitalists a temporary competitive edge, but would set a "bad" example for their own workers to follow. Behind the scenes, too, the most powerful men in English politics were watching developments, and the employers were poised, ready to launch a radical counteroffensive against the New Unions using the methods pioneered at Silver's.

During the 1930s in the United States, many employers adopted a "scientific" strikebreaking package, which became widely known as the "Mohawk Valley Formula." The formula was based on the methods adopted by the Remington Rand Corporation to crush a big strike at their Ilion, New York, plant.[96] Earlier, British employers might be said to have used the "Silvertown Formula." As I have written elsewhere:

The individual elements of both "formulae" were not original, but in both cases they were combined into a formidable strike-breaking package. The central elements of the Silvertown formula included the refusal of all offers of arbitration or negotiation and the transfer of work overseas or its "outsourcing" to other local factories. The firm also attempted to mobilize middle-class opinion against the strikers via the press, in particular by blaming the dispute on outside agitators. Silver's was also able to rely on the cooperation of the police, who used heavy-handed methods against the strikers. The police were also used to escort large numbers of scabs, who had been recruited in rural districts, through picket lines. Another innovation was the housing and feeding of the blacklegs inside the factory. Finally, the company made full use of the Metropolitan Police and Home Office solicitors to prosecute strikers.[97]

In the dying days of the Silvertown strike, the NUG&GL launched another strike at London's South Metropolitan Gasworks. If they were expecting a repeat of the historic victory at the Beckton Gasworks, they were disappointed. The specter of Silvertown remained. Under the direction of George Livesey, a man who was to play an energetic part in the employers' offensive over the next decade, the bosses put the package developed at Silvertown into action and the union suffered yet another bruising defeat. An important factor was the deployment of large numbers of police to protect blacklegs, although Livesey added a profit-sharing scheme to the mix. Two years later, the London dockers, hoping for a repeat of their 1889 strike, were defeated. Again, the employers had learned from the Silvertown experience. Scabs were fed and billeted aboard the *Scotland*, which was moored inside the docks, as had happened at Silvertown. Further strikes, most notably at Hull in 1893, were put down by police and soldiers, with gunboats anchored in the River Humber. Across Britain and Ireland, maritime workers were forced to register in shipping federation employment exchanges, and to agree to work with non-union labor.[98] The pattern was repeated in many other disputes across the country, notably in the national engineering dispute of 1897–98. As at Silvertown, another key weapon in the employers' armory was the courts. The *Lyons vs. Wilkins* case of 1896 outlawed even peaceful picketing and in early 1897 the ASE was fined £647 (over $1000)—an enormous sum for the time—for describing an engineering firm as "rat employers."[99] In 1901, in the famous Taff Vale judgment, a court ruled that employers could sue trade unions for damages resulting from strike action. The case, which was the handiwork of the Employers' Parliamentary Council, was intended to prevent strikes from ever happening. The judgment impelled trade unionists to look beyond syndicalism toward independent working-class political action. A year earlier, a number of union leaders had set up the Labour Representation Committee (LRC), but Taff Vale forced the others to break from the habit of working through the Liberal Party. As a result, the LRC grew into the Labour Party: something that recent right-wing party leader Tony Blair has tried to "spin" out of history by casting the break with Liberalism as a historical blunder and calling for a "Third Way" that jettisons any notion of working-class politics and socialism.

By the end of the 1889 strike, the Silvertown workers had few friends. As John Saville has shown, middle-class opinion had already swung against the New Unions by the last weeks of the London dock strike—at the very time that the Silvertown strike was beginning.[100] In the following decade, such opinion became hysterically anti-union. Nor did the Silvertown strikers enjoy the kind of financial support given to the dockers by local and overseas sources. In contrast, with scant support from established unions and elsewhere, the Silvertown strikers were starved back to work in what was the first battle in an employers' counteroffensive that was to continue past the turn of the century.

The Silvertown strikers were raw recruits to trade unionism: unskilled and semiskilled workers pitted against not only their wealthy and powerful employer but also the factory's disdainful "labor aristocrats" who refused to support the laborers' desperate struggle. Many of the Silvertown strikers were new proletarians, recently uprooted from the countryside in the great upheavals of the Industrial Revolution, the Enclosures, the Irish Famine, and the Highland Clearances. Over the course of the thirty-seven years of the factory's existence, however, others had put down roots in Silvertown. As a sympathetic journalist wrote in the London *Daily News*, "Silvertown is, in fact, a kind of close corporation, generation after generation of workpeople have lived all their lives at the one occupation. In cases not a few fathers, sons, and daughters all work for the firm."[101] This, no doubt, was an important factor in building solidarity, but it was also a weakness as it isolated the strikers. However, although they lost the 1889 battle, their numbers and cohesiveness were important in the ongoing construction of a strong industrial and political labor movement in West Ham. That movement was based on the development of a firm class consciousness that was stronger at this stage than farther west in the older districts of the East End, where workers tended to be employed in smaller enterprises.[102]

Making Feminist History

The Silvertown strikers also made feminist history; something which, curiously, Yvonne Kapp does not stress. As Professor Nick Buck observed in his doctoral thesis:

> The most striking feature of female employment in West Ham is the scale of its growth. It was rising much faster than male employment (e.g. male employment rose by 46% between 1891 and 1911, while female employment rose by 82%). Moreover it was shifting out of the 'traditional' female occupations of clothing manufacture and domestic and other service (64% of employed women in 1891, 42% in 1911) into other manufacturing industries (11.9% in 1891, 25.6% in 1911).[103]

In 1889, around 11 percent of Silver's workers were women. Under Eleanor Marx's guiding hand, these female workers were to found the first women's branch of the NUG&GL,[104] and were to stand shoulder to shoulder with the men in struggle. The NUG&GL was early on an exception to the rule in an age when many trade unions refused membership to women. The decision to admit them was made at a 5,000-strong meeting of men held near the Boleyn Tavern in Upton Park in mid-October 1889. After mounting the podium to an "enthusiastic reception," Will Thorne said that "down at Silvertown" there were many women workers who wanted to join the union and form their own branch. The outcome of the meeting was reported in a local newspaper:

> There might be those who believed in sect [sic] unions, but he did not. The men and women worked side by side, and why should they not all be Union members? . . . Some of the women were working now for a miserable pittance, scarcely enough to keep body and soul together, and he took it to be one of their principles to improve the lot of their sisters as well as their brothers. He wanted to ask them to show their opinions on these matters by a show of hands. A vote was then taken, and it was unanimously resolved, amid applause, to admit women into the Union.[105]

Eleanor Marx and the Silvertown women immediately acted upon the decision and for that reason alone the 1889 strike should be reckoned to have "made history." The Silvertown strikers and the wider East End NUG&GL membership had challenged a state of affairs in which the men are economically dependent on the masters, and the women are economically dependent on the men. The result is, the woman gets the beating the man should give to his master.[106]

The master was not beaten in this case, but the men and women had united against him in common struggle. It was a portent for the future. Working-class solidarity had trumped male chauvinism.

An Intransigent Employer

In learning the industrial ropes, the Silvertown workers undoubtedly made errors. It could hardly be otherwise. They were raw recruits to trade unionism, and the union they joined was itself brand new and lacked the resources to sustain a big strike for so long without substantial outside help. While the 1889 dockers' victory is justly celebrated today, we should not forget that the dockers were greatly assisted by huge financial donations from across the globe. Australia alone contributed some £30,000, which in today's currency is worth anywhere between £2.59 million and £31.1 million ($4.15 million and $49.86 million).[107] Not even a fraction of that sum trickled into the Silvertown strike fund. In the end, the Silvertown strikers were beaten more by hunger and lack of solidarity by established unions than by poor decision making or lack of determination. There was also an important downside to the "close corporation" of the workers noted by the *Daily News* journalist. With all of the wage earners employed in the Silver factory, and so many with little income during the strike, when donations petered out "their sole means of subsistence. . . [was] cut off."[108] The strikers were literally starved back to work on the old wages and conditions, a point admitted even by the implacably hostile *Essex Standard*.[109] It is also certain that this was the company's aim, for they rejected all offers of mediation to end the dispute. Gray was cheered on from behind the scenes by a ruling-class and middle-class opinion desperate to put an end to what they considered an epidemic of strikes led by socialist agitators. Those with a direct pecuniary interest in the outcome of the Silvertown strike included even the Marquess of Salisbury, the prime minister of the day, and a bevy of his fellow Tory and Liberal MPs.

Silver's won the battle, but the New Unionism, and the political developments it gave birth to, was to change the face of British society. Silver's itself eventually became a union shop. The 1889 strike leaders consoled themselves at the moment of their defeat that they had played

an honorable part in the continuing struggle for working-class emancipation—correctly as it turned out.

III.
Samuel Silver's Palace of Industry

⬦◆⬦

> Only the balefires are bright,
> And the flash of lamps now and then
> From a palace where spoilers sit,
> Trampling the children of men.[110]
> —ALGERNON SWINBURNE

UNTIL 1850, the district that became Silvertown was a vast and dismal stretch of marsh and tidal mudflats lying along the north bank of the River Thames, forming the southern section of the treeless Plaistow Marsh.[111] London—and the immense rotting pile of the older East End—lay to the west, over the River Lea. The district was almost uninhabited and consisted of "dead flats . . . marshes full of water rats, onions and greens, black ditches and foul drains."[112] At the beginning of the nineteenth century there was only one permanent building on the marsh, an old alehouse with a red roof known locally as the "Devil's House."[113] There was also a gibbet, which stood where the entrance to the Victoria Dock is today, "with ghastly corpses of so-called river-pirates hanging and rotting upon it, as a terror to evil-doers."[114] Superstitious locals saw evidence in this of a curse on the district, and later generations might have agreed.[115] The marsh was renowned for its bad climate, "proverbial insalubrity," and disease,[116] which had caused mass desertions from the garrison at North Woolwich during the Dutch War of 1667.[117]

To call this place a "greenfield" industrial site belies the nature of the terrain, yet such it was in economic terms in 1852 when Samuel Winkworth Silver relocated his waterproof clothing firm there from across the river in Greenwich. Silver acquired one acre of the marsh at the point

where the now long-vanished Ham Creek flowed into the Thames. It was
an appropriate choice for a waterproofing factory, for Silver had chosen
a miserably wet, muddy, and cold place. Much of the marsh lay seven to
ten feet below the mean high water level of the Thames and access to the
factory site was either via the old village of North Woolwich or from the
Barking Road to an ancient embankment that kept the tides and floods at
bay. From the landward foot of this wall of earth and rock, the observer
might see only the masts and rigging, funnels, and upper superstructures
of the larger ships plowing the Thames, and hear only the foghorns of the
smaller vessels. The local historian Dr. Pagenstecher tells us that "how
long since and by whom . . . [the marsh] was won from the river, it is
impossible to say," but he believed that the first earthworks were thrown
up by the Romans, or rather by the native Celts they pressed into labor.[118]
By the middle of the nineteenth century, a small hamlet had grown up at
North Woolwich, and in 1851 the North Woolwich and Royal Pavilion
Gardens were laid out.[119] These were within walking distance of what was
to become Silvertown, and were soon the only patch of trees and lawns in
the huge industrial area of the Golden Mile.

Sam Silver's family perhaps wondered about his judgment when he
relocated his factory to the Essex district that came to bear his name,
but the move from Greenwich was to prove astute. A few years earlier,
a railway engineer called George Bidder, acting on behalf of a syndicate
of businessmen, had bought up all the land from Bow Creek to Gallion
Reach from people who were probably glad to get rid of it.[120] The coming
of the railway to North Woolwich in 1847 and a steam ferry service across
the Thames from there to Woolwich proper in Kent prepared the way
for the industrial development of the marsh, and it is likely that Sam
Silver's keen nose had sniffed the way the commercial winds were blow-
ing.[121] Insider trading is not new. Silver's was not the first industrial firm
to settle at Silvertown proper.[122] In 1851, the Howard brothers had built
a small glass factory and wharf near the mouth of Ham Creek. The business did not prosper and Sam Silver bought the property, adding its two
acres to his existing one-acre block. He then purchased an additional five
acres.[123] The opening of the Victoria and Albert docks in 1855 helped the
business to prosper. The factory sat within half a mile of the docks, a mas-
terpiece of Victorian civil engineering that linked Silvertown to all corners
of the expanding empire with its cornucopia of commodities. Silvertown
was still a primitive place, however. As late as 1878, when the Lancastrian
manufacturer Henry Tate bought land at Silvertown for a sugar refinery,[124] a member of his family lampooned his decision in doggerel verse:

Is this man really sane?
He's bought up a marsh and a gasworks
At least seven miles out of town.
We'll either go down with swamp fever
Or the whole ruddy workforce will drown.[125]

Heavy Industry Comes to the East End

Nevertheless, Silver's and Tate's thrived. Here, the coal, india-rubber, gutta-percha, jute, cotton, kaolin, sulfur, iron and copper wire, and other essential raw materials for what was to prove one of Victorian Britain's most profitable enterprises could be landed almost directly into the Silvertown works. Humans, too, could be landed there from launches when the need arose. Just as important, the finished products could be shipped out directly to the world. The factory enjoyed five-eighths of a mile of river frontage, which was developed over time into wharves for the company's customized fleet. Sam Silver, of course, could have had no inkling of this in 1852, decades before the Electrical Revolution transformed British industry, but he was an acquisitive and ambitious man and he built solid foundations on the marsh.

The scale of his enterprise was something new for the East End. Ten or fifteen years later, Silver's and many of the other factories around it had grown into huge concerns employing many thousands of workers. These factories were, as Nick Buck has stressed, atypical of the East End as a whole. Further in toward the City, across Bow Creek, was the Inner East End—Whitechapel, Spitalfields, Stepney, etc.—old districts in which most industries were petty commodity producers catering for London consumption.[126] By mid-century, the few large-scale enterprises in the inner East End were in decline.[127] Buck notes that "linked to small firm size were many production characteristics of a pre-industrial type, particularly the low level of capital needed to enter the market, hence the large number of artisans on the borderline between being employers and employees and the low level of differentiation between the two classes."[128] As Gareth Stedman Jones notes, all except the richest employers lived close to, or even at, their place of business.[129] The Inner East End, Buck argues, thus "lacked a substantial urban bourgeoisie,"[130] and the working class was spread out over a large number of small enterprises and lacked class consciousness. Indeed, considers Stedman Jones, "the factory, with its large demands on space, its voracious appetite for fuel and its semiskilled labor force was quite inappropriate to London conditions."[131] In contrast, whereas industry in the inner East End had declined from the 1860s, West Ham had experienced "unprecedented industrial growth."[132] Silver's grew into a vast modern capitalist enterprise—the second-largest employer in the West Ham heavy industrial belt and the biggest on the Golden Mile—with high levels of capital investment. There was, of necessity, a marked differentiation between the classes; gone were the personal, paternalist relations between master and man characteristic of the small East End workshops. As the American super-capitalist Henry Ford once remarked, "A great business is really too big to be human,"[133] and this was true of Silver's. In the capitalist factory system, Marx and Engels wrote, "all feudal, patriarchal, idyllic relations" were torn asunder and there was "left remaining no other nexus between man and man than naked self-interest, than callous 'cash payment'."[134] This typified industry in the southern parts of West Ham where there was a marked concentration of large process, chemical, and engineering industries and a correspondingly lower number of "traditional London craft industries."[135]

The High Ratio of Fixed to Variable Capital at Silver's

The fact that Silver's managing director, Matthew Silver, was to prove implacably hostile to the NUG&GL is partly due to his individual psychological makeup and the hegemony of Spencerian individualist ideology in late Victorian Britain. There is a more direct reason for his obduracy, however, and this is to be found in the specific organic composition of the firm's capital. Capital, Marx argued, could be broken down into two categories: fixed, or constant capital, and variable capital. By the former, he meant investment in plant, machinery, and raw materials. By the latter, he meant the proportion paid to workers in the form of wages after the extraction of surplus value.[136] The ratio of the two components is not identical across industries. Light industry has a relatively small proportion of capital investment in plant and equipment, whereas a high ratio is found in heavy industry such as Silver's. In fact, Silver's invested huge amounts of capital in its factories. The firm was forever introducing new technology, and it became Britain's foremost electrical and telegraph company. Not to do this meant that it would lose market share to competitors at home and abroad. Because of the relatively low ratio of fixed capital, employers in light industry were generally more willing to make compromises with their workers, although this does not mean that some of them were not ruthless. However, the limits within which production was profitable were considerably larger than in heavy industry. This had direct consequences for the comparative intensity of the class struggle between the sectors. In 1939, the French leftist Daniel Guérin attributed the rise of fascism in Italy and Germany in great measure to the financial support of heavy industrialists and bankers with a stake in their industries. These capitalists and financiers bankrolled the fascists, despite all Hitler and Mussolini's plebeian rhetoric and petty bourgeois support, because they saw them, correctly, as battering rams with which to crush the workers' movement in a time of crisis.[137] It also helps explain the earlier implacable response of employers such as Silver's to the New Unions. To make consistent profits, given their high outlays on machinery, raw materials, cable-laying vessels, etc., Silver's had to extract the maximum possible surplus value from their laborers. This meant that unions had to be excluded from the plants at all costs, particularly during economic downswings; and on the factory floor despotic rules and harsh supervision prevailed While we know with the benefit of hindsight that Silver's was a consistently profitable firm even through the 1890s depression, its huge capital investments were always a gamble.

By 1892, Silver's had a ratable value of £14,560, second only among West Ham factories to the Great Eastern Railway Workshops at Stratford, which was valued at £21,750 and almost twice the value of the third largest, the Thames Ironworks in Canning Town. In 1878, Tate's sugar refinery had a ratable value of £8,250. Keiller's jam factory was rated at £1,000 in 1879, and the Thames Ironworks and Shipbuilding at £8,108 in 1846. The Victoria and Albert docks had a combined ratable value of £48,375 in 1884, but these covered an enormous area and were an unsophisticated business with little mechanization and huge numbers of casual employees.[138]

These material conditions were to have a big impact on working-class consciousness in West Ham. Stedman Jones and others have argued that the culture of the unskilled and semiskilled workers of the inner East End had tended to be apolitical. If anything, they preferred to vote Tory because that party favored some degree of protectionism for British industry over untrammeled free trade. Inner London, it is true, had boasted a radical political culture, particularly among artisans, who looked to Tom Paine and other iconoclasts, and were notably "atheist, republican, democratic, and fiercely anti-aristocratic."[139] That, too, had tended to be swamped by waves of imperialism and jingoism, exacerbated by government repression. In contrast, working-class consciousness was to develop quickly in rapidly expanding and heavily industrialized West Ham,[140] where the workers were to flock to the New Unions and socialist parties. As Marx put it, consciousness is a reflection of social being. In this respect, West Ham was similar to pre-revolutionary Petrograd, where the Bolsheviks found their greatest levels of support in large factories.[141] (There are many reasons why workers in large factories develop class consciousness. These include close proximity to other workers, the detailed division of labor making workers interchangeable and homogenous, and the machine-dictated pace of work.) Diana Banks-Conney observes that although one of the two constituencies in Bow and Bromley in the inner East End elected Labour MPs from just prior to the First World War, their tenure was not continuous, and the party did not have a majority on the local council until after the Second World War. This was unlike West Ham, which elected Britain's first socialist MP to Westminster in 1892 and its first socialist council before the end of the century.[142]

From Low- to High-Tech Industry

All this was to come. Initially, Silver's was a modest and relatively low-tech enterprise, a light industry devoted to the manufacture of waterproofed cotton fabric, essential for the manufacture of the once-ubiquitous British "mac" or rubberized raincoat.[143] Silver's manufactured many thousands of these. "One of the useful novelties of the season," a fashion journalist noted in 1883, "is the 'Silvertown Waterproof,' which has a very silky appearance, is extremely light and portable, and folds up into a very small space" and "is an invaluable companion by sea or land."[144] The waterproofing trade was a logical extension of Silver's traditional business. The family had run a haberdashery in Cornhill in the City before shifting to Greenwich in 1844 and thence to the wasteland across the river.[145] According to one source, Silver's was originally "colonial and army agents, clothiers and outfitters,"[146] which suggests a substantial business with imperial links. Waterproofed cloth was to remain one of Silver's key products, but it was eclipsed by other, more profitable, goods.

By 1864, the business was buoyant enough for the Silver family to transform it into a public limited liability company, re-dubbed the India-Rubber Works and Telegraph Works Company Limited. It was already a sizable firm; its initial share issue of £500,000 would be worth around £772 million as a proportion of GDP in 2010 values (around $1300 million).[147] Silver was well connected; the provisional committee of the new public company included Sam Mendel, one of Manchester's foremost cotton merchants, and William Fenton Hugh of the Great Western Railway.[148] Lt. Colonel Hugh Adams Silver and John W. Willans served as joint managing directors at this time,[149] but at the beginning of 1866, a new man called Matthew Gray replaced them as sole managing director[150] (or CEO in today's terms). He was to remain in the post for the next thirty years, when one of his sons took over. One suspects that with the firm's entry into heavier industry, Gray's older and more amateurish predecessors were out of their depth.

Matthew Gray, Captain of Industry

Gray's appointment was based on the Silver board's appraisal of his solid "commercial knowledge" and his perceived ability "to manage the entire undertaking." The board was satisfied that "judging from his antecedents" he was well "qualified for the post,"[151] and so he proved to be. Sam Silver remained as chairman of the board, with Gray eventually taking over in his later years. Some accounts have the firm merging with Thomas Hancock's rubber and gutta-percha business at Smithfield at this time, but there is no mention of this in the company minutes.[152] Likewise, a claim that George Henderson was managing director of Silver's from this time until 1886 also has no basis in fact.[153]

The board must have been delighted with their new recruit. Gray proved to be a shrewd, intelligent businessman who was not afraid to take calculated risks to advance the company's interests. And his gambles were successful. He was also to prove a ruthless class warrior when the company's interests and those of the employing class as a whole demanded it. These interests coincided perfectly with his own, for he became a major shareholder in the firm and if not in the front rank of Britain's wealthy, he was at least in its second. According to the contemporary socialist press, Gray had one thousand shares in the company at the time of the strike in 1889.[154] We know little about him from the terse company records, and he eschewed personal publicity. He appears to have worked his way up from the shop floor, whether at Silver's or in some other firm it is impossible to say. A number of newspaper articles describe him as an engineer,[155] so it is possible that he began his working life as a fitter (a machinist in American terms) rather than as a middle-class professional engineer. It was to this presumed early personal blue-collar history, perhaps, that Gray owed his relish for bare-knuckle industrial relations fighting. Strike committee activist Fred Ling told a factory-gate meeting in 1889 that men like Gray "who had risen from the ranks were the worst tyrants."[156] Gray appointed his five sons as departmental managers in the Silvertown Works and, nepotism or not, they proved themselves capable organizers and businessmen. William Gray, for instance, oversaw the firm's contract for the installation of electric street lighting of Brussels in 1894.[157] Christian Gray was instrumental in the recruitment of scab labor during the 1889 strike, and Robert K. Gray took over as managing director from his father toward the end of the century.[158] Another son, Matthew Hamilton Gray, was a prominent member of the Institute of Mining and Metallurgy[159] and a key professional engineer at the Silvertown Works.

Matthew Gray *père* proved himself a phlegmatic and ruthless man during the 1889 strike. If we can say "like father, like son" he slept easy at night. A reporter for the *Essex Standard* interviewed Gray's son Chris at Colchester during the 1889 strike and described him as "a man in the prime of life, pleasant, and good-humoured, inclined to be reticent, but certainly bearing no outward signs of any particular worry or anxiety."[160] Pleasant or not in personal life, Matthew Gray and his sons were brutally inflexible in their resolve to win the 1889 dispute, and would brook no arbitration or compromise. Gray epitomized what Marx had in mind when he quipped, "While the miser is merely a capitalist gone mad, the capitalist is a rational miser."[161] Silver's was in business to make profits, nothing more and nothing less, and Gray was determined to maximize them whatever the cost to his employees. Moreover, Gray must have been under great pressure from the ruling class as a whole not to yield and thus open the floodgates to a surging tide of wages demands and unionization across British industry.

Diverse Manufactures

From the start, Silver's was possessed by a relentless urge to expand, take over, renew, and diversify. By the time the company was floated in 1864, it had branched out far beyond waterproofing into a variety of rubber and rubber-based products. These included ebonite, a very hard form of rubber that was in great demand for domestic articles such as combs and pens, and for industrial applications such as electrical insulators for which we use hard synthetic plastics today. Silver's also used ebonite to make acid pumps, batteries, telegraph insulators, soda-water corks, and musical instruments such as bassoons, clarinets, oboes, and piccolos. Indeed, the firm's range of products was astonishing and also included rubber railway buffers, valves, hose and tubing, washers, electrical batteries,[162] electric motors and generators, switchgear and electrical instruments, electric lighting systems,[163] tennis balls, and footballs—400,000 of the latter per season by 1900—and solid cycle and cart tires.[164] When Dunlop's lost their patent for pneumatic bicycle and vehicle tires, Silver's added those products to its repertoire, making its "Persan" brand at its French factory at Persan-Beaumont near Paris.[165] Much later, after merging with the Akron-based rubber giant B.F. Goodrich, the firm made "Silvertown" tires, although these were apparently manufactured in another factory at Burton-on-Trent and in Akron, Ohio. Silver's also used rubber's close cousin, gutta-percha, in enormous quantities. Unlike some other golf ball brands, for example, Silver's golf balls contained a core of gutta-percha in preference to rubber.[166] The star product in the Silver firmament, however, was insulated electrical and telegraph cable, which it began to make in 1864, initially using india-rubber insulation before switching to gutta-percha.[167]

A Web of Electricity, Steam, and Iron

By moving into cables, Silver's positioned itself to take advantage of the market in a nineteenth-century industry comparable in importance to the twenty-first-century telecommunications business. We take the telegraph for granted today, but in the nineteenth century, its invention was a gigantic leap forward in communications technology, comparable in the sweep of history with the invention of the wheel. Indeed, the electric telegraph has been described as "the Victorian Internet."[168] Until Samuel Morse perfected it in the 1830s and '40s, the transmission of information had always been dependent upon terrestrial modes of travel such as human runners, horses, elephants, donkeys, or ships. It took months for vital information to reach the other side of a continent or to the antipodes. The optical telegraph or semaphore, which dated from 1794, was cumbersome and dependent on daylight, fine weather, and unobstructed lines of sight. Using Morse's dot-and-dash code, messages sent along electrified copper cables could reliably reach any part of the world almost instantaneously, regardless of atmospheric conditions, terrain, intervening seas and oceans, seasons, or the diurnal cycle. In 1855, confounding the skeptics, Isambard Kingdom Brunel's mighty steamship the *Great Eastern* laid the first transatlantic cables from Ireland to North America. By the end of the nineteenth century, the globe was crisscrossed by over 200,000 miles of submarine cables in addition to those on dry land, and Silver's had manufactured perhaps a quarter of these.

The submarine cables were of immense geopolitical significance, in particular for the administration of the European colonial empires. For this reason, the construction, maintenance, and operation of the "All-Red Line" of undersea cables hooking up Britain's colonies to London was massively subsidized by the British government; a policy entrenched after the Indian Mutiny of 1857 had underlined the need for rapid communications in the far-flung empire.[169] As Daniel Headrick reminds us in his fine book *The Tentacles of Progress*, "The web of power that tied the colonial empires together was made of electricity as well as steam and iron."[170] The All-Red Line, it was boasted, only touched dry land in British possessions; the bulk of it was submerged below the seas. It is easy to forget in today's world of silicon chips and optical microfibers just how revolutionary the telegraph was. Even eighty-odd years after its invention, it was still imbued with an aura of wonder, as the following passage illustrates:

> In a large building near London Wall a well-lit room . . . is just getting into its stride. A steady clacking of typewriter keys, staccato drumming from queer electrical instruments, the plopping of leather cylinders falling from pneumatic tubes into wire cages compose the metallic medley that never ceases day or night. Over seventy men and women sit at desks, ranked row on row, bent and intent; for they are serving the great Atlantic cable that for three thousand two hundred miles lies like a swollen serpent on the bed of the ocean, while messages of wealth and ruin, of hope and despair, of friendly greeting and commercial agreement flash along the mysterious length of it.[171]

Many of the "queer electrical instruments" and the cables themselves would have been manufactured at Silvertown. Silver's was the preeminent British cable contractor, laying and manufacturing cables for a variety of British and foreign telegraph operating companies. The firm also invested heavily in these companies itself. By 1900, Silver's had laid 40,000 miles of ocean cable.[172] In 1887, the *Telegraphist* noted that Silver's had laid the 6,300-mile cable from Galveston, Texas, to Valparaiso in Chile; the 5,400-mile line from Cadiz in Spain, via the Canaries to Luanda in Africa; three other cables from Marseilles across the Mediterranean to Algiers; 1,700 miles of cable off the West Coast of North America; plus others across the Caspian Sea, and off the coasts of Florida and Canada.[173] Silver's had started to gear up the Silvertown Works for cable manufacture in 1864 and in 1867 was awarded its first cable-laying contract for the line from Key West to Havana for the Western Union Company. While Silver's manufactured the cable for this first contract, they chartered a specially fitted-out ex-Mediterranean fruit trade vessel, the SS *Dacia*, from the Bright Company to lay it. Encouraged by the success of the project, Silver's purchased the vessel three years later, along with the SS *International*, which was used immediately to lay new telegraph cable from England to the Channel Islands. In 1881, Silver's bought another ship, second only to the SS *Great Eastern* in size among cable-laying ships, and renamed her SS *Silvertown*. Four years later, they completed their fleet with the purchase of a smaller vessel, the SS *Buccaneer*, which they used primarily for maintenance work on cables in shallow ocean waters.[174] The firm even manufactured torpedoes and torpedo wire that the Royal Navy could use to defend the empire's global cable network.[175]

The Electrical Revolution

By the 1870s, the firm that had begun as a haberdashery was at the cutting edge of Victorian industrial technology. It had jumped from retail and petty commodity production to heavy industry. The first wave of Industrial Revolution was based initially on the stationary steam engine, and from the 1840s, efficient steam-powered railways enabled a second wave. In the 1880s, following the invention of the alternating current induction motor, a third quantum leap occurred, and Silver's was quick to exploit the opportunities opened up by the new electrical industry; indeed, it was a logical move given its presence in the electric telegraph business. Silver's began to manufacture electric motors and dynamos, along with a variety of precision electrical instruments and switchgear, electrical cables, and insulators. The same period also saw the emergence of domestic, industrial, and municipal electric lighting systems as reliable and safer alternatives to gas light. Again, Silver's was on hand to make and install such systems, as was the case for Brussels in 1894 and in the electrification of the tramways of British cities such as Glasgow. By the 1880s, Silver's had established itself as one of the world's premier rubber, electrical, and telegraph firms.

Business was very lucrative. In 1914, their aggregate subscribed capital (ASC) amounted to £1,150,000 (or around £654,350,000—or over $1 billion—in today's values. In comparison, for the same year the mean

ASC of 284 incorporated British electrical manufacturing companies was £170,000,[176] or around £96,730,000 in today's values.[177] Silver's had mutated into a high-tech industrial giant with few rivals in the specialized field of telegraph cables and the new electrical industry. The business required huge amounts of investment capital. The first three specialized ships alone cost the company £192,000 by 1881, or over 38 percent of its share capital. For the times, this was a vast sum; it would be worth £225 million today as a comparative share of GDP,[178] and this was over double the total mean ASC of other British electrical firms. Melanie McGrath was only half right when she wrote, "There never was any silver in Silvertown,"[179] for though the workers saw very little of it, Silvertown's factories and docks created enormous profits for the shareholders.

Few other companies were prepared to take the risks run by Silver's, or had the capital reserves to do so, which as A. A. Foster surmises, explains why the firm had few serious competitors either in Britain or overseas.[180] Given that contracts for cable laying came, in Matthew Gray's words, "in fits and starts," Silver's operated as a conventional shipowner between contracts, carrying cargoes of grain, sugar, and at times, coal. They were also prepared to accept bundles of shares in other telegraph companies in partial payment for laying their cables. They did so, for instance, in 1883 when they took £131,000 in debenture stock (certificates of loan or loan bonds) and £131,000 in fully paid-up shares in payment from a Spanish company for laying the line between Spain and the Canary Islands. In 1885, they accepted £75,000 in shares in the West Africa Telegraph Company for cable laid between Africa and Europe. Though this helped the company to get orders, it reduced Silver's working capital and when the price of raw materials skyrocketed just before the Great War, Silver's failed for the first time to pay a dividend to shareholders.

This was unusual, however. In 1875, the firm's share capital stood at £470,000, although this was reduced because of buying into the West Coast of America Telegraph Company. Nevertheless, as Foster tells us, Silver's was "consistently profitable until 1910," regularly paying its shareholders a 10 percent dividend.[181] The firm's February 1888 general meeting, for instance, declared a tax-free dividend of ten shillings a share, approximately £43.40 in 2010 values using the retail price index as a guide, or £211 based on average earnings.[182] The half-yearly meeting of July in the same year resolved that "an interim dividend of 5 percent, or ten shillings a share, tax free, payable on or after 20th inst., be now declared."[183] The three-month strike in 1889 did not dam the river of profits, and the same was true of the even longer engineers' strike of 1897–98.

Silver's was always prepared to be bold and fortune favored them. In an era that preached the virtues of the free market, the colossal cable-laying undertakings had been carried out by private enterprise.[184] The overseas telegraph firms' operations were, however, heavily subsidized by the British government for the strategic reasons sketched in above. When combined with the firm's willingness to take great risks, the result was a profit bonanza, which continued even during the darkest days of the 1890s depression.

The Gutta-percha Shed

Today few people, perhaps except for dentists and historians, have heard of gutta-percha, but in Victorian times, it was a household word. Used in a myriad of domestic and industrial applications, it was the Victorians' plastic. A cousin of india- or hevea-rubber, it is derived from the thick sap of certain Southeast Asian trees, most notably the taban, or *Pallaquium gutta*, which grows wild in the tropical rainforests. The Malays had long used it for whips, and knife and tool handles, but for many years their European conquerors regarded it as merely an inferior form of inelastic rubber. In time its positive qualities became apparent. Workable when soaked in hot water, it rapidly hardened at normal temperatures and was extremely water-resistant. It was highly prized in the electrical and tele-graphs industry, where its superior qualities as an insulator, impermeable in salt and fresh water, saw it replace india-rubber, particularly for sub-marine cables.[185]

Harvested under primitive conditions in the jungles and often riddled with impurities, gutta-percha landed on the docks at Silvertown after a long ocean voyage from Singapore. At Silvertown "in a dark shed," wrote a journalist from the *Standard* who visited the works in 1869, one could "observe large heaps of what looks like a compound of cork and wood. That is gutta-percha in its natural condition."[186] In other warehouses, great coils of copper and iron wires were stored, awaiting their marriage with gutta-percha. Other storehouses contained bales of Indian jute and calico, and large barrels of sticky black tar, brought in from the nearby Beckton and Silvertown gasworks. "Leaving the dark shed," continued the man from the *Standard*, "we are introduced to an ugly machine that, whizzing round in a very spiteful manner, is cutting up the gutta-per-cha into shreds, and it looks very much as if it would like to perform the same operation on any incautious visitor who came within range of its teeth."[187] The gutta-percha, which usually arrived in the factory in a filthy condition, was then masticated, heated, and strained in a number of great machines and water baths until it reached the strict levels of purity demanded by the industry.

Brute Power and Precision Machines

The *Standard* reporter was not technically minded. Had he been so, he would have perhaps made the point that Silver's was among the most high-tech of industries in the world. By 1887, the factory had expanded from the original modest one-acre property, to take up fifteen acres, ten of them covered by the firm's workshops, the rest occupied by storage yards, wharves, and the like. Put another way, the factory occupied a site roughly equivalent in size to about seven soccer fields, or an area with a perimeter of 800 by 800 meters, or almost 2,700 by 2,700 feet. At night, it blazed with incandescent lights. Factories, streets, and houses in British cities at the time were gas-lit, but from 1885 Silver's was illuminated entirely by electric light, "the installation being one of the finest private ones in England" as a writer for the *Telegraphist* observed at the time.[188] The system initially consisted of 140 arc lights and 1,300 incandescent lamps of between 2,000 and 3,000 candlepower each.[189] With no electrical generation and distribution grid in England at the time, the electricity was generated in Silver's own on-site powerhouse. Moreover, all of the generating plant, switchgear, cables, instruments, and fittings had been made on-site in the company's own workshops and installed by their own engineering crews. The era of outsourcing, lean production, and "just-in-time" methods lay far in the future. However, though Silver's used electricity to a greater degree than most manufacturers, the works still depended heavily on coal-fired steam power, provided in 1887 by 47 steam engines and 31 Lancashire boilers, a formidable array of industrial firepower charged by an army of stokers.[190] The generating plant, too, relied on coal-fired boilers.

Such was the brute force motor power of the factory, but this only gives us a partial picture of Silver's capabilities, for this was also a precision electrical engineering works as well as a mass producer of simpler industrial and domestic goods. Cocooned from the gathering economic depression by government subsidies and riding the crest of the telecommunications wave though Silver's was, the firm could not afford to sell substandard telegraphic and electrical equipment if it wished to continue

in business for the long haul. Silver's might have been the biggest company in the business, but slipshod work would mean they would lose
market share to their competitors, which included the smaller W. T.
Henley's just downriver at North Woolwich. Strict quality control was a
religion in the high-tech temple of the Silvertown Works; products were
laboriously tested and retested to ensure the highest standards. Thus,
noted the *Telegraphist* in 1887:

> In all parts of the world the word "Silvertown" is accepted as a guaran-
> tee of good sound workmanship. The success of the Company may be
> traced to the scrupulous care with which every article manufactured is
> examined and tested before being sent out of the works.[191]

And so it was. "Scrupulous care" started with the quality of the copper
wire for the cables, which had to be at least 96 percent pure; the greater
the purity the greater the conductivity of the finished cables, essential for
the clear transmission of messages over the wires. The copper arrived
at the works in great coils, much of it from the mines of Cornwall and
West Cork via the smelters of Swansea. Inside Silver's, the copper coils
were mounted on massive spindles and twisted together, seven strands at
a time, into thick cables on powerful machines of the firm's own design
and manufacture. Next, the cables were drawn repeatedly through baths
of heated and liquidized gutta-percha and Stockholm tar to apply several coats of this mixture, according to specifications, and using apparatus
patented by Silver's.[192] The gutta-percha was essential protection against
leakage of electricity and input of seawater, ordinary rubber having been
found to deteriorate too quickly on the deep ocean beds. While the gutta-
percha was still pliant, the cables were drawn through a die and any air
bubbles were squeezed out in steam-jacketed cylinders. The coating had
to be uniform and was minutely inspected for any breaks or holes that
would impede transmission. Next, because the gutta-percha was still pli-
able and might deform under pressure or handling, the cables were drawn
through great baths of refrigerated water worked by horizontal engines
The two-mile-long lengths of cable cores were then finished and were
again wound mechanically onto large bobbins or calendars driven by powerful engines. They were then retested electrically with delicate reflecting
galvanometers of Sir William Thomson's design in yet another tank room
where the water was kept at a constant 75 degrees Fahrenheit. Afterward,
they were wound with several layers of jute and again tested before being
tightly wound again with iron wire on specially built machines. Finally,

the cables were coated with a cold, sticky, tar-based composition originating in the nearby gasworks, and then tightly wrapped in hempen tapes or
cords. The finished cables, which resembled enormous thick black snakes,
were then ready to be laid on the ocean floor, protected against rocks and
other submarine hazards by the multiple layers of cords, pitch, and iron
wire. They were stored as two-mile lengths in huge cylindrical tanks and
transferred as needed to similar tanks aboard the company's fleet of ships,
which between them could carry 12,000 tons of cable, sufficient to stretch
out for a distance of roughly 11,000 nautical miles across the ocean beds.

Laying the Cables

Nautical cable laying was a huge undertaking that had confounded the
skeptical critics. The cables spanned the wide oceans, and the first transatlantic cable, laid in 1857, was 1,852 miles long and weighed 2,000 tons.[193]
The lengths of cable lying in the vessels' holds were spliced together
mechanically aboard ship, the machines equipped with a special braking
mechanism to prevent the cable from being payed out too quickly or slowly
on the turbulent ocean and uneven sea floor. The enormity of the cable-
laying task is brought home when it is borne in mind that it took the cable
three hours to sink to the ocean floor at a depth of 2,000 fathoms. If the
ship was traveling at nine knots, the distance from the vessel to the point
at which the cable reached the bottom was twenty-seven nautical miles.[194]
At either end of the sea cables, on dry land such as at Newfoundland and
Waterville in Ireland, sat the cable stations, which housed sophisticated
electrical instruments, many of them manufactured at Silvertown, operated
by small armies of operators. The telegraphists and maintenance workers
at Waterville were better looked after than their Silvertown counterparts.
Their solid houses stand to this day in good repair and sit in pleasant
gardens on the Kerry coast. According to knowledgeable locals, even
when they were first built the houses boasted indoor baths and bathrooms.
Remarkably, all of the machinery needed to produce this huge range of
cables and other goods was itself crafted in the company's extensive state-
of-the-art carpenters', instrument makers', and engineers' workshops.[195]
The firm was a model of vertical and horizontal integration.

In 1889, the Silvertown Works was a showcase of British industry.
Business was booming, defying the generally depressed state of the economy. Silver's was a radically innovative firm, an early player in the electrical
revolution that was beginning to transform the face of British industry.

Silver's at this stage was not, of course, run on Fordist lines, but the logic of mass production was implicit in the factory's operations. Silver's was quick to seize on new American mass production techniques in the closing years of the century. The firm steadily generated fabulous riches for its seventy-two shareholders, many of them luminaries of the British political establishment, with which Silver's enjoyed synergic bonds. Paradoxically, the only year in which the firm failed to make a profit was 1911, during the expansive phase of a new long wave of capitalism (roughly 1896–1919),[196] a year when people the Cockneys would have thought of as "toffs" rioted outside City banks in their greed to buy shares in rubber companies.[197] The price of raw rubber had rocketed from three shillings and ten pence a pound to twelve and eleven pence, rising 277.17 percent, and the firm made a net loss of £39,457[198]—the equivalent of £3.1 million today using the retail price index, or £25.8 million as a share of GDP.[199] The soaring price of a commodity crucial to the Silvertown Works was temporarily crippling, but the company had enough "fat" to ride out the lean year and profit rates were restored thereafter when the new plantations in Asia came onstream and rubber prices tumbled. Nor did the big strikes significantly affect the bonanza. In 1889, the year of the first great strike, Silver's made a net profit of almost £58,000—the equivalent today of £4.98 million using the retail price index as a guide, or £59.8 million as a share of GDP.[200] Adding just over £25,000 brought forward and deducting an interim dividend of £20,800 paid in July of that year, there remained a disposable balance of slightly more than £62,000, a tidy sum for the times.[201]

Much of the credit for Silver's remarkable expansion was due to Matthew Gray, who had proved to be an innovative and forward-looking manager. His factory had come into its own at the zenith of the Empire, and was riding the crest of the wave of the electrical revolution. Not only did Britannia rule the waves, she also ruled the greatest empire in history, in part due to the girdle of wires stretched under the seas, connecting Whitehall and the India Office with the remotest corners of Victoria's realm. Silver's was strategically crucial to the entire imperial enterprise, a fact that cannot have been lost on Lord Salisbury's Tory administration. However, this glittering success came at a steep price for the firm's workers.

IV.
Great Sacrifice, Great Barbarism
❖❖❖

> The growth of civilization means the growth of
> towns and the growth of towns means, at present,
> a terrible sacrifice of human life.[202]
> —*THE TIMES,* 8 October 1868

> One is forced to conclude that the Abyss is literally
> a huge man-killing machine.[203]
> —JACK LONDON

> To be born English is to win first prize in the
> lottery of life.[204]
> —CECIL RHODES

SAMUEL SILVER'S CATHEDRAL of industry sat on the outer eastern edge of a colossal city. Victorian London was a city of great enterprise, industry, culture, and invention. As Roy Porter reminds us, "The nineteenth century acknowledged London as the centre of things: the creation in 1884 of the Greenwich Meridian, marked by a brass rail inlaid in concrete, crowned it as the prime meridian—zero degrees longitude— whence all the continents spread out east and west."[205] Smoky, teeming, vibrant, and creative, it was the largest and richest capital city in history. Its great industries were fed by an expanding empire, which was protected by the world's most powerful navy and armies of Highlanders, Tommies, Askaris, and Sepoys. In turn, these industries exported their diverse wares to the world. London's wonders eclipsed those of the ancient world: powerful steam locomotives puffed to the corners of the British Isles; iron steamships plowed the dirty Thames to unload their cargoes of spices, metals and ores, fruits, meat, tea, wool, indigo, cocoa, timber, grains, coffee, sugar, cotton, ivory, coal, fish, rubber, and whatnot on the quays of its enormous artificial dock basins. The City of London's banks were stacked with piles of gold and silver coins, ingots, and currency notes—for London was the banking and financial capital of the world. The city's poets, novelists, composers, and artists formed a glittering constellation of talent. Its central streets were lined with opera houses, art galleries, teaching hospitals, libraries, and universities. At the Royal Botanic Gardens in Kew, Joseph Hooker and his team of botanists worked in tandem with the government to nourish the seeds of future plantation plenty, including the rubber so important at Silver's Works. Its philosophers, scientists, inventors, medical men, and engineers were in the vanguard of progress and knowledge. The great metropolis was in "real time" communication with the remotest reaches of the Empire via an immense girdle of submarine and aerial telegraph wires, many of them spooled out by Silver's customized ships. Who could not but marvel at this great city in the valley of the Thames? In 1889, Silver's great works, the most advanced of their kind, epitomized the marvel that was Victorian industry. And yet there was a chill darkness at the heart of all this wonder and bounty: the somber contradiction between Victorian London's splendid material wealth and high culture on the one hand, and a barbarous system of industrial and social organization on the other.

Think of the Darkness

Bertolt Brecht's words "Think of the darkness and the bitter weather / The cries of pain which echo round this world,"[206] were written about this city in which even beggars were held to ransom. "The capital," in the words of the economic historians Ball and Sunderland, "was like Wilde's Dorian Gray. The proud architectural and cultural face of Georgian, Victorian, and Edwardian London existed because of the hidden picture that was the inner suburban industrial districts and the poverty associated with them."[207] William Cobbett cursed it as "the Great Wen"[208] even before its period of unparalleled expansion, and John Ruskin was horrified by "the great foul city of London . . . rattling, growling, smoking, stinking— a ghastly heap of fermenting brickwork, pouring out poison at every pore."[209] The city had experienced explosive unplanned growth during

Victoria's reign. It was, Patrick Geddes later wrote, a "polypus"—"a vast irregular growth without previous parallel in the world of life—perhaps likest to the spreading design of a great coral reef,"[210] but, we might add, quite without the purity of those vast natural calcareous accretions. There were two Londons, Asa Briggs reminds us: "one dark and mysterious, the other dazzling and ostentatious."[211] William Crook remarked that the same sun, which never set on the Empire, never rose in the dark alleys of the East End.[212] From the security of a Hansom cab, Jack London shuddered at the scenes where "as far as I could see were the solid walls of brick, the slimy pavements, and the screaming streets,"[213] from whence "strange, vagrant odours came drifting along the greasy wind, and the rain, when it falls, is more like grease than water from heaven."[214] When London inquired about how to get there, his friends, comfortable in the West End, replied: "'But we know nothing of the East End. It is over there, somewhere.' And they waved their hands vaguely in the direction where the sun on rare occasions may be seen to rise."[215] In this city, the classes were largely segregated into zones every bit as sharply delineated as those in colonies with a color bar.

What Walter Benjamin wrote of class society in general was epitomized by the city on the Thames:

> The cultural heritage is part and parcel of a lineage which he [the historical materialist] cannot contemplate without horror. It owes its existence not only to the toil of the great geniuses, who created it, but also to the nameless drudgery of its contemporaries. *There has never been a document of culture which is not simultaneously one of barbarism.*[216]

It has always been so with cities in class society. The intellectual brilliance of ancient Athens, the pomp and riches of ancient Rome, and the wonders of Angkor, the greatest city of antiquity, were all founded on the "nameless drudgery" of the slaves. "Even in fabled Atlantis / The night the ocean engulfed it / The drowning still bawled for their slaves," wrote Brecht.[217] As in ancient Athens, Angkor, or Brecht's Atlantis, so in Victorian London: the wealth of the few depended on the unceasing and ill-rewarded toil and misery of the many. Sensitive middle- and upper-class Victorians were uncomfortable with the dark knowledge of the East End lurking just downriver but most chose to ignore it, or justified it in one way or another if confronted by its existence. As Brecht's Jonathan Peachum put it, "I discovered that though the rich of this earth find no difficulty in creating misery, they can't bear to see it."[218] Others had "a mission / To purge us of the seven deadly sins," the recipients of middle-class "good works" might have noted.[219] Beatrice Webb was not wide of the mark when she declared that much of the middle-class "social work" in the London slums was "a secularized version of Christian guilt and atonement."[220] Less altruistic was the trade in "misery tourism" in which toffs descended on the East End to experience a frisson of dirt and poverty firsthand, or to pay for "a bit of rough" with a Cockney girl or boy prostitute. In 1884, the *"British Weekly* Commissioners"* reported one egregious example of slumming:

> A noble lord, who shall remain nameless, created quite a sensation last season in a West End drawing-room. "Only think," he said, "I've actually seen a woman making a match-box!"[221]

Nor should we overlook the brutal origins of much of the cargo landed on the London quayside. This was the era of "high imperialism," a time in which British industry and commerce sank a deep economic taproot into the colonial and semi-colonial soil.[222] Much of the vast flow of tropical commodities into London depended on super-exploited colonial labor. Even after the formal abolition of slavery by the British Parliament in 1833, British industry depended on commodities produced by slave labor in countries outside of the Empire. This was particularly true of sugar, cotton, sisal, and indigo from the Americas. The rubber for Silver's factory, too, was extracted from the forests of Africa and Latin America by half-starved Brazilian *seringueiros* and coerced indigenous collectors. Later, it was harvested by indentured coolie plantation labor.[223]

A Palace in the Mud

London's contradictions manifested themselves geographically in the contrast between the opulent West End and the penurious East End, (though other great pockets of poverty also existed elsewhere in the metropolis). A short journey from the City, wrote Jack London, brought one to a region that was "one unending slum."[224] By late-Victorian times, this vast benighted area stretched on beyond "traditional London" to the borough of West Ham, where urbanization and industrialization were occurring at fantastic speed. Nowhere was this more so than at Silvertown in the south of the borough where Samuel Silver's palace of industry rose from the Thames mud, dwarfing the slums around it, its cavernous machine halls echoing with the throb of huge engines, the sky blackened with its reeking smoke. In Silvertown, great culture and invention coexisted in counterpoint to great barbarism and wretchedness. The sacrifice of which the *Times* writer wrote was made on the altar of the god of profit: the victims were the workers whose nameless drudgery created "the glory of England." Silver's management and shareholders would have applauded Cecil Rhodes's boast that "to be born an Englishman is to win first place in God's lottery." Silver's employees might have begged to differ; the dice were loaded against them and there was a huge gulf between Silver's high-tech factory and its bleak surroundings.

The electric lights of this industrial Taj Mahal blazed out over a bleak workers' suburb that had sprung up with the marsh weeds. Silver's had sunk enormous sums of capital and expertise into the works, but there was little money to spare for the laborers. It was a case in point of what Edward Aveling and Eleanor Marx had meant when they wrote, the "factory-chimnies [*sic*] that Radical politicians call 'the glory of England' are in truth, the curse of England."[225] By 1889, a forest of such chimneys rose over Silvertown, the smoke blackening the sky and coating the workers' hovels in layers of grime. The Cockneys craved bright colors and flowers because of the grey monotony of their world; the only patch of open green space between Silvertown and North Woolwich was the Royal Victoria Gardens. The Thames flowed past largely hidden behind the embankment and a wall of factories. Decades later, the Silvertown writer Melanie McGrath observed that the Victoria Gardens were "the only place to the east of the Lea, aside from Lyle Park, where there is an unimpeded view of the river water."[226] As for the River Lea, there were no fish to catch in its waters, only diseases.

The lives of the Silvertown laborers were blighted by chronic destitution and systemic violence. In Queen Victoria's reign, 32 percent of Londoners lived below the poverty line. Old age—should one live that long—would prove a nightmarish coda to a life of grinding poverty. One-third of the weekly wage earners of England died destitute or on Poor Law relief,[227] and the vast majority of London's aged paupers—the "submerged tenth"—lived in the East End.[228] For many, old age meant incarceration in the dreaded "spike"—the workhouse—an institution that dated back to medieval times. In 1885, the social reformer Charles Booth estimated that 35 percent of the population of the East End was destitute.[229] Will Thorne sorrowed and raged over the "pitiable sight" of "poor, ill-clothed children" shivering in the biting winter wind on West Ham's Barking Road.[230] According to Jack London, 55 percent of East London's children died by their fifth year.[231] In Silvertown almost one in ten died in infancy. The figures point to a yearly holocaust of Cockney children.

Silvertown: An End-of-the-World Place

By all accounts, Silvertown was a place apart. Although only six miles downstream from the Pool of London, it had—and in some respects still has—an air of isolation, strangeness, and remoteness. This was due, the *Daily News* noted, to its being "virtually an island because of the docks and the river." It was an ugly place. "Its dreariness cannot be denied, though when the weather is very favourable there are some admirable views to be obtained beyond the river of the hospital at Greenwich, the arsenal at Woolwich, and . . . Shooter's Hill."[232] For Eleanor Marx, who came to know Silvertown well during the 1889 strike, it was an "end-of-the-world place,"[233] though she passionately defended the honor and interests of its inhabitants. A 1907 study of West Ham reported that Silvertown was "distinct in character" from the rest of the borough: "a large area with few inhabitants" because a "great deal of space is used for industrial purposes." The West Ham socialist councilor Joe Terrett has left us a grim pen portrait of Silvertown at the turn of the nineteenth century:

> In the south of the borough are Victoria and Albert Docks . . . and beyond that is the industrial district of Silvertown with its collection of immense factories and wharves fronting on the River Thames—a more desolate region, contrasted with which St. Helens or Widnes seem beautiful townships by comparison. The atmosphere is blackened with the noxious fumes of chemicals, and the stench of bone-manure and soapworks, and the only sounds are the shriek of railway engines and the mournful foghorn toots of the steamboats coming up the river.[234]

The workers' houses occupied a central strip, close by the factories, "interrupted by the graving dock" observed the Fabians Howarth and Wilson,[235] and hemmed in by the marsh and river. Today, there is little to remind us of the past in Silvertown. Part of the suburb was torn down in 1912 when work began on the King George V Dock, and included the local Catholic church, whose "tall spire [was] visible to all the ships" plying the river.[236] More of it was flattened by an explosion in a local explosives factory in 1917, and the area is said to have been so severely bombed during the Blitz that the old bonds of community largely perished along with the dead. What Hitler failed to achieve, slum clearance finished.

"A Disgrace to Civilization"

During Victorian and Edwardian times, many of West Ham's residents were casual laborers, picked up if they were lucky at the dock or factory gate for a day's work. Permanent workers—and it must be owned that much of Silver's workforce was in this category—were known locally as "staid men."[237] As for the employers, wrote Dr. Pagenstecher, "most ... who draw their wealth from the teeming factories have left the neighbourhood to dwell in more fashionable quarters,"[238] a fact confirmed by Alderman Terrett.[239] This was in sharp contrast to the custom in the older East End, where the small employers lived close to their workshops—and their workers. Silver's head offices were located in Cannon Street in the City, and managing director Matthew Gray lived across the river in Kent's leafy Lessness Park,[240] a world away from Silvertown's mud, smoke, and smells. The managers would have made their way to the works first-class by means of the railway, which ran through Silvertown to North Woolwich, and it is not likely that they paid the suburb itself much attention. It was a place to hurry through, shudder at, and forget. The famous Australian socialist Frank Anstey, who was born in Silvertown, might have recalled that there were no "silvertails" in Silvertown!

The residential streets and connecting roads of Silvertown were unsealed tracks laid out on soft alluvial mud, up to ten feet below the Thames high water mark. They were often deeply plowed up by carts, making them "so impassable in bad weather that the people cannot avail themselves of their privileges," wrote a reporter in 1881. He concluded that "the conditions of the waste lands, and the rude [illegible, but possibly tracks] that are called roads are a disgrace to ... civilization."[241] They were not the only disgrace. Silvertown had sprouted up like mushrooms after rain, a testament to the Victorian authorities' laissez-faire indifference to town planning and the appetite for profit of those who controlled them. In 1857, Charles Dickens complained that because Silvertown lay outside of the City of London's jurisdiction, town planning regulations did not apply: the inhabitants were free "to possess new streets of houses without drains, roads, gas or pavement."[242] Nor did things improve much during the next few decades. Silvertown was out of sight and out of mind. "Who is responsible?" asked the *Daily News* rhetorically, and answered, "What is everybody's business is nobody's business."[243] In that laissez-faire age mud, disease, death, ignorance, and poverty were individual problems, not the concern of society as a whole. For Herbert Spencer, the father of Social Darwinism and the celebrity philosopher of his times, it all came down to biology: human society was governed by the law of the "survival of the fittest."[244] The poor deserved their fate and attempts to change their conditions of life and work flew in the face of natural selection, the medieval dogma of Fate recast as "science" in an industrial age. As Karl Marx observed, "Capital ... is reckless as regards illness or premature death of the workers, unless forced to pay heed to these matters, forced by social compulsion."[245] There was precious little of such compulsion in Queen Victoria's Britain. The authorities reserved compulsion for the dragooned and maltreated poor.

By all accounts, Silvertown stank, even in the nostrils of Londoners accustomed to the stench of an atmosphere containing "dust loaded with fecal matter, hot air, sewer gases, and smoke," which metastasized into the infamous London fog. Sometimes of a "bottle-green color, sometimes pea-soup yellow," the smog included "fuliginous matter" such as ammonium sulfate, which "crystallized on window-panes in tree-like patterns."[246] Grace Foakes, a docker's daughter from Wapping, recalls, "It is hard to imagine what a London fog was like" at the turn of the nineteenth century when

> everyone had a coal fire, factories sent out great clouds of sooty grime, ships and tugs were driven by steam, their funnels belching out great quantities of thick black smoke. Winter would bring to the river such fogs as you do not see today. The air was so thick and yellow that you could not see where you were going . . . [and] big black pieces of soot would settle everywhere.[247]

Even half a century later, "unliftable black smog" reduced visibility along Silvertown's "Sugar Mile" to "a mere foot," and the passenger ferry between North Woolwich and the Kent shore sometimes drifted blindly, narrowly avoiding collisions with seagoing vessels.[248] The stench of Silvertown's lanes must have been stomach turning, but there was no collective will or power to change it—that was only to come later with the development of working-class political organization and the takeover of West Ham's local government by socialists such as Thorne and Terrett. Otherwise, the authorities acted only when they could no longer avoid doing so, either from embarrassment or fear of the spread of contagion from the poor to the rich.

Islands of Liquid Filth

In 1858, the "Great Stink" and associated cholera epidemics finally forced the Disraeli government to confront London's drainage and public health problems. By 1865, the celebrated engineer Joseph Bazalgette had constructed huge connector sewers and pumping stations to channel the city's sewage to outfalls at Beckton and Crossness. Silvertown did not benefit from Bazalgette's visionary scheme, however, even though the Beckton outfall was close by, for at the time West Ham lay beyond the boundaries of Greater London. Even after 1893, when most of West Ham was connected to the northern London outfall sanitary sewer, Silvertown's domestic wastes still ran straight into ditches alongside the residential streets or rotted in cesspools.[249] Indeed, as late as 1900, its sewage flowed into the marsh and street gutters. In that same year, Archer Crouch wrote that "the habitable area [of Silvertown] consists of islands of liquid filth, surrounded by stagnant dikes."[250] The suburb was also periodically flooded with salt water when high tides and heavy rains caused the Thames to overflow the embankment. One doctor wore sea-boots to visit his patients. Even in "normal" times, noted the *Daily News*, the residents waded in mud and water in rain, or were "smothered in dust" when it was dry and windy.[251] Duncan Barrett and Nuala Calvi's book on Silvertown in later times records the dismal effects of the great flood of January 1953:

> At one a.m. the watchman at North Woolwich Pier reported that the Thames had reached a dangerous level. Less than an hour later, six feet of surplus water was spilling out of the Royal Docks and onto the streets of Silvertown, where it was flushed into the local sewers and back up into the lower lying neighbourhoods of Custom House and Tidal Basin. . . . On Monday morning, after much pumping from the local fire brigade, the waters had receded. But they left a carpet of thick black mud on the streets, and in the downstairs rooms of many people's houses. The local residents mopped their ruined homes down and dragged what little furniture they owned out onto the streets, rinsing it with buckets of water and trying to avoid the rats that had been washed up from the sewers.[252]

Seventy or eighty years earlier, such floods were even more devastating, and the means of ameliorating them much more primitive.

Dust Heaps for the City's Rubbish

Much of the stench of Silvertown came from the smoke and fumes of the factories. As a Newham History Workshop booklet observes, nineteenth-century West Ham—the borough of which Silvertown forms a part—"unlike London . . . had no laws controlling offensive trades."[253] Alderman Terrett resented his borough being "the dust-heap on which the metropolis shoots its rubbish,"[254] but the situation was not new. East London had always been a dumping ground for the wastes of noxious industry, and three hundred years earlier the economist Sir William Petty had shuddered at the "fumes, steams and stinks of the whole easterly pile."[255] What was new was the scale of the pollution; the air of Victorian London was fouled with "soot and tarry hydrocarbons," twenty-four tons of which were dumped every week on each square mile.[256] The polluting heavy chemical factories of West Ham were concentrated in Silvertown and nearby suburbs, the lighter ones in the north with the exception of the great railway workshops. The smoke of the heavy chemical industries contributed to the thick green "London Particular" fogs,[257] which often blanketed Silvertown. One dark day in 1860, lost in the fog, the unfortunate Mr. Talbot, the manager of the Silvertown creosote works, lost his way, slipped on the slimy dockside cobbles, fell into the water and drowned.[258] He was not the first or the last to do so—many dockers and seamen perished in this way[259]—but nothing was done to curb the factories' foul breath or the exhalations from domestic coal fires. Elsewhere in London, the smog was said to "grip the throat and set the eyes watering,"[260] but in Silvertown it literally burned the linings of throats and lungs. A 1907 account reported that "the inhabitants of Silvertown complain greatly of the fumes and smells from some of the factories," and that the emissions were so caustic that they corroded machinery in local factories.[261] Silver's contributed mightily to the smoky pall, its dozens of great furnaces belching clouds of smoke and smuts. The rubber vulcanizing process at Silver's also discharged sulfur dioxide and hydrogen sulfide, the latter known to schoolchildren as the rotten-egg gas in stink bombs.

By 1857, wrote Charles Dickens, Silvertown had become "quite a refuge for offensive trade establishments turned out of town; those of the oil-boilers, gut-spinners, varnish-makers, printers' ink-makers, and the like."[262] Other firms produced creosote, naphtha, and other coal-tar products. Odam's chemical manure works, Silvertown's second-oldest factory, manufactured nitrates, phosphates, and superphosphates from the corpses of diseased cattle, a business that dated from the rinderpest epidemic of 1866, when thousands of infected beasts were herded to the knackery for slaughter, a throwback to a London City ordinance of 1371.[263] The horror of the rendering works is conveyed in Barrett and Calvi's description of John Knight's soap works as seen by the workers at the adjacent Tate & Lyle sugar refinery:

> From their vantage point on the top floor, the Blue Room girls could see the swarm of overfed bluebottles that buzzed constantly around the rotting pile [of dead animals]. Every so often, the poor men would appear whose job it was to shift the putrid mound, and as they shovelled away, rats measuring at least a foot long would come scurrying out, only to be chopped in half by the men and added to the top of the pile.[264]

On windy days coal dust blew from Cory & Son's on the foreshore, where "a battery of hydraulic cranes and a floating derrick unload[ed] coal directly into barges."[265] The anchored mother barge measured 270 by 90 feet and boasted its own plant to produce gas for lighting,[266] and Cory's handled two-thirds of the two-and-three-quarter-million tons of coal imported by sea each year into London.[267] Other local factories produced vitriol, asphalt, benzene, candles, jute bags, matches, cube sugar, syrup, and jams, their chimneys belching smoke and odors. "We used to have sweet and sour," recalled an old resident of adjacent North Woolwich; "Knight's would make you gag . . . then there was Tate and Lyle's sweet, sickly smell." Worse still, she would sometimes wake in the night and think there was a cesspool in her room.[268] Woe betide anyone unfortunate enough to fall into the Thames, for the pollution was "absolutely atrocious" and at low tide the banks would be strewn with "bones, horses' heads, and stuff like that," she recalled, because "they used to dump it straight in the river," causing a terrible smell.[269]

Fires and Accidents

Fires and explosions were relatively frequent occurrences in Silvertown's factories. One broke out at Silver's in 1864, just before the firm became a public company.[270] In April 1880, a "terrible" fire raced through the premises of Burt, Boulton & Hayward, manufacturers of tar, creosote, pitch, naphtha, and benzene,[271] killing eleven workmen before it was extinguished. The blast sounded like "a clap of thunder" to seamen aboard ships in nearby Victoria Dock,[272] and resulted from a blocked worm in the condenser of a creosote still.[273] Observers warned of further disasters and another "great fire" broke out at the Anglo-Continental Guano Works in early 1886,[274] and a "fire of enormous magnitude" swept through the Manhattan Wharf in Silvertown on the night of Thursday, 9 June 1887, igniting 80,000 gallons of oil stored in drums.[275] In August 1897, a thirty-two-year-old laborer named Joseph Gardiner was roasted to death in molten sulfur when a boiler blew up at Silver's. The explosion occurred when a fitter, acting on the instructions of his supervisor, was experimenting with pressures in the steam lines.[276] Less than two years later Keiller's Silvertown jam factory was partly destroyed by huge gas explosions,[277] though it was repaired and for decades afterward made the well-known "Branston" pickles and other preserves. Worst of all was the huge explosion at the Brunner Mond munitions factory on the night of 19 January 1917 when fifty tons of TNT ignited, causing around seventy deaths and hundreds of serious injuries. The blast sent tremors as far away as Burton-on-Trent in the Midlands and was considered the world's largest-ever peacetime explosion, greater than the immense explosion triggered by British army sappers at Messines Ridge on the Western Front in 1917.[278]

Clearly, these factories were hazardous places, even more so since the workers' houses were crammed next to them, as the Dockers' Union noted angrily after the 1917 explosion. As we shall see, there were many other hazards inside Silver's and the other factories. The *Standard* reporter cited above was fearful of the sharp teeth of the masticating machine that shredded the gutta-percha, and not without reason. Although there is no record of any visitor being maimed by this or similar machines at Silvertown, accidents must have been a common enough fate among the employees, and compensation was at the management's pleasure, not a legal right, and niggardly at that. The Factory Act of 1875 did prescribe a number of long-overdue reforms, but much of the machinery of the age was unguarded and a trap for the tired, unwary, inexperienced, or merely unfortunate worker.

One such worker was Henry Reed of Silvertown, a married man with four children, who lost four fingers and part of his right hand in an accident at Silver's Works in 1886. Six years later, "after a few words," Reed attacked Christian Gray in the street in Silvertown, wounding him in the throat. Afterward Reed fled into a field near the Silvertown railway line and slashed his own throat "to the bone from ear to ear with a razor." Shortly before, Chris Gray had given orders to foremen that Reed was not to be reemployed after he had allegedly gone on a drunken spree and absented himself from work.[279] Reed's wife, Henrietta, however, insisted that he had been off work due to illness, not the drink. The coroner recorded a verdict of "suicide while of unsound mind."[280] Given the bleak future facing the dismissed one-handed man, perhaps it was a rational decision, although it left his widow and children without hope of support.

Breakneck Growth of West Ham

This was the heyday of the Industrial Revolution, a helter-skelter era in which society was turned upside down in the upheavals of what Karl Polanyi called "the Great Transformation." The countryside was fast being depopulated, and the "surplus" population forced off the land was sucked into the ever-growing cities without heed to planning for social needs. Nowhere was this growth so fast and sustained as in London's Outer East, in particular the borough of West Ham, of which Silvertown was a key part. According to a collective of local historians, West Ham's growth between 1871 and 1901 was unique: "Such change over so short a period has probably never been experienced elsewhere, certainly not in Britain," they wrote.[281] "One hundred years ago in 1886," their pamphlet continues, "West Ham was the place where everyone wanted to be, or so the statistics tell us. People were moving into the area from every corner of England, from Scotland, Ireland, Wales, and from other parts of the globe."[282] As a result, West Ham became the largest industrial area in southern England.

After 1880, there were said to be so many immigrants in Silvertown that "English-born people were in a minority." There were Silvertown schools early in the twentieth century where all the teachers were Irish.[283] This was the childhood experience of the elderly lady mentioned earlier, whose cane-wielding teacher, Biddie O'Shea, was a Hibernian immigrant.[284] The little girl's favorite hymn was "Hail, glorious St Patrick," and the avuncular parish priest, known affectionately as "Father Fitz," was a Fitzpatrick from Ireland.[285] The Catholic parochial school may have been an improvement, however, on the leaky "wooden lean-to" classroom built by Silver's at midcentury to teach the Three R's during the week and the Gospels on Sunday to Protestant children.[286] As a number of writers have stressed, over half of London's dockers were either Irish-born or of recent Irish origin, Ben Tillett among them. The famous match girls of Bow were also largely Irish-born or of Irish extraction, as Louise Raw has demonstrated.[287] Unfortunately, anti-Irish feeling had deep roots in the East End,[288] a diversion from the class system that immiserated workers of all ethnic backgrounds and creeds. The Irish, Scottish Highland, and rural English diasporas provided able-bodied laborers for the East End's docks and factories. Poor food and hygiene would render their children and grandchildren less fit for the demands of industry; but no matter, there were more where they came from when they succumbed.

Rack Rents, Dry Rot, and Open Sewers

With no planning regulations, this flood of humanity was forced to find shelter as best it could. Wages were higher in London than the provinces, but the advantage was largely cancelled out by higher rents. House-rent, James Rogers informs us in his *History of English Labour*, was "the most formidable item in modern, the most trivial in ancient times."[289] Rents had risen steadily across Britain during the Industrial Revolution, and the poor were forced to pay a higher proportion of their incomes on rent for hovels than the affluent classes spent for their mansions.[290] Silvertown rents also appear to have been higher than in other parts of working-class London, but they did not usually translate into solid and salubrious housing.

The first houses in Silvertown were probably built by Samuel Silver in Twyford and Winchester Streets for favored employees, adjacent to the factory.[291] Some other employers later built solid houses at Silvertown for their workers, Howarth and Wilson note, with gardens, "bay windows, well-lighted stairs, and a grate as well as a copper in the wash-house." These houses were let at 7/6d per week in the early twentieth century, and were said to have rented out at 9 shillings ($1.73) before they were damaged by the big floods of 1888. Rents varied with the demand, and during the construction of the Albert Dock (opened in 1880) some houses in West Silvertown were let for up to 14 shillings ($2.70) a week.[292] The houses had originally been "built for the better sort of carpenters, steve-dores and dock gaffers," the social historian Roy Porter claims.[293]

Such dwellings, it must be stressed, were atypical and the rents were in any case beyond the reach of casual laborers and the unskilled work-ers in the local factories. They had to make do with what they could get, and as the years passed houses intended for five or six people became rookeries for dozens. Although the 1891 Public Health Act prescribed (an inadequate) 400 cubic feet of space per person (two hundred less than provided to soldiers in barracks), the law was massively flouted.[294] Many more houses were thrown up by the "hundreds of small jobbing builders who operated in the [West Ham] area," write Howarth and Wilson, adding that "the majority [of these] possessed neither experience nor financial stability."[295] Not surprisingly, much of the housing stock in the district was substandard, with floors rotting from the damp ground, and scanty natural light inside. The provision of damp courses and windows would have meant extra expenditure and less profit for the builders. Overcrowding was the norm, with several families occupying the four-room houses without gardens that were standard. Beds were often "nursed" on the "relay" system—that is, occupied in rotation by workers on different shifts—a sure recipe for the spread of disease. Howarth and Wilson had also heard of beds tucked away under staircases[296] in order to wring the maximum amount of space—and rents—from the little houses. Walter Drummond of the Stevedores' Union told a mass meeting during the Silver's strike that a nearby house had recently housed twenty-four people in four small rooms.[297] Today, Silvertown old-timers recall a time when up to six children slept in one bed.[298]

The majority of the district's houses lacked bathrooms and gardens, and were plagued with leaky roofs, rising damp, and vermin. Lavatories drained into cesspools or directly into the streets or marsh, and many tenants had to make do with earth closets. Charles Dickens, who visited in 1857, recorded: "The houses are run up at a cost of only £80, and are mere band-boxes placed on the ground."[299] Public facilities seem to have been little better. When it rained, the local schoolteacher was forced to unfurl an umbrella inside her classroom for protection against leaks.[300] What the Fabian investigator Mrs. Pember Reeves found about washing facilities in inner East London would also have applied to Silvertown: "In none of the bedrooms are any washing arrangements. The daily ablutions, as a rule, are confined to face and hands when each person comes downstairs." Children would receive a weekly bath in shared water, the mother might manage it once a fortnight, and the father would use the public baths when he could afford it. Moreover, "two pennyworth of soap may have to wash the clothes, scrub the floors, and wash the people of the family, for a week."[301]

Nor did things improve of their own accord as the nineteenth century drew to a close. In 1901, C. F. G. Masterman, who later became the Labour MP for West Ham, wrote that in the borough "I have myself seen during the past year the creation of hundreds of houses of so cheap and nasty a character that not only are they hideous to look upon, but are even at the start very doubtfully fit for human consumption—yet no-one raises a finger to prevent this state of things."[302] All this meant that the southern areas of West Ham, including Silvertown, contained "*perhaps the largest area of unbroken depression in East London.*"[303] When the conservative Mayor of West Ham proposed a resolution of sympathy for Queen Victoria's death, two ILP councilors, Scott and Godbold, moved the following addendum: "[The Council] desires to express its sympathy with all those families living in single rooms in West Ham who have members of their families dying of consumption."[304] Nothing much changed over the years. One old-timer recalls growing up in Silvertown in the 1930s and never seeing a bathroom until he was evacuated to Somerset during the Second World War. Hands and faces were washed in the kitchen of his parents' three-room flat, occupied by eight people.[305]

"Fever and Ague Abound"

The etiology of disease was imperfectly understood in Victorian times, but even if one subscribed to the "miasma" theory of infection, it was clear that Silvertown, built on marshy soil below river level with open sanitary sewers running alongside terrace rows, was a death trap. In 1857, Dickens noted that the ditches behind the terrace rows "are nothing more than cesspools."[306] Almost fifty years later, little had changed. Archer Crouch remarked that "fever and ague abound" in Silvertown.[307] In 1886, Thomas Drake, the Medical Officer of Health for West Ham, reported:

> The death rate for West Ham will compare very favourably with that of any other town of similar size and with the same class of population, which consists in a large proportion of the working classes, many of whom are often ill-provided with the means and comforts necessary for robust health, and who work in the vitiated atmosphere of factories, and whose dwelling houses are frequently crowded.[308]

In 1906, Silvertown suffered infant mortality rates of 181 deaths per 1,000 live births compared with 141 per 1,000 in West Ham's central ward.[309] Twenty to thirty years earlier, up to one-quarter of all babies in huge swathes of the East End died at birth or shortly afterward.[310] By way of comparison, the UK's rate between 2005 and 2010 was 4.91 deaths per

1,000, and that of war-devastated Afghanistan during the same recent period was 135.95 per 1,000. The recent infant mortality rates for some of Africa's poorest and most war-torn countries, Rwanda, the Central African Republic, Somalia, and the Democratic Republic of the Congo were, respectively, 100.15, 105.38, 106.67, and 115.81 per 1,000.[311]

Lurking behind the statistics was a universe of human pain and sorrow. Grace Foakes, who grew up in the East End at the turn of the nineteenth century, recalls the life and death of a baby brother in simple but moving language:

> It was a boy and Mother named him Wilfred. We were allowed into her room to see him. I remember my mother telling me to be specially careful with him. "He hasn't come to stay," she said. "He's only lent to us for a little while." Wilfred was a poor weak baby and, on thinking about it now, I believe he had no chance of living. When he was six weeks old he was taken into Great Ormond Street Children's Hospital, and within a few days we had news that he was dead.[312]

Around four in ten of all children in West Ham died before they reached five years of age.[313] The survivors of early childhood diseases such as whooping cough were likely to suffer "lasting ill-effects in the form of susceptibility to tuberculosis and general weakness of the respiratory system."[314] Even twenty or thirty years later, conditions for children were grim. In 2000, an elderly woman remembered that only the kindness of a man in a bowler hat who gave them his lunch every day ensured the survival of herself and her siblings. Her crippled father never had shoes, worked intermittently as a bartender, and died aged forty.[315] Nor was survival into adulthood a guarantee of a long life; in 1889, according to Walter Drummond, the average life span of a worker "on the marsh" in Silvertown was thirty-five years.[316] There were many deaths from infectious diseases, many of them directly due to polluted water supplies, exacerbated by overcrowding, overwork, and malnutrition. Bedbugs and lice were facts of life, no matter how diligently the people strove to exterminate them with boiling water, soap, or kerosene. These conditions sapped the bodily defenses of the inhabitants, particularly the very young and the elderly. Typhoid and cholera were common, and simple diarrhea carried off adults and children alike in the summer months. As London's first Medical Officer of Health, Shirley Forster Murphy, pointed out in the 1890s, districts such as West Ham provided with water from the River Lea were more likely to suffer higher mortality rates than those

supplied by the Thames. The problem was that the reservoirs and fil-
ters of the East London and New River companies were unable to cope
during floods when filth was washed from upstream.[317] There were also
periodic smallpox outbreaks of "alarming proportions," and epidemics of diphtheria, whooping cough, scarlet fever, typhus, and measles,
which spread rapidly amid the crowded terraces. Deprived of milk, many
infants developed rickets and walked all their lives with a characteristic
bow-legged gait. Medical treatment was scarce and mostly too expensive
for those who fell sick. Decades later, malnutrition was still common in
Silvertown. One elderly resident recalled a childhood in which, "when
you went to bed you'd go to bed with tears in your eyes for something to
eat, and you had to wait until the next morning, two thin slices of bread
was all we could afford."[318]

There were no infirmaries in, or close to, Silvertown in the 1880s:
the nearest were the London Fever Hospital in Islington and the Poplar
Hospital.[319] A visit to the doctor cost in the region of a shilling and a home
visit 2/6d plus the price of medication,[320] a large sum from an unskilled
worker's pay packet. In 1888, Matthew Gray brought the matter to the
attention of Silver's board of directors, and proposed to build a small
house in or near Winchester Street by the works to act as a dispensary in
order to "render better medical & surgical assistance than was now available." He planned to employ "a young doctor, who would pay no rent"
for lodgings above the dispensary, "and receive a salary of £100 a year
as a retaining fee."[321] Presumably, he would derive the bulk of his income
from patients' fees. It was a small step forward, but given that the appalling rates of disease were primarily due to poor sanitation, overwork, bad
nutrition, and slum housing, and best tackled by improved public health
measures, it was not likely to be efficacious.

Booze, Sin, and "Podsnappery"

Alcoholism was also a problem. Some "breadwinners" in the East End
squandered their earnings on drink, and alcohol played a prominent part
in the horrible scenes of domestic and communal violence recounted by
Jack London in his *People of the Abyss*. Other writers are more nuanced.
Charles Booth offered a view that differed from common accounts:

> Anyone who frequents public houses knows that actual drunkenness is
> very much the exception. . . . Go into any of these houses. Behind the

bar will be a decent middle-aged woman, something above her customers in class, very neatly dressed, respecting herself and respected by
them. The whole scene is comfortable, quiet and orderly.[322]

Though such a wholesome picture may well be unduly optimistic, it
is a useful antidote to the common middle-class view of the East End as a
gin-soaked hell. It is likely that Mrs. Elizabeth Cundy, the twenty-seven-
year-old Somerset-born proprietor of the Railway Tavern and Coffee House
(a.k.a. Cundy's) on Connaught Road, Silvertown, was one such "decent"
publican.[323] She was a supporter of the 1889 strikers, donated to the strike
fund—and persuaded the brewery to do likewise—and allowed them use
of her premises as a permanent strike headquarters. Union leader Will
Thorne spent most of his life in West Ham and warned against "highly
exaggerated" stories about the working class and drink. "We did have our
jollifications," he admits, "but they were not as bad as people make out."[324]
The prominent clergyman Augustus Stopford Brooke claimed that there
was little drunkenness and no dishonesty in Silvertown, although he was
perhaps putting the best face on matters in an impassioned sermon in support of Silver's strikers.[325] Mrs. Pember Reeves bears him out. From her
observations, married men living on the kind of wages paid to London
workers simply did not have the money to spend on alcohol and many
were in fact teetotalers. "Drink," she insisted, "is an accusation fatally easy
to throw about. By suggesting it you account for every difficulty, every
sorrow. A man who suffers from poverty is supposed to drink."[326] That
being said, some of the early East End workers' leaders were certainly
fond of the drink. Ben Tillett, it is said, sometimes had to be led to the
podium after a drinking bout, and by 1910 Will Thorne's militant Scottish
friend Pete Curran had drunk himself to death. Thorne himself "signed
the pledge" for a while, but was never a heavy drinker.[327] The evidence is
decidedly mixed. Years later, an elderly North Woolwich resident insisted
that men were regarded as "sissies" if they did not drink.[328]
Nevertheless, there was a thinly veiled ideological stance akin to Dickens's "Podsnappery"[329] in many accounts of East End drinking. If drink
was the cause of poverty, then poverty resulted from the moral turpitude
of the working class, according to a common syllogism. George Sims, to
his credit, warned against this simplistic view, avowing that "poverty is
equally the cause of drink."[330] D. J. Davis, the chairman of the West Ham
ILP, agreed. "It was not the drink that made men wretched," he argued,
"it was because they were wretched that they drank."[331] Today's opinion
holds that alcoholism stems from the interaction of environmental and

inherited genetic factors, so Davis's observations were a timely riposte to the lurid tales of the slummers and ideologues. Such tales continue to this day when guides regale the thousands of tourists who join "Jack the Ripper" excursions to Whitechapel with sensational accounts of the gin-soaked East End of 1888.

Maximum Income Paid to the Newest Apprentice

Prostitution, too, was widespread in the East End. The Royal Pavilion Gardens, which lay alongside the embankment between Silvertown and North Woolwich, were so "notorious for prostitutes and other anti-social persons" in the late 1880s that they were closed down. They reopened, refurbished and sin-free—or so it was hoped—as the Royal Victoria Gardens,[332] the women presumably plying their ancient trade elsewhere. Booth considered that prostitutes made up "a large standing army whose numbers no one can calculate." His estimate of those who worked at it full-time in London was between 60,000 and 80,000. Again, the vice was usually seen through the prism of middle-class respectability—and hypocrisy. Instead of confronting the social system that spawned it, "do-gooders" could focus on individual "fallen women," inevitably with a stiff dose of religious moralizing. One prominent Victorian do-gooder was William Gladstone, the Liberal politician who served four terms as prime minister and spent many hours proselytizing among the women of the East End streets. In fact, many women had little choice but to enter the trade, or it was at least a tempting alternative in which a young woman could expect to make more money in one night than in a month in a sweatshop. As Booth drily remarked, it was "the only career in which the maximum income is paid to the newest apprentice."[333] So the moralists preached, and middle- and upper-class sex tourists and frustrated locals were happy to visit the gardens. These customers were never seen as the problem, and were rarely molested, arrested, or preached at by the moralists. The East Enders may have smiled wryly at Bertolt Brecht's admonition:

> . . . first sort out the basic food position
> Then start your preaching: that's where it begins.
> You lot who preach restraint and watch your waist as well
> Should learn for all time how the world is run:
> However much you twist, whatever lies you tell
> Food is the first thing. Morals follow on.

So first make sure that those who now are starving
Get proper helpings when we do the carving.[334]

Strong Bonds of Community

In his autobiography, Ben Tillett lamented the "lurid descriptions" of
East End life that sapped "the self-respect of the casual worker"[335] and
that we should counterbalance bourgeois views with the very real social
solidarity of the working people of Silvertown. One example of this
occurred during the 1889 strike when, according to the union supporter
Stopford Brooke, "half-starving girls gave their meal tickets to married
women who needed them more than they did."[336] Despite the poverty and
the bleakness of their lives, the men and women of Silvertown made the
best of things, and enjoyed strong bonds of community. "Silvertown, to
me," reminisced the woman cited earlier, "will always be a happy memory.
Silvertown, with all its smoke, smells, docks and factories! And yet to me,
always a feeling of affection and loyalty. There I was born ... and lived my
whole childhood." There is no doubt that she wrote from the heart. Her
memories—admittedly always the fondest in life's twilight—derived from
the strong sense of community in a place that, as she points out, "from
its very position . . . was a little world of its own."[337] Another East Ender,
looking back seventy-odd years to her childhood, spent a few miles away,
recalled, "They were happy days in that close-knit community. The feeling of belonging out-classed everything else. There was poverty, disease,
dirt and ignorance, and yet to feel one belonged outweighed all else."[338]
An elderly Silvertown resident recalled that every street in Silvertown
had a midwife, a knowledgeable woman who would be summoned when
labor pains began.[339] Another told of how her father, who had regular
employment in a local foundry, would insist that his children take meat
gravy from their Sunday lunch to their neighbors to ensure they had more
than just plain potatoes to eat.[340] Silvertown's workers and their families
were not just passive victims of the industrial system. They were flesh-
and-blood human beings who sorrowed and hoped, swore and fought,
loved and hated, enjoyed themselves when they could at pub knees-ups or
their teetotal equivalents, dreamed of a better life for their children, and
bore adversity with simple stoicism and a very Cockney, Irish-influenced,
irreverent and ironic sense of humor.

Solidarity was neither an esoteric doctrine nor a luxury for the
East Enders; it was an essential part of life. Grace Foakes wrote of her

neighbors: "If you know anything about Londoners, you will know that they believe in helping each other."[341] People "would help each other out all the time" recalls an old Silvertown resident—it was a system of mutual aid that needed no organizational structure.[342] In 1889, one well-known account related the life of the fiercely independent East End "factory girl" and her strong bonds with friends, family, and workmates:

> She shares her last crust of bread with a girl out of work and "cried her eyes out" over the grave of a fellow-worker. Among no other class of young women does there appear to be so much camaraderie, such a strong instinct that all must pull together, such a commune of food, clothes, and halfpence as among the factory-girls of the metropolis.[343]

As in Bryant & May's at Bow in 1888, so too in Silvertown in 1889, where the workers—male, female, young and old—were prepared to make common cause against those who profited from their misery.

V.
A Time of Hope

❖❖❖

> Oh, God! That bread should be so dear,
> And flesh and blood so cheap![344]
> —THOMAS HOOD

NOWHERE WERE THE HARSH lessons of life more cruelly felt than in the East End and in Silvertown in particular. Life was vicious and short, but the rare Cockneys with a taste for Scripture may have found solace in the biblical injunction that "there shall be no reward for the evil man; the candle of the wicked shall be put out."[345] The socialists among them would have realized, however, that no supernatural agency would help them. More prosaically, these marsh dwellers may have felt that the will-o'-the-wisp, "a fair day's pay for a fair day's work," was within their grasp. Buoyed up by recent union victories, the strikers took action with great optimism and verve. They did not ask for much, but the stakes were higher than they perhaps imagined. As Frederick Engels explained to Jules Guesde in Paris, laying out the consequences of success and failure:

> In Silvertown, a London suburb, Mrs. Aveling [Eleanor Marx] is conducting a strike . . . in Messrs. Silver's works where rubber goods, etc., are produced. The strike, in which three thousand working men and women are involved, has been going on for ten weeks and has every prospect of success. That it should succeed is important, for its failure would mean the interruption of the long series of successes scored by the workers since the dock strike, and would spell victory for the English employers whose rapidly dwindling confidence would thus be restored.[346]

The battle lines were drawn that hot Indian Summer: the union marshaled its pickets; the company prepared for a long siege. The workers faced a formidable adversary in Silver's managing director, Matthew Gray, who sat grimly resolute in his Cannon Street offices. Behind the scenes, powerful men watched, anxious that there should be no repeat of the outcome of the dockers' strike. The middle classes, too, were becoming increasingly uneasy over union power. A hardening of attitudes was discernible in the columns of the *Times*. Initially fairly sympathetic to the dock strikers, by mid-September the paper had become openly anti-union. By December, it was demanding strong action against strikers and "paid bullies." In a Christmas Eve editorial, notes John Saville, the paper "exhorted employers to take the lead in encouraging and organising an anti-union force in their own industry, and once again reproved the police for their alleged passivity in the face of mass picketing and intimidation."[347] The Silvertown strike broke out just as middle-class opinion began to turn, fearful of what the press portrayed as the organized intimidation of "free laborers" fomented by outside agitators and "loud-voiced bullies."

In the midst of this industrial turmoil, the weekly meeting of Silver's board of directors took place on Thursday, 12 September 1889, at the company's City offices at 106 Cannon Street. It was another hot day by London standards, with the temperature rising into the high 70s and hardly falling below 60 degrees during the night. Old Man Samuel Winkworth Silver was in the chair as usual, apparently unruffled by events. Also in attendance were the Hon. Henry Marsham, Matthew Gray, and his eldest son, Robert K. Gray, along with the company solicitor, a man named Hutchins. The company secretary, William Tyler, took the minutes. Messrs. W. Scott and W. Henderson were absent. If there was any anxiety in the hearts of these men, it is not reflected in the minutes. The board had had a great deal of business to discuss in recent weeks. They had recently secured a number of new deep-sea cable-laying contracts, including for new lines between Argentina and Europe via Ascension Island, along the west coast of Africa, and off the Japanese coast.[348] Silver called the meeting to order and the men worked their way down the agenda paper to Item 8, which is tersely recorded as follows:

> Silvertown Labourers—A letter dated Sept. 11, signed by three delegates, with reference to a demand for an advance of wages, was read. Mr. Gray having explained the nature of the demand, it was decided to leave the matter entirely in his hands.[349]

The Yardmen's Demands

The three delegates represented the company's yardmen; unskilled and semiskilled men, laborers employed to carry machine parts, cables, rubber, copper, and other raw materials around the yards and wharves outside of the factory buildings; to shovel coal; sweep up rubbish; to maneuver heavy loads; and to fill and empty carts and railway wagons. Their central demand was for a pay increase, although yardman Harry Stone also mentioned in a letter to the *India Rubber Journal* that they wanted an undercover lunchroom as they worked outside in all weathers and that "however bad the weather is, the yard labourers have to take their meals in the open air (wet or dry)."[350]

Leaving aside for the moment the justice or otherwise of the pay claim, discrepancies remain as to exactly how much the workers were paid and how long they worked to earn it. With no laborers' union in the plant, there was no collective bargaining, so pay and conditions were at the pleasure of the management. Company secretary Tyler claimed that the yardmen were paid £1/6/6d ($5.11) for a 63-hour week, which implied an hourly rate of $5\frac{3}{4}$d (9 cents). He never retracted this claim and always insisted that Silver's workers were well paid. Harry Stone disputed Tyler's arithmetic, claiming that he personally worked a 59-hour week for £1/3/4$\frac{1}{4}$d ($4.50), which works out at around $4\frac{3}{4}$d (8 cents) an hour, a penny less than the sum Tyler claims.[351] Stone was a literate and thoughtful man and it seems reasonable to accept that he knew exactly what he was paid each week, especially as his family had to live on it. The discrepancies do not stop there, as there does not seem to have been a uniform rate for yard laborers. It seems likely that Stone was one of the more skilled men in the yard and was paid accordingly. According to the *Labour Elector*, the yardmen's normal working week was 59 hours and hourly rates varied between $3\frac{1}{2}$d and $4\frac{1}{2}$d ($4\frac{1}{2}$ and 7 cents) per hour. The paper added that the men's demand was for $5\frac{1}{2}$d (9 cents) an hour.[352] The wages situation appears to have been even more complicated, given that Harry Stone claims to have already been paid that amount.

Very little industrial work can be classified as being entirely unskilled and levels of expertise varied among the yardmen and the workers in the factory as a whole. There is no reference in extant accounts to the new trade of electrician, but it seems clear that they too must have been employed in the factory, although the newly formed Electrical Trades Union does not appear to have recruited members there at this stage. What is likely is that the three farthings an hour increase generally accepted as the workers' demand was an average figure. The idea bandied around in the press at the time and repeated in some memoirs that the yardmen's demand was for the dockers' tanner—sixpence an hour—does not appear to have been strictly true. It made a good story, however, and did underline the fact that the yardmen had been inspired by the example set by the dock laborers. For its part, Silver's was happy to accept publicly that their workers were seeking the tanner. Their workers, they argued, were for the most part in continuous employment and thus did not deserve an increase that was meant to compensate dock laborers for irregular hours and casual employment. This argument was an exercise in what we today would call "spin": truth appears to have been an early casualty in the class war that was breaking out in Silvertown.

Without a recognized general union in the plant, the strike developed haphazardly. At this stage the yardmen's sectional interests motivated them; their demand for a pay increase did not apply to the unskilled and semiskilled workers on a factory-wide basis. Having handed in their petition, the yardmen settled down to await a reply. They did not have long to wait. At their meeting on 12 September, the directors had given Gray a free hand to act as he saw fit and he acted quickly. Whether this was due to panic or calculation we will probably never know for the company minutes are, as usual, terse, but he must have been mindful of the context of the demand in a climate of widespread industrial unrest. Nothing in his subsequent behavior, however, suggests that Gray was anything other than cool-headed. Perhaps, he reasoned, the company was making healthy profits and he might buy the loyalty of the yardmen and play them off against other workers in the factory if he granted them what was after all a trifling increase. Whatever the reason, he had a notice posted at the main gates informing the workers of his decision to grant the yardmen's demands, at least in part. The yardmen must have been jubilant, the rest of the workforce envious.

The Round Robin

That day, Friday the 13th—an auspicious day for the superstitious—was an even warmer day than Thursday, with the temperature nudging 80° F after a muggy night. The docks were still strikebound, and it was in this hothouse atmosphere that the news of the yardmen's pay increase spread around the factory. If Gray had thought that he had brought the matter to a satisfactory conclusion, he was soon to be disabused. Sometime over the weekend of 14 and 15 September, workers in the electrical shop petitioned Gray for an extra $\frac{3}{4}$d an hour, an increase similar to that which he had granted to the yard laborers.[353] The idea swiftly caught on throughout the vast factory. Will Thorne recalled that the entire non-craft workforce signed a "round robin" to management asking for the same increase.[354] In his report to the next board meeting, held on Thursday, 19 September, Gray estimated that "about one-third of the hands at Silvertown had applied for an increase of from $\frac{1}{2}$d to 1d an hour, averaging 15 percent advance." He added that a general wage increase would cost the company about £13,000 a year,[355] the equivalent of roughly £1.2 million today using the retail price index, or as much as £13.5 million as a share of GDP. The strikers estimated that if their demands were granted, it would cost the company an extra £11,000 per annum (or around $17,630) in wages.[356]

Silver's board members must have thrown up their hands in horror at the prospect, although granting such an increase would still have left the company with a clear profit of almost £45,000 for the year— today equivalent to anywhere between £3.88 million using the retail price index or £46.6 million (around $74 million) as a share of GDP. Exactly what discussions took place within the management at this time, we cannot say. The company's minutes provide only the barest outline of decisions, and neither Gray nor any other personage on the company side has left an account of the strike. Much communication, we can be sure, was verbal and went unrecorded. However, from this time on, Gray was intransigent: he would neither negotiate directly with the strikers nor accept outside offers of arbitration. He dismissed organizers of the NUG&GL and other union bodies as outside agitators with sinister hidden agendas. Whether Gray's resolve was stiffened by messages from shareholders, politicians, and other industrialists is a matter of speculation, but it fits perfectly with John Saville's perception of the growing determination of the employers and middle classes to resist union organization and wage claims.

What is clear, however, is that any increase in the company's wage bill would have to be met from profits and share dividends. Granting a general pay increase in response to the organized demands of the workers would set a precedent, open the door to union organization in the factory, and erode shares. The unionized workers at the nearby gasworks in Beckton had, under Will Thorne's leadership, secured a substantial shortening of working hours, so perhaps Silver's workers would soon demand the same. The board had given Gray a free hand in the dispute, but even if he did not consult directly with the powerful men behind the scenes, he must have been mindful that they would watch developments closely. He also had the wind in his sails, confident of the turn of the tide in middle-class public opinion. The workers, if they did not know already, would soon realize that they had taken on one of the richest and most powerful firms in the country, and that standing behind it was an array of the most influential men in British economic and political life. A workers' victory at Silvertown would set an example for the working class as a whole and would increase the power of the New Unions; in this respect, both the strikers and Silvers were proxies for a broader class struggle. There can be little doubt that Silver's could have well afforded to grant the modest demands of the strikers. The ruling class had demanded a line in the sand and Gray's hand wielded the stick that drew it.

Conduit to the Highest Levels of Power

The most direct conduit between Gray and the most powerful men in the British political establishment was Henry Marsham, a Kent blueblood who sat on Silver's board of directors. Marsham's brother Charles, the third Earl of Romney, was at the time the Lord-in-Waiting (Government Whip in the House of Lords) in the Tory administration of Prime Minister Lord Salisbury.[357] Salisbury associated with figures such as William Collison, who shortly afterward headed up the strikebreaking National Free Labour Association, and even the unsavory Kelly-Peters Gang and the "Eyeball Busters," East End criminal elements who specialized in roughing up trade unionists.[358] Salisbury, no doubt, keenly followed events at Silvertown. Romney, too, must have known MPs such as Francis Charteris, who had founded the Liberty and Property Defence League in 1882, a lobby group of landowners and industrialists animated by a hatred of socialism, democracy, and unions.[359] Salisbury, who came into the world as Robert Arthur Talbot Gascoyne-Cecil, was himself a shareholder in the firm, a fact revealed by both the socialist *Labour Elector* and the pro-business *India-Rubber Journal*. The fact was widely repeated in both the press and by speakers at union rallies. Curiously, Yvonne Kapp claims it was not true,[360] but Salisbury himself appears never to have denied it and it would have been foolish of him to do so, given that the share register was open to public scrutiny. Unfortunately, that document does not appear to have survived, or at least it is not held with other company documents at the London Metropolitan Archives, so the *Labour Elector*'s account is the main source of information.

The register would make interesting reading and must have read like something out of *Who's Who* or *Burke's Peerage*. Silver's epitomized the lopsided distribution of wealth in class-ridden British society. As Jack London observed a decade or so later, "five hundred hereditary peers own one-fifth of England; and they, and the officers and servants under the King, and those who compose the powers that be, yearly spend in wasteful luxury . . . £370,000,000, which is thirty-two percent of the total wealth produced by all the toilers of the country."[361] Quite a number of these had a direct pecuniary interest in Silver's.

When Lord Salisbury died in 1903, his estate was valued at £310,336. In today's terms, that was at least £26 million (retail price index) and as high as £441 million as a share of GDP. A sizable proportion of this considerable fortune may have derived from his gilt-edge shares in Silver's. His descendant Robert Gascoyne-Cecil, alias the 7th Marquess of Salisbury, continues the family tradition of right-wing Tory politics, having served in a number of positions in the House of Lords, and testifies to the enduring influence of the establishment "gene puddle." His eldest son Robert Edward "Ned" William Gascoyne-Cecil, Viscount Cranborne, promises that the line might "stretch out to the crack of doom," to borrow a line from Shakespeare's *Macbeth*.

There were seventy-two Silver's shareholders in 1889, and the *Labour Elector* published the names of some of the most prominent of these, comprising "Prime Minister and Jew, Gentile and Lawyer—aristocratic members of the Lords and Radical members of the Commons—Great unpaid and dissentient Liberals, Reverend and Medical Sweaters."[362] Current and former board members, besides Henry Marsham, Sam Silver, and Matthew Gray, included Neil Bannatyne, W. Scott, Major Darwin, Sir Charles Rich, J. Buchanan, Charles H. Moore, the MP and big-game hunter, Colonel Alexander Weston Jarvis MP, J. G. T. Child, Henry Davidson, General Green, H. A. Hankey, P. N. Bernard, Dr. Beattie, Abraham Scott, C. H. Junes, Major Rufrell, C. W. Robertson, J. Mellor, Captain Petty, John W. Willans, Justinian Petty, J. H. Mackenzie, and Robert Henderson.[363] In 1889, the prime minister held twenty-seven £10 shares, the approximate value of which is given below. Other parliamentary shareholders (with the number of shares they held in 1889 given in parentheses) included Richard Burdon Haldane, the Member for Haddington in Scotland and later the one and only Viscount Haldane of Cloane, (10); Andrew Grant, another Scottish Member of the House of Commons (224); Edmund Robertson, the Member for Dundee and later the first and last Baron Lochee of Gourie (41); W. B. Barbour (120); and

Mark J. Stewart (120).[364] In addition prominent shareholders included Lady Hobhouse "of Bruton St W" (16); the Earl and Countess of Egmont (38); the musicologist and composer Sir John Stainer and his wife, Lady Stainer (150); Sir Philip Rose (Disraeli's executor) C. E. Lewes and John Sebag Montefiore (jointly 150); C. J. Prideaux, Q.C. (50); and James Williamson, J.P. (80).[365] Those whose shareholdings the *Labour Elector* does not quantify, included the meddlesome Oxford mathematician Professor Bartholomew "Bat" Price; Reginald Capel; the Irish peer Viscount Monck (a former Governor-General of Canada); Lieutenant Colonel Sir William Wallace; and Earl Russell, of the family that produced the well-known philosopher Bertrand Russell.[366]

In 1888, Silver's board of directors transferred large bundles of shares in the West African Telegraph Company to a number of well-placed nominees of the Eastern and South African Telegraph Company. Prominent among them was Sir Daniel Gooch, telegraph engineer, chairman of the board of the Great Western Railway, and Tory MP for Cricklade. Gooch had also been a member of the anti-union majority on the 1867 Royal Commission into Trades Unions. He received 2,000 shares. Sir John Pender, K.M.G., received 3,000; Sir James Anderson, 3,000; and John Denison Pender, 1,500. Charles Burt and John George Griffiths received 100 each. George Draper got 314; and Lewis Wells, William Payton, and Henry A. Saunders each got 300.[367] There was also, the *Labour Elector* charged, "quite an army of gentlemen of the blackcloth [priests] among the shareholders." The paper threatened, "It would be well for them to know that their names are known," calling on them to "go to see the strikers at Silvertown, and investigate matters for themselves and not long would they be in doubt of the justice of the men's demands."[368] These "Reverend Sweaters" included the Anglicans E. Davis (20 shares); Dr. Frost (30); C. Brooker (number not stated); and W. H. Williams (80); along with the Catholic priest C. Moore (6 shares). Another Anglican divine, Henry Latham, held 120 shares.[369] The somewhat eccentric Master of Trinity College, Cambridge, and author of a treatise on angels, Latham was an adroit player of the stock market who built a large house named Southacre in the town's outskirts with the proceeds of his stock exchange gambling.[370] None of the priests appear to have taken up the paper's invitation to visit Silvertown to see for themselves the conditions in which the blessed meek lived and labored. Indeed, the clergy by and large ignored the plight of the strikers; the sole honorable exception, as we shall see, being the Reverend Stopford Brooke, a radical Irishman.

Fat Dividends Paid Regularly

Silver's was one of the most lucrative industries in the land, regularly paying fat dividends to shareholders. According to A. A. Foster, from the time it was floated in 1864 the firm regularly paid out a 10 percent dividend, except for 1904 when it was reduced to 5 percent, and in 1911, when "for the first time in its corporate history," it paid no dividend and made a net loss of £39,457 due to a 277 percent increase in the cost of raw rubber.[371] Calculating the value of one £10 share in today's prices is problematic. However, as a share of per capita GDP, it would be worth £5,970, using other measures around £1,000. The value of Prime Minister Salisbury's shares, therefore, could be as low as £27,000 or as high as £161,290 and that of his yearly dividends as low as £2,700 or as high as £16,122 in today's terms. Cleric Henry Latham's 120 shares netted anything between £37,200 and £62,100 in yearly dividends.[372] In February 1890, immediately after the Great Strike, the company still paid a dividend of 10 shillings a share, the same amount as a junior female laborer's weekly wage. Again, it is difficult to say exactly what this would be worth today. Using the retail price index it would be worth £41, but using per capita GDP, £298, and share of GDP, £496. Clearly, whatever method of computation is used, Silver's shares were, as the fictional East End "wide boy" "Arfur" Daley might later have put it, "a nice little earner," and this during a period of general economic depression. Gray himself was a wealthy man with a huge pecuniary interest worth the equivalent of anything between £298,000 and £496,000 in yearly dividends. In addition, in 1889 each of the directors received a minimum regular remuneration of £2,000,[373] worth anything up to £2,000,000 today for each. Contrary to common misperceptions, the colossal incomes of today's bankers, speculators, and CEOs are nothing new. Those who produced Silver's wealth, however, labored long and hard for paltry wages, and the socialist *Commonweal* was not far off the mark when it accused Silver's of being "one of the worst sweating firms in London."[374]

"Works Altogether Closed"

Monday 16 September dawned gloomy and overcast, and by the afternoon a thick fog had settled over London. When the workers arrived at the factory gates that morning, they were confronted by notices that informed them that Gray had withdrawn his previous offer to the yardmen, and had also flatly rejected the demands of the workers in the electrical shop. According to the *Stratford Express,* the notices declared that "any men dissatisfied with their existing pay should go to the cashier's office at four o'clock to be paid off." Almost "all of the yard labourers did so, and left work," the report continued, adding that "it is said that they were informed they would not be employed again."[375] As a result, discontent seethed. The 280 striking yardmen were soon joined by 700 or 800 workers from other sections of the factory.[376] Two days later, in the early evening of 18 September, a day of brilliant sunshine after an early frost had heralded the end of the Indian summer, Matthew Gray summoned the remainder of his employees to a factory meeting at which he reiterated his refusal to grant any pay increases.[377] He warned that there would be no pay increases or changes to conditions, and that those who did not like it were free to leave and seek employment elsewhere. Gray claimed to pay more than the average for similar firms and advised the workers to be content with what they had. One imagines that he also mentioned that it would be an easy matter to find replacements for strikers at a time of mounting unemployment.

If he believed threats would intimidate the remaining workers, he was wrong. By Thursday afternoon, reported the *Stratford Express*, the works "were altogether closed,"[378] with "2,000 men thrown out of work," added the *Times.*[379] In fact, as John Burns told a strike meeting the following weekend in Hyde Park, the factory was "still at work upon the execution of orders,"[380] but with a much reduced workforce. A small number of company "loyalists" and staff employees maintained some production, but the great furnaces and engines steadily fell cold and silent. Samuel Silver later admitted to shareholders that "almost all of the Company's workpeople went out on strike in the middle of September and remained out from 10 to 12 weeks."[381]

If they had misgivings, the workers must have drawn courage from developments on the docks. The following day, Friday, 20 September, the dock strike ended in victory for the union. The East End celebrated, with "the names of [strike leaders] Burns and Tillett on every tongue," reported the *East and West Ham Gazette.*[382] There were frosts most mornings by now, hinting at the coming harsh winter, but the Silvertown workers toasted the remarkable victory of the despised casual dockers over the powerful establishment. The London Dockers' union now boasted 18,000 members and had given hope to other downtrodden laborers that change was on the way. There were great victory parades through the East End, with brass bands, flags and banners. Even the heavens smiled, it seemed, with the sun streaming down from a cloudless sky. In Silvertown, wedged

between the Thames and the Victoria and Albert docks, the atmosphere
must have been electric.

VI.
"They Want My Life's Blood"
-◆◆-

> Political Economy regards the proletarian . . . like a
> horse, he must receive enough to enable him to work. It
> does not consider him, during the time when he is not
> working, as a human being. It leaves this to criminal
> law, doctors, religion, statistical tables, politics, and the
> beadle. [383]
> —KARL MARX, 1844

> The company's horses [are] better fed and sheltered
> than their workpeople ... [Silver's] could not get a good
> horse under £30 or £40, but they could get a good
> workman at $4\frac{3}{4}$d an hour.[384]
> —BEN TILLETT

INDUSTRIAL DISPUTES, as both Matthew Gray and the strikers' leaders
realized, are in part won by the side that better mobilizes "public opinion."
Press attitudes to the New Unionism varied in line with the political pre-
dilections of the paper's owners. The twice-weekly *Stratford Express*, for
example, was generally sympathetic to the strikers, but the *East London
Observer* was firmly on the employers' side, and the *Times* waxed vocifer-
ous in its opposition to the New Unions. Matthew Gray proved himself an
industrial autocrat, but he was sensitive to his image in the newspapers.
Middle- and upper-class readers formed the bulk of the readership of the
daily papers, yet even before the 1870 Education Act literacy levels were
surprisingly high among working-class children and adults.[385] Silver's

sent a steady stream of letters to the press, justifying their hardline stance, designed to undermine public support for the strikers.

As the strike dragged on, the layers of lies and obfuscations were steadily peeled back for any who cared to look. The strikers also enjoyed the full support of the left-wing weekly the *Labour Elector,* and the Radical *Reynold's Newspaper* was sympathetic. Although Engels and Eleanor Marx considered H. H. Champion, the former artillery officer who nominally edited the *Labour Elector,* to be "dodgy,"[386] the paper transcended the abstract Social Democratic Federation (SDF) style speechifying. Champion had founded the paper to oppose the dictatorial and sectarian Henry Mayers Hyndman's influence but had accepted money from Tory and Liberal sources in order to do so. Champion's contemporary, E. Belfort Bax, believed that Champion "developed a tendency for political intrigue with a view, as he in all probability sincerely thought, of obtaining immediate results in the improvement of the condition of the working class and in general progress." However, Bax adds, "the habit of intrigue" led him into behavior which "no considerations of political expediency or anything else could . . . morally justify."[387] When the Tory gold ran out control of the *Labour Elector* passed to an editorial board that included Tom Mann and John Burns.[388] Under their direction, the paper provided invaluable information and analysis from the point of view of the workers as opposed to bystander commentary and abstract declarations of the need for socialism. Despite its murky origins, it became a prototype, perhaps, of George Lansbury's socialist paper, the *Daily Herald.*

The Strikers' Demands

The mainstream press initially simplified the workers' demands, although, to be charitable, it is likely the inexperienced strike leaders had difficulty in drawing up a coherent log of claims that would cover a broad range of job classifications, levels of skill, and existing pay differentials. Even if the strike were successful, most of Silver's workers would still not receive the dockers' tanner, a fact that highlights management's disingenuous argument that their permanent workers ought not to receive hourly pay rates commensurate with casual labor. Stranger still, if the company secretary William Tyler was to be believed, the workers already received most or all of what they were demanding. While Tyler endlessly asserted that "no able-bodied labourer employed by us receive[s] less than $4\frac{3}{4}$d an hour,"[389] the available evidence undermines his claims. According to the *Stratford*

Express, workers in the india-rubber shop received on average only four-pence an hour, with some of the more highly skilled men earning $4\frac{1}{2}$d.[390] The *East End News* reported that male wages across the plant varied from $2\frac{1}{2}$d to $4\frac{3}{4}$d an hour "and in some very exceptional cases $5\frac{1}{2}$d."[391] If Tyler's claims were true, the india-rubber shop workers would all be making at least sixpence an hour, the sum demanded by the Strike Committee for the most highly skilled operatives. The phenomenon of workers striking to demand what they were already being paid is a puzzle indeed. Tyler, though, was adamant. Silver's board of directors had been asked for an interview, he continued, "by a few of our workpeople, and by agitators who have never been in our employment, and have made themselves conspicuous by misstatements and abusive language." As a result, he concluded, "of course the Directors cannot consent to such an interview."[392] There was no "of course" about it: Silver's was acting in bad faith and had absolutely no intention of negotiating even if the "agitators" had tugged their forelocks respectfully in the presence of their alleged "betters."

The London Trades Council Inquiry

More facts became known as a result of the inquiry of a delegation sent to Silvertown by the London Trades Council. The LTC was the peak union body in the city. Moribund during the 1860s, it was resuscitated in 1873 during a period of parliamentary anti-union activity.[393] By 1889, it was in the main a sluggish body of respectable craft unionists headed up by its conservative secretary, George Shipton, with a minority of more activist delegates. The dock strike had passed the council by, although it had played a mediating (as opposed to organizing) role during the 1888 match-women's strike. That the council had bestirred itself to display any interest in the strike at Silvertown was in large part due to the efforts of the socialist Tom Mann, who had recently been sent to represent the Battersea branch of the Amalgamated Society of Engineers (ASE) on the body. Much of its time had been taken up with discussion of matters such as the sugar bounty,[394] and they had sidestepped an early request by Ben Tillett for assistance for the dock strikers.[395] At Mann's instigation, an LTC delegation met the Strike Committee in its headquarters at the Railway Dining Rooms on 30 November, a fine but very cold day. Its findings were reported dispassionately the following Monday in the *Times*. The Strike Committee's Mr. Parker was in the chair and a large number of workers attended, including some women and girls.[396] Gray, true to form, refused to meet with the delegation,[397] although he could scarcely term the staid and respectable George Shipton a dangerous "agitator." The delegation closely questioned a number of workers from various departments about their wages and conditions. Their testimony, as reported by the conservative *Times*, amounted to a withering indictment of the company. Mr. Cowley from the cutting shop testified that the young men in his section were receiving between tuppence and thruppence an hour. Some adults got fivepence, and the highest paid, the leading hand, got sevenpence, which worked out at £1/16/9d for a 63-hour week (less if the strikers' claim of a 59-hour working week was the case). Mr. Hobbs, of the telegraph department, claimed that his section's calendar hands, responsible workers who operated large winding machines, got $4\frac{1}{2}$d an hour. His colleague Mr. Eiffe said that half of those employed in the shop got fourpence, whereas company secretary William Tyler had claimed the hands as a whole got over $5\frac{1}{2}$d an hour. A twenty-five-year-old laborer named Wyatt testified that although he had worked for seven years in the telegraph section and was "competent to do any of the work in the department," he was paid only fourpence an hour. Another mill hand said he was twenty-one years old and got $4\frac{1}{4}$d an hour, and that of 259 men in the telegraph section, not one got as much as fivepence an hour. Fifty percent got $4\frac{1}{2}$d and "a good sprinkling" as little as fourpence, he claimed.[398]

"Starvation Wages"

It was pay such as this, no doubt, that Walter Drummond had in mind when he claimed Silver's paid "starvation wages . . . so low that it was impossible for any man to bring up a family respectably on them."[399] Piecework was a common feature. Huge and wealthy though it was, Silver's had turned cheeseparing and petty diddling with the rates into an art form. The Reverend Stopford Brooke claimed that older workers could expect particularly shabby treatment. They would be threatened with dismissal but told that they could stay if they accepted a ha'penny less an hour.[400] Given that the alternative was most likely the workhouse,[401] an institution they had every reason to hate and fear, they had no choice but to accept. They were thus robbed far beyond the norms of wage slavery in the factory. A simple calculation shows that each such older person swindled in this way saved the company half a crown a week or £6/10/ a year, 65 percent of the dividend paid on one share.

The worst pay rates in the factory in that most patriarchal of ages were reserved for female workers. William Tyler estimated that Silver's employed about 350 women and girls—around 11 percent of the total workforce—and claimed that they earned on average 13/5d for a fifty-four hour week.[402] Again, his claims were at odds with the workers' testimony. Girls in the telegraph department told the LTC delegation that they worked 59 hours for between 7/5d and 9/10d a week, or 1½ to 2d (2 to 3 cents) an hour, and that even the forewoman received only 14 shillings a week, or less than thruppence an hour. Mrs. Curtis, a widow who worked in the sundries shop, said there were about one hundred women in her section and they nearly all got 9/10d a week or tuppence an hour. When learning the job, they got five shillings a week, or just over a penny an hour, while 11/1d (2¼d an hour) was the highest wage paid to any non-supervisory female employee in the shop.[403] The company also offered a production bonus they called "exertion money" to the five "girls" they judged to have worked the hardest in any one week. According to Stopford Brooke, this came from a kitty of 12 shillings put aside by the company for the purpose.[404] For their pains, the five girls who qualified would receive an extra 2/4¼d in their pay packets that week. To cap it all off, the girls were not paid if there was no work for them to do, but were still expected to remain on the job without pay and were sacked if they went home.[405] When this is factored in, average hourly pay rates were even lower than those quoted by either the strikers or Tyler. For single working women with dependents, life was an endless, losing struggle. Stopford Brooke gave the example of a widow with a large family who was employed on a piecework basis at Silver's. Her average weekly income came to 14 shillings, but one week, he declared, "she put on a desperate spurt and earned 14/6d." Her supervisor thereupon docked her half an hour's pay because he felt this effort proved that she had been previously underworking. "They want my life's blood," Brooke quoted this "poor creature" as saying.[406]

Remarkably, Silver's claim to pay higher wages than many other London firms seems to be valid, up to a point. According to the authors of the book *Toilers in London*, the average wage of a London "factory girl" in 1889 was between 4 and 8 shillings a week, with wages increasing somewhat "when they become young women."[407] This does not prove, however, that Silver's was the paragon of Tyler's fancy. Higher rents in Silvertown cancelled out higher wages. As Eleanor Marx, speaking at a mass meeting in Silvertown, put it, the strikers were "simply asking for the elementary right to live," and if the management's claim to pay higher wages than other employers were true, "it was high time the workmen of other firms came out."[408] The employing class themselves were aware of this and feared that another New Union victory could result in a snowballing effect.

What Were These Wages Worth?

Working out how much such wages were worth in comparison with those of today is a difficult task. A simple calculation shows us that tuppence an hour for 59 hours adds up to slightly less than ten shillings a week; or £40.7 for the same number of hours in 2010 using the retail price index as a guide. Female trainees would take home the equivalent of £20.35 in 2010. In 2012, the minimum wage rates (male and female) in the United Kingdom for a 40-hour week were £243.2 for those aged 21 and over; £199.20 for those aged 18–20; £147.20 for those aged 16–17; and £104 for apprentices.[409] Though direct comparisons can be misleading, it is clear that Silver's paid subsistence wages—just enough to live on so that the operatives could report for work each day and perform their duties. In 1895, the same girls would have to work five hours to buy a quartern (large) loaf of bread, and a one-mile trip by cab or on the underground would set them back sixpence, or six hours' work. The 11 shillings per week received by the highest-paid female worker in Mrs. Curtis's shop added up, roughly, to £28 per year; the 36/9d received by the comparatively well-paid leading hand in Mr. Cowley's section added up, roughly, to £95/11/- for over three thousand hours of toil, a fraction of the equivalent 2012 minimum wage for forty hours' work. In 1891, a general laborer in Britain could expect to earn slightly less than £69 per annum and a fitter £107.[410] In comparison, according to another source, an Anglican curate could expect to make £300, and membership of the "comfortable classes" in the 1870s required an income of at least £400 a year.[411] In 1891, a surveyor or professional engineer could expect to earn around £380 for a year's work.[412] Silver's claim to pay good wages does not withstand scrutiny in the light of such comparisons, particularly when we take large amounts of overtime into account, along with high rents.

In her PhD thesis on the East End labor movement, Diana Banks-Conney cites some interesting statistics compiled by Henry Mayhew regarding the cost of living in London at the beginning of the twentieth century. Mayhew divided the results of his surveys into four categories of family: B, C, D, and E. For the purpose of the exercise, in all categories, the family consisted of a husband, wife, and three children. We will only look at Category B, which consisted of the poorest London families. This category averaged a total expenditure of £5/1/8½d over a five-week period or £1/0/4d per week. These families spent the following amounts per five-week period: food, £3/0/9½d; beer and tobacco, 1/11¾d; fire and light, 10/½d; rent, £1/1/6d; washing and cleaning, 3/3¾d; clothes, etc., 11d; education and medicine, 5¾d; insurance, etc., 2/8¼d.

The average male wage paid by Silver's in 1889 was approximately £1/2/0d per week, or £5/10/0d per five-week period. We should bear in mind here that Silvertown rents were considerably higher than in other parts of the metropolis. Though there was some slight inflation during the 1890s, £1/2/- was worth only £1/4/- in 1902, so the comparison is reasonably valid as an estimate.[413] Clothing and repair was particularly expensive. According to an article published in *Nineteenth Century* magazine in 1888, the prices of some common household items were as follows: an overcoat, £1/15/-; an umbrella, 7/6d; a flannel shirt, 3/-; a pair of boots, 10/6d; a man's suit, £2; repair of boots, 6 shillings.[414] According to the same article, the average weekly expenditure of a British household in 1888, including the cost of meat, bread, vegetables, flour, fruit, butter, tea, coffee, cocoa, sugar, soap, candles, paraffin, coal, beer, clothing, and rent, came to £1/10/4½d.[415] There was no money for luxuries. The docker's daughter, Grace Foakes, recalls that in Edwardian London toys were "very poor and cheap by today's standards. One could buy a doll's china tea set for 6¾d and a baby doll cost you the same. A box of wooden-cube bricks, complete with pictures, cost 6¾d as well, and a clockwork train set cost 1s 11¾d," but "even at these prices they were too dear for the likes of us. The only toys we possessed were given to us at Christmas time."[416] For the rest of the year, children had to improvise or use their imaginations, as Grace and her sister did, pretending that a wonderful doll's pram and a beautiful doll inside a shop window were theirs. One day, "alas ... the doll and the pram were gone. We cried all the way home, mourning for toys we had never possessed."[417]

It is clear from such evidence that the Silvertown workers would have had little or nothing left over at the end of each week and would have had to make do with less than the "average" consumption. Henry Mayhew's estimate of working-class rents in London, too, comes to around one-fifth of household expenditure, and the *Nineteenth Century*'s to one-sixth, but in Silvertown rents commonly amounted to between one-third and one-half of a worker's wage, an "enormous" amount, conceded the *Times*.[418] There was a correspondingly smaller amount left over to spend on essential items. With no savings to fall back on, the strike would have been a grueling experience. The company itself owned a number of houses in Silvertown and rented them out to employees, presumably at market rates, so they must have been aware that they were paying less than a living wage to their employees. A junior female, it will be recalled, earned less than 10 shillings a week, the average adult male £1/2/-, or around £25 and £57 respectively per annum on the basis of a 59-hour week.

The shadow of the pawnbroker's three brass balls hung heavy over Silvertown. Many families could only house and feed themselves by pawning domestic items, and nothing much changed over the years. As one elderly Silvertown resident recalled of her childhood years in the 1930s, "Few women could manage for the whole week on the money given to them by their husbands even if they were endlessly resourceful; the money/wages was not adequate to support a family. Debts would pile up and most often possessions would be pawned to raise a small amount of money just to buy food till the end of the week." A neighbor added, "We used to pawn the old man's suit on the Monday. We would pawn anything, suits, saucepans, my dad's best boots. They would go in on a Monday and get them out Saturday; we did not get much for them but enough to get a bit of food for the week. . . . My mum used to take her wedding ring in every Monday morning to be pawned and wear a brass curtain ring all week."[419] Another old Silvertown resident remembered that many children walked barefoot even during winter and if they did have shoes the soles would be hanging off or worn through, revealing toes sticking out of the holes in their socks.[420] If this was the case forty or so years after the strike, with workers enjoying the benefits of established trade unions, what must it have been like in the late 1880s?

The Blood of Living Labor

In stark contrast, each of the six or seven company directors received a minimum of £2,000 a year, a sum that would take a factory girl eighty years to earn and an adult male laborer over thirty-five years, both periods beyond the workers' average lifetimes. Put another way, one director's annual salary would pay the yearly wages of eighty girls or thirty-five male operatives. The lucrative regular dividends paid to the firm's seventy-two shareholders depended on the super-exploitation of the factory laborers. As Marx put it in the famous "gothic" passage of *Capital*, a man such as Matthew Gray was merely capital personified. His soul is the soul of capital, which has a vital impulse of its own, the impulse towards self-expansion, towards the creation of surplus value towards making the constant factor of capital (the means of production) absorb the greatest possible amount of surplus labour. Capital is dead labour, and like a vampire, can only keep itself alive by sucking the blood of living labour. The more blood it sucks, the more vigorously does it live.[421]

Matthew Gray was constrained by the demands of capital, the *raison d'être* of which was the production of more capital by extracting it from labor. In the strike, he was also governed by the class imperative to hold the line against the proliferation of wage increases. He could ignore the consequences of his actions as a normal, indeed necessary part of life, and the pain of others is usually easier to bear than one's own. The Anglican theological orthodoxy of the time also insisted that the social system was divinely ordained. It does not seem coincidental that in 1848, a year in which the specter of revolution was haunting Europe, Mrs. Cecil Frances Humphreys Alexander had published her collection of *Hymns for Little Children*. One of the hymns is the well-known ditty "All Things Bright and Beautiful," one verse of which encapsulates the socio-religious Tory dogma of the age:

The rich man in his castle,
the poor man at his gate,
He [God] made them, high or lowly,
and ordered their estate.[422]

To this way of thinking, the lot of the poor was to endure what was God's will. Strikes and unions were unnatural disruptions of a legitimate system mandated by Heaven.

The Strikers' Log of Claims

The strikers' demands boiled down to a brief log of claims, summarized in *Justice*, the SDF's official weekly newspaper. The workers wanted a general pay increase of $\frac{3}{4}$d an hour, "save for some exceptions." The minimum hourly pay for warehousemen was to be 5d; for packers, 6d; for yard laborers, engineers' laborers, and bricklayers' laborers, $5\frac{1}{2}$d. Timbering work such as in excavations and pile driving was to be paid at the rate of $6\frac{1}{2}$d—"that being the casual contractors' pay throughout England." Stokers and boiler cleaners were to be paid a minimum of 6d. The union also demanded proportionate increases in pay for piecework, and for women, girls, and boys in all departments. Overtime pay for work after 5 p.m. was to be paid at time and a quarter and work on Sundays and holidays at double time. The workers further demanded the abolition of the hated rule refusing payment for time worked to anyone omitting to put in a ticket at the start of the day. This rudimentary timekeeping system was much resented by the workers, who could forfeit up to a day's pay for forgetting to lodge their tickets. Finally, the workers stipulated that they would only return to work on the basis of no victimizations of strike activists.[423] As the *Daily News* pointed out, these demands were "not very exorbitant."[424] The moderate log of claims also bears out the observation of the legendary American labor leader Mother Jones that "all the average human being asks is something he can call home; a family that is fed and warm; and now and then a little happiness; once in a long while an extravagance."[425] However, for the company, negotiations with the Strike Committee would have been tantamount to recognition of the NUG&GL as the collective bargaining agent of the laborers. Matthew Gray was determined to exclude the union from the factory so as to keep wages at a minimum and the workers at his mercy. Maintenance of high profits depended upon a system of industrial despotism and long hours of work that effectively shortened the lives of the laborers. What we know of the work regime at Silvertown and elsewhere in Victorian Britain suggests that the workers were subjected to panopticon-like surveillance, hemmed in by petty rules and regulations and fined if they broke them. There was no personal liberty and no free association in Samuel Silver's machine halls and workshops. In theory, the workers enjoyed Blackstone's "absolute rights of every Englishman." In practice, as privates in an industrial army they were dragooned and regimented by Silver's omnipresent "non-coms" and subalterns, who were charged with wringing the very last drop of surplus value from them. Tied to their machines, the workers' lives epitomized what J. P. McKay described as a "dull routine of ceaseless drudgery and toil . . . a torment of Sisyphus . . . [in which] the toil, like the rock, recoils perpetually upon the wearied operative."[426] Silver's board was determined to keep it that way.

"More Like a Machine than a Man"

The content of the workers' log of claims hints at working conditions in the factory. There was no extra pay for overtime, despite a nominal ceiling on the working week of 59 hours, according to the workers, and sixty-three to sixty-three-and-a-half hours according to William Tyler in a letter to the *East End News*.[427] In late November, the Reverend Stopford Brooke delivered a sermon in the Bloomsbury Congregational Church in which he claimed, "No overtime [pay] is allowed, because the directors say the men earn enough without it."[428] The nominal working day in the factory was from 6 a.m. to 6 p.m., with one-and-a-half hours for unpaid meal breaks, but as the *Stratford Express* pointed out, the working hours "were really much longer." In the india-rubber shop, for instance, men regularly worked for 70 to 80 hours a week for fourpence ha'penny an hour. However, should a worker miss two half hours of work in a week, he would be sent home for the day, and, moreover, would be required to come in so that he could be sent home on pain of even greater penalties.[429] Without a collective agreement and without union protection, there were no ceilings on overtime and the workers were expected to work whatever overtime was demanded of them at no more than their hourly base rate.

Though it might have been exceptional, a case was cited of a man in the ebonite shop who had worked 124 hours in a single week and got "not a penny extra in overtime pay."[430] Michael Henry of the Coal Porters' Union, speaking at a factory gate meeting, dared Matthew Gray to deny the facts of the case, and made good his promise to produce the man, who stood up on the platform and said "he was the man who had worked 124 hours."[431] It is an astonishing tale. The man started at 5 a.m. on a Monday morning and worked through until 12:30 on Tuesday morning. He was back in the factory at 6 a.m. on Tuesday and worked through until midnight. The following morning, Wednesday, he started work at 6 a.m. and worked until half an hour after midnight on Friday morning: an unbroken stretch of forty-two-and-a-half hours. He returned at 8:30 on Friday morning and was "last seen working at four o'clock on Saturday afternoon," declared Henry.[432] An article in the *Labour Elector* declares that the worker in question

> looked more like a machine than a man created in a God-given image, and his appearance was sufficient to have moved the hardest heart with pity, and if no other instance of sweating had been discovered, this affords ample justification for the efforts of the Strike leaders to help and raise the oppressed.[433]

"Tyranny and Illegality"

With no union to protect him, the unfortunate ebonite worker had little choice but to comply with such outrageous demands on his time and health. Such long hours of arduous labor meant a short life. The exact nature of the man's occupation is not recorded, but ebonite manufacture involves work in high temperatures, and the molten sulfur used in the process is inherently dangerous. This was especially so for a man deprived of sleep. Although this case might have been an unusually excessive example, the company ordinarily showed little concern for the general welfare of its employees. How they coped with the results of overwork was not the firm's affair, for when a worker had outlived his or her usefulness or decided to leave, there were countless others to replace that worker. As Marx put it, "In the days of classical Rome, the slave was bound in chains; the wage worker is bound to his owner by invisible threads. The appearance of independence is kept up by means of the perpetual change from one wage lord to another and by the legal fiction of the contract."[434] Life was a treadmill, death the only escape, trade unions the only means of amelioration—should they be recognized, which was not the case at Silver's. Should they seek to escape by changing employers—itself difficult during a developing economic slump—it was a matter of substituting one "wage lord" for another possibly worse one. Bad treatment was not a matter of individual injustice, but one that derived from the contracts that bound the worker to the master.

Stopford Brooke accused the company of treating its workpeople "like machines, and not like human beings," and according to the pro-business *India-Rubber Journal,* he "gave some striking instances of tyranny and illegality dealt out to them."[435] The cumulative effect of these instances was an early grave, possibly via the workhouse, paupers' ward, or asylum, for, as Marx put it, such a system "prolongs the workers' period of production during a given time of his life, by shortening his life as a whole."[436] There seemed to be no limits to the firm's greed. One particularly hated requirement was the ticket rule, a rudimentary timekeeping and surveillance system denounced by the Strike Committee as being "as illegal as it was arbitrary." The rule required each worker to put his or her ticket in a box at the entrance of the works each morning. If they omitted or forgot to do so, they would be sent home and would lose pay for the entire time worked. In one instance, the Strike Committee noted, a worker forfeited nine hours' pay in this way.[437] Whether he or his children went hungry as a result was not the employer's concern.

"Good and Healthy Workshops?"

The contradiction between the interests of management and workers was just as stark when it came to actual working conditions on the factory floor. According to the company secretary, "our workshops are large and well-ventilated and lighted, and our appliances are of the best."[438] The yardman Harry Stone half-agreed with this. "Mr. Tyler tells you that they have good and healthy workshops," he wrote, "that we grant."[439] The reality, however, is not as rosy as Stone concedes. He was contrasting conditions inside the factory with those of the yardmen outside in all weathers. Probably the conditions in the instrument shops and cable-making sections were as clean and healthy as any in Victorian England, if only because of the demands of the precision manufacturing processes involved. Elsewhere, the reality was somewhat different.

Rubber factories are notoriously dangerous and unhealthy places to work. The workers had to contend with a witch's brew of chemicals including molten sulfur, sulfur dioxide, and hydrogen sulfide, all of which were extremely detrimental to their health. Other common chemicals—some of them carcinogenic—included naphtha, benzene, and carbon bisulfide. Rubber and gutta-percha manufacturing also involves extremely hot working conditions. The workers' testimony to the London Trades Council delegation undermines the company's claims that Silver's was a healthy place to work. Mr. Eiffe testified, "Where he worked the men had to strip themselves naked, as there were five boilers with steam up under the place where they stood."[440] Continuous exposure to high temperatures can result in heatstroke and even death. However, the claim, attributed to Michael Henry of the Coal Porters' Union, of a boy being forced to work in temperatures of 196 degrees F is not credible, as the boy would have been boiled alive like a lobster. More likely, Henry said 96 degrees and was misquoted. There seems little reason, however, to doubt Henry's allegation that the foreman concerned, a Mr. Herbert, made the boy work in extreme heat and then put him in a cold room "with only a coat thrown over his shoulders."[441] Stopford Brooke told his parishioners of young men working in temperatures of 120 degrees, and alleged that if they took advantage of the rule allowing them an hour's wait before going into cold rooms, "they were discharged at the end of the week without reason given."[442] Harry Stone also qualified his initial agreement with the company regarding the yardmen's working conditions.[443] The yard gang worked outside year-round, in snow, hail, rain, wind, and sunshine, with perhaps a sack thrown over their shoulders for protection, an irony given that Silver's was still a manufacturer of waterproofed cotton cloth.

"Horses Better Fed and Sheltered"

As previously mentioned, Walter Drummond of the Stevedores' Union claimed in a factory gate address that the average life span of a Silvertown worker was thirty-five years.[444] According to Robert Woods and Nicola Shelton in their study of mortality in the Victorian era, males born in England and Wales between 1838 and 1854 could expect to live 39.9 years, females 41.9. The corresponding expectations for 1871–80 were 41.4 and 44.6.[445] Given the poor nutrition, bad sanitation, overwork, and unhealthy working conditions endured by workers "on the marsh," Drummond's estimate rings true. The dockers' leader, Ben Tillett, surely only exaggerated a little when he told a mass meeting of strikers and supporters on Clerkenwell Green that "the company's horses [are] better fed and sheltered than their workpeople," and added that Silver's "could not get a good horse under £30 or £40, but they could get a good workman at $4\frac{3}{4}$d an hour."[446] Indeed they could. If their employees did not like it, any number of others were desperate for work. The socialist W. Stephen Sanders recalled that in the winter of 1888 the streets of London echoed with the "doleful chants" of long processions of unemployed men:

We've got no work to do-oo-oo,
We've got no work to do-oo-oo.
We're all froze out poor labouring men
And we've got no work to do . . .

The men were parading for "the collection of coppers from people who were themselves only a hair's-breadth from the edge of the same abyss of misery."[447] Many others could be found, in Cockney argot, "carrying the banner," homeless and tramping the streets all night, regardless of the weather or the season.[448] In such circumstances, the unemployed, as Marx believed, really did "belong to capital no less absolutely than if the capitalists had bred the members of this [reserve] army [of labor] at their own cost."[449] Small wonder, therefore, that Silver's treated their horses more solicitously than their workers.

VII.
The Strike Gains Momentum

◆◆◆

> [The Silvertown strike] is a revolt against oppression: a protest against the brute force which keeps a huge population down in the depths of the most dire depredation, for the benefit of a knot of profit-hunters ... [it] is a strike of the poor against the rich.[450]
> —WILLIAM MORRIS, 1889

EMPLOYERS FACED WITH strikes often claim—and some perhaps even believe—that their workers have been led astray by outsiders with sinister agendas. Politicians and conservative pundits echo such claims. Samuel Silver informed shareholders:

> As regarded the strike at Silvertown . . . [the shareholders] had not far to seek for its exciting cause. The dock movement took place in the vicinity of their works, and affected a number of the labourers there. These men were instigated by the clamour of professional agitators and several irresponsible advisors.[451]

The corollary of such claims is that otherwise "loyal" workers are coerced or tricked into striking. In this vein, William Tyler wrote to the press complaining that "the majority" of the workers "have been intimidated into leaving their work, having when going to their meals to pass through the crowd, who hissed and groaned at them, and used violent language. In some cases they have been hurt, but will not give evidence, lest worse should befall them."[452] While it would be foolish to deny instances of assault or threats of it against blacklegs, it simply beggars belief that "the majority" of employees could be prevented from going to work for many weeks by a handful of militants. Nor is it credible that the militants could force the workers to tramp distances of up to twenty miles to and from union rallies in other parts of London against their will. One wonders also what magical powers "unprincipled agitators" must have possessed in order to prevail upon strangers to quit their work without good reason. In reality, the central leadership of the strike was home-grown and though outside labor organizers did come to Silvertown, they were responding to requests for help from the Silver's workers themselves. The company's claims were at best patronizing and at worst insulting to those they employed. Tyler's claim that the dock strike had "unsettled the minds" of some of the workers implies that they were like children. Given that the Victorians believed that to "spare the rod was to spoil the child," the remedy could only be chastisement.

Fred Ling, Rank-and-File Union Leader

Although none of the rank-and-file strike leaders rose to national prominence in the labor movement, most of them were intelligent, courageous, loyal, and resourceful people. Preeminent among them was Frederick Ling, who worked as a stoker at Silver's.[453] A colorful stump orator, Ling declared at one mass meeting that "the capitalist's money compounded but the workers' stopped at simple interest."[454] He remains a shadowy figure about whom only tantalizing snippets of information survive. Where and when he was born is unknown, but it is possible given his long association with Silvertown that he was born there. At the time of the strike he lived at 3 Frederick Terrace, Wilton Road,[455] but later moved to 3 Mecklenburgh Terrace,[456] and still later to Albert Road in Silvertown East.[457] He was the founding Secretary of the Silvertown branch of the NUG&GL, which was created during the strike,[458] and he held the position until the end of June 1906.[459] He may have died shortly after the latter date[460] and if so he outlived his old foe Matthew Gray by five years.[461] Given his great energy during the strike, it is likely that Ling was a comparatively young man, but one old enough to have developed as a class-conscious militant. It is also possible that he had already joined the union as an individual before the 1889 dispute began, but this is speculation. The newspaper record shows that Ling became an accomplished orator during the strike, and he appears to have possessed considerable organizing skills. He was also a socialist, or became one during the strike. In 1890, during the agitation for the eight-hour day initiated and led by the NUG&GL and Eleanor Marx's Bloomsbury Socialist Society,[462] he is quoted in the *Stratford Express* as advocating:

> Labour should be represented in Parliament by one of their own clique, and Mr. Keir Hardie was the man they were putting forward. . . . They all knew that the employers might promise an eight-hour day one week and take it away the next, therefore they wanted an act of Parliament that should enforce an eight-hour day.[463]

Ling remained a comrade of Eleanor Marx after the strike when his house was used as the main union meeting place in Silvertown. He took to the spirit and methods of the New Unionism with great enthusiasm. In many ways, he epitomizes the forgotten rank-and-file militants who rallied to the cause of unskilled labor and kept the flame burning through the dark days of the 1890s depression. Blacklisted after the strike and heavily fined[464] in what appears to have been payback by Matthew Gray, life cannot have been easy for him, but he did not abandon the struggle.

The Strike Committee

Leadership of the strike was vested in an approximately thirty-strong Strike Committee, which operated from rooms above the Railway Tavern and Tea Rooms on the corner of Constance Street and Connaught Road opposite the Silvertown station. Also known as Cundy's after the landlady, the twenty-eight-year-old, Somerset-born Elizabeth Cundy, the pub lingered on until 2008 when it fell victim to urban blight and Council rooming house regulations, and died. Despite its sad end, the pub was for many years a center of social life for local dockers and factory workers. Although a reporter for the *Times* found the premises to be "dismal,"[465] the chances are that Cundy's fitted the rosier picture painted by Charles Booth cited earlier.

Some of the names of the Strike Committee members can be found in contemporary newspaper accounts. The first chairman was a man called William Scrine (of which more later), the treasurer was a worker called Thomas Reed, and the secretary, chosen because of his penmanship skills, was a man called Arthur Hillier. Other members included John Buck, H. Girling, C. Rudd, J. Brown, R. Machon (or perhaps Mahon or McMahon), W. Cartwright, a man named Atkins, another named Wright, and Mr. Stewart, who was said to act as chief marshal at demonstrations, perhaps because of his physical strength. George Bateman, who later took over as chairman and remained in the position until the very end of the strike, appears to have been a competent and committed unionist. By the time Will Thorne and the other "outside agitators" arrived on the scene, Ling and his comrades already had the strike well organized, with the influence of the dock strike readily apparent in their predilection for picket lines, flags and banners, street marches, bands, and mass meetings, which proceeded despite the increasingly autumnal weather of plummeting temperatures, bracing winds, and downpours.

Two weeks after the beginning of the strike, the great majority of laborers had quit work, mostly willingly, although some were laid off. Four hundred were still at work by that time, Ling reported, but most of them had agreed to strike once they had finished some piecework. The main aim, Ling added, was to close down the coal shop,[466] essential for raising steam for the boilers and the machinery still running. The firm's turners and smiths, all of whom appear to have been ASE members, had also either been locked out or had struck work in sympathy with the laborers, and were receiving dispute benefit from their union. The fitters, carpenters, and instrument makers remained on the job, however, and this was to cause an ugly internecine dispute with the laborers.[467]

Digging In for a Long Struggle

On the other side of the picket lines, Matthew Gray was digging in for a potentially long struggle. Although he reported confidently to the directors on Thursday, 26 September, that "things were in much the same state as when the Board met last," this was not quite the case because he revealed that he "had arranged to increase largely the production of electric-light wires at the Company's Persan Works."[468] This was a smaller factory, which employed around three hundred workers, situated on the River Seine near Paris. Persistent rumors were also circulating around Silvertown that Gray was dismantling machinery and shipping it to the French factory. According to reports in the *Stratford Express* and elsewhere, the firm's engineers, working without laborers, were carrying out this work.[469] Will Thorne said at a factory gate meeting that the export of the work to France highlighted the need for the working class to organize across frontiers.[470] In this, Thorne was well ahead of his time, for the internationalist objective of cross-border unions still has not been achieved over 120 years later. Other well-grounded rumors suggested that Silver's was contracting out work to other London engineering and electrical firms.[471] Gray certainly took advantage of the opportunity created by the strike to remove old machinery and install new equipment while the factory was largely out of production; another reason, perhaps, for him to be in no hurry to settle the dispute. According to an intriguing article published in the *Labour Elector* toward the end of the dispute, Gray was also prolonging the strike as part of a design to rig the share market. The article alleged:

> It is frequently stated, and generally regarded as correct, that Mr. Gray is keeping up the lock-out for his own ends in order to depreciate shares in the company, and thus force them on the market. Already, it is said, there have been cautious inquiries from an unknown buyer. If this is so, it would be well for the other shareholders to ascertain the facts and take steps to stop any little plot of Mr. Gray's or any other person, to rig the market.[472]

Irritated, Silver's board of directors referred the matter to their solicitor, Mr. Hutchins, with a view to possible legal action.[473] The article, however, had been cunningly constructed. The editor made an apology of sorts, stating that it was "a correct report of a statement made at a public meeting," but with the caveat that "it will be noted that we did not assert its correctness, but, on the contrary, expressed doubts as to its veracity."[474] Silver's did not pursue the matter after the "apology," either because they were advised that a libel case was not likely to succeed, or because they feared further publicity might lend credibility to the story. Over a century later, we will probably never know whether there was any truth in it. Whether it harmed the firm is a moot point. Supporters of the strikers would have welcomed its publication, but with hardening attitudes toward strikes in the middle classes, it would have been easy for them to dismiss it as scuttlebutt. Probably the *Labour Elector* strongly suspected Gray of financial chicanery but lacked solid proof, and the carefully worded article was a way of warning the strikers that they were facing an unscrupulous foe who was in no hurry to negotiate. The workers, for their part, were determined to fight on, despite admissions by the Strike Committee in late September that no early end to the dispute was in sight.[475]

"Resolutely Refuse to Yield"

On Saturday, 28 September, a fortnight into the strike, Fred Ling presided over a large meeting of workers and their supporters in the cul-de-sac outside Silver's factory gates. Tom McCarthy of the Stevedores' Union exhorted the strikers to emulate the dockworkers "in resolutely refusing to yield." Tom Walsh of the Sailors' and Firemen's Union also spoke, along with Walter Drummond. Strike relief was paid out, with men receiving 5 shillings each and boys and girls getting two-and-sixpence. These were not princely sums, but a number of other unions had pledged to contribute funds, and the strikers were actively collecting in working-class neighborhoods. The next day, a Sunday, the strikers and their supporters marched through the City and crowded into Hyde Park, appropriately near the stump of the Reformer's Tree in Hyde Park for another rally, with Fred Ling again in the chair.[476] The keynote speakers included the silver-tongued Cockney John Burns, who had been a central leader of the dock strike, and Will Thorne, the militant socialist leader of the NUG&GL. Thorne announced to loud cheers that his union had just sent £250 to the strike fund,[477] around £22,000 in terms of its purchasing power today.[478] Over on the other side of the park, another rally of East End workers was in progress. These "malcontents," sniffed a reporter for the *Standard*, "consisted of East-End tailors—the undersized, ill-fed, and ill-clothed German and Polish emigrants whose presence in this country has called the 'sweating' system into existence."[479] This was surely victim blaming with a vengeance, but the 6,000 tailors fought on to win partial concessions after six weeks on strike. Led by the socialists Lewis Lyons and Woolf Wess of the *Arbeter Fraint* (Workers' Friend) group, they were seeking a ten-and-a-half-hour day.[480]

Will Thorne: Not Eloquent, but Sincere

One can imagine the scene that autumn day in Hyde Park: the huge crowd milling around the speakers' platform, footsore from the long march across central London from Silvertown but full of hope; the leaves turning brown, red, and yellow and falling from the fine old trees; the weather fine, too, but with a hint of winter's chill in the air. When Will Thorne came to the platform, two thousand pairs of eyes fixed upon him, a plainspoken man yet one who could inspire and lead with the force of his personality and his burning convictions. Thorne spoke with a flat West Midlands accent—for he was a Brummie (a native of Birmingham, or "Brum") who had made his way to London and found work in the giant Beckton gasworks—and though he lacked the silver tongue of John Burns or Tom Mann, he radiated a powerful intensity of emotion and honesty.

W. Stephen Sanders has left us a pen portrait of him when he was an impassioned young agitator burning with anger at the abuses dished out to his class, before he became "the big burly figure" who long sat at Westminster as Labour MP for West Ham. He was, Sanders tells us, "slight and fine-drawn through the heavy labour of his arduous calling" at the Beckton furnaces. Earlier in 1889, at a meeting of the Battersea branch of the Social Democratic Federation, of which both were members, Sanders heard Thorne speak:

> He came . . . straight from the retort house with the murk of that fiery place burnt into his features. Round his eyes were dark rings of coal-grime, and his hands were, and are still, gnarled and knotted by the handling of the charging-tools. His voice, as I remember it, was not strong, and his words were not eloquent, but his obvious sincerity was more convincing than fine phrases.[481]

The Silver's strikers must have hung on Thorne's every word. Raised in poverty, his father dead after a drunken brawl, Thorne was illiterate when he arrived in London. It could scarcely be otherwise, for he had started work for a rope and twine spinner at the age of six. Acutely aware of his own ignorance, he had a thirst for knowledge and a passion for justice. Before his arrival in London he had already distinguished himself by leading labor agitation in a Midlands gasworks.[482] In London, he learned to read and write, tutored by his friend and comrade Eleanor Marx. With his keen intelligence, he might have chosen to turn his back on his fellows but he chose the path of class liberation. The same might be said for his fellow stoker Fred Ling, the NUG&GL Branch Secretary, whose talents also stretched far beyond what was necessary to wield the charging tools in Silver's boiler house.

John Burns, Cockney Militant

Thorne's fellow speaker John Burns was a powerful, if theatrical, orator. A fitter (machinist) by trade, a member of the Battersea branch of the Amalgamated Society of Engineers, and a Londoner born and bred, he spoke broad Cockney, with all its glottal stops and colorful colloquialisms. His speeches were informed by a keen intelligence. Frederick Engels was justifiably worried by what he saw as his craving for popularity,[483] and Hyndman dismissed him as "a self-seeker,"[484] but Burns was a gifted organizer and a speaker who could hold his listeners spellbound.[485] Stephen Sanders, who knew him well from their days in the Battersea branch of the SDF, recalls the full-bearded Burns as a "powerful and vibrant" orator, and has left us this summary of his talents and nature:

> His appearance was bucolic; in humour, good temper, and shrewdness he was a typical Londoner, but redeemed by his burning Socialist faith from the tolerant cynicism which characterises the average Cockney. He had received no education worthy of the name; this deficiency, however, was, to a great extent, made good by his mother wit and natural ability.[486]

Burns, Sanders continues, had "a talent for epigrammatic and telling phrases" and—possessed of a "striking and magnetic personality"—he could "sway and control great working class audiences."[487] Although he later drifted away from his roots and became a Liberal cabinet minister—confirming Engels's suspicions—he had been of great service to the working class.

Another "outside agitator" was the Scot Pete Curran, a close friend of Will Thorne's who was earning his living at the time as a steam hammer operator across the river from Silvertown at the Woolwich Arsenal.[488] Often victimized and blacklisted, Curran remained "bright and cheerful," Thorne tells us, and was an indefatigable activist who "excelled as a public speaker—eloquent, witty, sometimes sarcastic, and capable of delivering sledgehammer attacks of logic." He was also a member of the SDF and later served on the national executives of the ILP and the Labour Party, as well as acting as chairman of the General Federation of Trades Unions and as a fraternal delegate to conferences of the American Federation of Labor.[489] The strikers could draw heart from the support of men such as these, although some men, including Curran, nursed their own demons, for he "probably drank himself to death" according to the historian Derek Matthews.[490] These were heady days, however, crammed with marches and stirring speeches, many of them hard up against the railway line that bisected Silvertown. They must have terrified and angered the bourgeois.

Slinking Out the Back Door

On Tuesday, 1 October, two days after the Hyde Park rally, on an otherwise nondescript autumn morning, the strikers staged their largest meeting to date in front of the factory gates.[491] A reporter from the *Labour Elector* found the strikers "very hopeful" at the meeting. He met Will Thorne and reported him to be "a simple, unassuming man and a capital speaker who had entirely gained the confidence and esteem of the men."[492] The strike, Fred Ling announced to loud cheers, had already lasted sixteen days and he was "hopeful of a settlement." He was, however, putting the best face on things because the previous week the Strike Committee had traveled to Cannon Street in an unsuccessful bid to talk to the directors. Ling gave a fighting speech. Gray had "slunk out of the office three minutes before the strikers got there," he declaimed, to cries of "Shame!" from the strikers. However, though Gray might well have sneaked out the back door,[493] he was obdurate rather than cowardly and simply saw no good reason to meet the deputation. Another speaker was the flamboyant Irishman Michael Henry of the Coal Porters' Union, who "emphatically asserted, backed up by the enthusiastic cheers of the men, 'that we are going to win' this strike.'"[494] Much later, Will Thorne recalled Henry as "a journalist, novel writer, and a smart platform orator." Henry had formed the Coal Porters' Union with workers employed to unload colliers at the docks. Although another Irishman, Jim Connor, later ousted him as union secretary,[495] Henry was a prominent figure in the early years of the New Unions and worked hard for the Silvertown strikers. He blasted the directors in his usual colorful style, describing them as "Mr. Gray and his five puppies." Silver's was raking in profits of £160,000 a year, he claimed to the outrage of the crowd, and was contracting out work to other London firms. Silver's was a powerful firm, he acknowledged, but collective action by the individually weak could bring their foes to their knees. In his native Ireland, he declared, the Land League's boycott movement had achieved great things. His own parents had been evicted from their farm thirty years ago, but the grass was growing over it as the landlord could find no one unprincipled, foolish, or brave enough to take it over. That, thundered Henry, was the kind of resolve that the strikers needed to win their dispute![496] His words would have struck a chord with those in the crowd whose forebears had crossed the water to escape famine, oppression, and poverty, and there were many of them in the East End, where third-generation immigrants were known as Irish Cockneys.

Although Mr. Donald of the Labour Union believed that if Silver's could have got the work done cheaper in France "they would have done it long ago," we do know from the company records that Gray *had* transferred work there early on in the dispute. The highlight of the two-hour meeting was Ling's announcement that a number of impoverished young women "lured down from Manchester" by Silver's to work as strike-breakers had gone home. The Strike Committee had bought them tickets and escorted them to the railway station, where they parted on cordial terms, for the chances are that the women had come to Silvertown in good faith. It was a heartening act of solidarity and the meeting concluded in high spirits, with the strikers and their supporters afterward parading the streets of Silvertown with banners held high behind a brass band.[497] The morning after the big rally, 150 workers in the coat shop, where the cables were sealed in rubber or gutta-percha, walked off the job to the cheers of the pickets. Significantly, some 120 of the new strikers were females. The union also approached the mayor of West Ham, Alderman Hay, with a view to his acting as an arbitrator in the dispute, which he readily agreed to do.

The morning of Thursday, 3 October, dawned dull and overcast, with rain clouds scudding across the sky, but the strikers rallied again at the cul-de-sac leading into the main entrance to the works. Will Thorne was again in fine form, regaling the workers with an amusing tale of how an under-manager called Wood was planning to fire the factory's boilers. Thorne, a stoker himself, remarked with professional pride that Mr. Wood would have many boilers to attend to, and as he would not get up much steam, the machinery would not revolve too fast. In fact, he said, laughing, such a novice boiler-man might well cause an explosion! Thorne also lambasted what he saw as the hypocrisy of the numerous clergymen who held shares in the company, and stressed that since the strike had been widely reported in the press they could not claim to be unaware that sweat labor provided them their dividends. On a more ominous note, Thorne drew attention to the matter of the carpenters, engineers, and instrument makers who were still working in the factory with their respective union's support. He believed that because Silver's had been planning to replace old machinery for some time that the artisans were only working until their unions called them out. He reasoned, somewhat optimistically, that the company could not hold out for three days longer. Walter Drummond also spoke, but in a harbinger of things to come, the wintry skies opened and torrential rain prompted an early adjournment of the meeting.[498]

Capital Attendance in Victoria Park

Meanwhile, over in Cannon Street in the City, secure from the elements behind thick brick walls, the weekly meeting of the Silver's board was in session. Had Will Thorne been privy to their discussions, he might not have been so sure that an early end to the strike was in sight. Matthew Gray reported the "position as to the strike to be unaltered" and the meeting went on to discuss the contents of another letter to the press, "to be signed by the Secretary, stating the facts as to the pay & treatment of the Company's workpeople." This "settled and ordered to be distributed," the meeting passed on to other matters.[499] The following day, Friday, 4 October, was cloudy, cold, and "very miserable," and it perhaps matched the bitter mood of the strikers picketing outside the works, for company secretary Tyler's letter appeared in a number of newspapers that morning and must have dashed any hopes that Silver's was on the verge of surrender. Nevertheless, the strikers were determined not to give in. Showers fell throughout Saturday, and it was "bitterly cold," but this failed to dampen the enthusiasm at a huge mass meeting in Victoria Park. The *Stratford Express* recorded that although the "gravelly soil was as wet as it possibly could be," there was "a capital attendance," estimated at 10,000 people, including contingents of dockers, lightermen, tailors, and painters, who marched into the park behind their banners from the nearby streets. They were joined by a detachment from the Phoenix Brothers, an Irish nationalist society. The strikers must have been grateful to have so many friends.

John Burns, himself until recently a member of the ASE Executive Council, mounted the platform and excoriated the carpenters' and engineers' unions for refusing to call out their members. Michael Henry attacked the establishment worthies on the company board and among the shareholders, singling out Prime Minister Lord Salisbury in particular as the butt of some vintage Irish mockery. Walter Drummond again drew attention to the unsanitary living conditions of the workers in Silvertown, many of whom were crammed family upon family in four-room houses. West Ham councilor Alderman Phillips deplored the company's conduct of the strike, and called upon Gray to negotiate in good faith for the welfare of the district as a whole. Phillips was dismayed that the district's small shopkeepers and other tradesmen were suffering a slowdown in trade because of the dispute.[500] The next day, Sunday, 6 October, was dry and warm, but it was not a day of rest and recreation for the strikers. A large body of them walked to Stratford and there paraded through the streets behind a fife-and-drum band, collecting money for their relief find and listening to streetcorner speeches.[501]

Tussy: Chief Orator at Silvertown

The star of the day was a passionate, dark-haired, young woman whose burningly eloquent words were soon greeted with loud applause. Some of the strikers and their supporters probably remembered her from the dock strike. She was an unknown quantity for others, but she was soon to win them over. Unlike Burns, Tillett, Mann, Thorne, and the other New Union leaders, she was of the educated middle class, but the workers soon learned to trust her. The big lesson of the current strike, she avowed, was the need for unity: the skilled and unskilled must work together for the common good and the men and women at Silver's should "work together in combination." The woman, noted the *Stratford Express*, was Mrs. Aveling,[502] but she is better remembered today as Eleanor Marx, the feisty, independent-minded daughter of Karl Marx. At the time her father was relatively unknown in Britain, and she earned the respect of the people of Silvertown as a result of her own qualities. That she was able to do so as a Jewish woman in a pervasively sexist and anti-Semitic era is further testament to her talents and strength of character. Marx, who lived at 65 Chancery Lane in the City, was to spend most of her waking hours for the next two months in Silvertown, so much so that she cancelled her regular Sunday afternoon visits to Frederick Engels's house, and dropped out of sight for her less political friends altogether. Engels informed her sister, Laura Lafargue, that since the Dock Strike "Tussy," Eleanor Marx's nickname among family and close friends, "has become quite an East Ender, organising Trades Unions and supporting strikes—last Sunday we did not see her at all, as she had to be speechifying both morning and night." Some writers have accused Engels of patronizing her on account of these remarks,[503] but in fact he was full of admiration for his young friend and comrade who had immersed herself in the actual class struggle. Eleanor Marx was at the forefront of a working-class upsurge that Engels had longed to see for many years—and one that he must have regretted her father had not lived to witness. "These new Trades Unions of unskilled men and women are totally different from the old organisations of the working-class aristocracy," he enthused, "and cannot fall into the same conservative ways."[504]

Tussy, never one to do things by halves, launched into the Silvertown strike with all the considerable enthusiasm she could muster. After the German socialist Clara Zetkin visited Laura Lafargue in Paris, after staying with friends in London, Lafargue wrote to Engels that "Mme. Zetkine and her boys were here yesterday: she gave me news of Tussy whose agitation she is very enthusiastic about, especially her getting up on tables and chairs to harangue the Silvertown women strikers."[505] A sympathetic journalist who heard Marx speak in Silvertown has left us with a word picture of a "figure [who] deserves the praise that has not been entirely her reward":

> Anyone who saw and heard some of the hundred rough impromptu meetings which were held hard by the railway lines that go running through the streets of Silvertown will have been struck by the dark, energetic Jewish face, the clear silvery voice, the graceful and fluent speech of the chief orator—a woman.[506]

Eleanor Marx was the common-law wife of Dr. Edward Aveling, himself a socialist, who was also to become deeply involved in the Silvertown strike and in the affairs of the NUG&GL. She was no man's appendage, however, and she had earlier that year proved her caliber during the dock laborers' strike. Ben Tillett recalls that "another of the helpers at [the dock union] headquarters, doing the drudgery of clerical work as well as more responsible duties, was Karl Marx's daughter, Eleanor, the . . . wife of Edward Aveling." She was, he added, "brilliant, devoted and beautiful" and "a vivid and vital personality, with great force of character, courage and ability."[507] Tom Mann believed her to be "a most capable woman," who "possessing a complete mastery of economics . . . was able, alike in conversation and on a public platform, to hold her own with the best." Furthermore, Mann adds, "she was ever ready . . . to give close attention to detailed work, when by so doing she could help the movement."[508] We should not lose sight of the fact that Eleanor Marx made her mark on the world despite the ideology of a profoundly sexist era in which women were belittled as the "weaker" sex. As Arthur Field insisted at the time of her untimely death in 1898, she would be remembered "not because she is the daughter of Karl Marx, but because she is Eleanor Marx."[509] Despite their many disagreements, Henry Hyndman conceded with respectful generosity that "she would have done great things had she lived."[510]

Equal Rights for Women

Eleanor Marx's great contribution to the strikers' cause, and to the labor movement as a whole, was her dogged insistence on equal rights for women workers. Olga Meier, in her commentary on a collection of the

Marx sisters' family correspondence, draws attention to Eleanor's instinctive feminism: she "simply assumed she was an equal human being and
that was that."[511] Moreover, she was to be a pioneer in the organization
of working women, and, as Meier adds, "she was at her happiest when
she could be of service to the unskilled and semiskilled workers."[512] Her
feminism was linked indissolubly to her socialism: "Women," she insisted,
"are the creatures of an organized tyranny of men, as the workers are the
creatures of an organized tyranny of idlers." Women and the workers as
a whole had to emancipate themselves. Though women would find allies
among good men, their liberation could only come from their own actions;
women could not hope that emancipation would come from "man as a
whole."[513] Though she championed the idea of building women's union
branches, she was not what we might call today a radical-feminist sepa-
ratist. Nor did she wish to accept only an "auxiliary" role for the women
strikers. In her first speech at Silvertown, she stressed the necessity for
workers' unity: male and female, skilled and unskilled, of whatever nation-
ality or creed. Marx was extremely popular with the union members of
both sexes and they called her "Good Old Stoker,"[514] perhaps because of
her fiery speeches. In one of these, to loud applause,

> she . . . appealed strongly to the women. They must form unions and
> work in harmony with the men's trade unions. As the dock strike had
> taught them the lesson that skilled and unskilled labour should work
> together, so the present strike should teach them a further great lesson,
> that they could only win by men and women working in combination.
> The capitalist was using women to underwork men and that would
> be the case until women refused to undersell their brothers and hus-
> bands.[515]

It was apparent, however, that women were at the bottom of the industrial pile. There had been women in British factories since the start of
the Industrial Revolution, and their numbers were growing. This was
true of the large new factories springing up on the fringes of the East
End; in addition to Silver's, places such as Keiller's jam factory and the
sugar refineries in Silvertown. Over one-tenth of the workers at Silver's
were women and they were in the majority in some departments.[516] Their
wages were set at a fraction of those of men, even for identical work, and
the "women's work" they usually performed was undervalued and underpaid. (This was a system later described by sociologists as the sexual
division of labor or gender segmentation of the workforce.) From the

capitalists' point of view, patriarchy was a great boon: employing women on substandard rates helped depress wages and boost profits. For Eleanor Marx, the struggle of working women was indivisible from the struggle for workers' rights and socialism, and although she was very aware of "her own special constituency of women,"[517] she was very critical of "bourgeois feminism." In a polemical article published in the Vienna *Arbeiterinnen-zeitung* (Workingwomen's Newspaper) in 1892 she declared:

> We can understand, sympathise, and also help if need be, when women of the upper or middle class fight for rights that are well-founded and whose achievement will benefit working-women also . . . [but] if every demand raised by these women were granted today, we working-women would still be just where we were before. Women-workers would still work infamously long hours, for infamously low wages, under infamously unhealthful conditions; they would still have only the choice between prostitution and starvation.[518]

She went on to give examples of contemporary English middle-class feminists who had opposed the raising of wages and the shortening of working hours, even where women worked long hours for scandalously low pay in appalling conditions. "We see no more in common between a Mrs. Fawcett and a laundress," she argued, "than we see between Roth-schild [the banker] and one of his employees."[519] (Marx was referring to Dame Millicent Garrett Fawcett, who, under her "married name" of Mrs. Henry Fawcett, was prominent in the Victorian women's suffrage movement.)

Marx fiercely rejected any suggestion that men should protect women as the "weaker sex." After the "Bloody Sunday" rally in Trafalgar Square in November 1887, she stated that "no woman who enters such a move-ment as this has the right to ask—and so far as I know not one does ask—for different treatment from that dealt out to the men by whose side she is fighting, simply because she is a woman." In the same letter, she lashed out at the official hypocrisy in which an alleged concern for "the fairer sex" concealed violent misogyny: "My experience on Sunday was that women were singled out by the police, and received a good deal more than their fair share of blows."[520] She was also scornful of the hypocrisy that allowed married men to have mistresses while expecting their wives to remain faithful.[521]

Champion of Socialism

Eleanor Marx's father, had he lived, would have been proud of her contribution to the East End workers' struggles. As her biographer Chuschichi
Tsuzuki has noted, "Among the daughters of Karl Marx, Eleanor alone
grew into a fighter dedicated to a cause, a brave, ingenious, never-tiring
champion of Socialism." She was an enthusiastic supporter, too, of Irish
emancipation, something she perhaps picked up from Annie Burns, the
Irish "factory girl" who became Frederick Engels's life partner.[522] Such a
stance must have resonated with the large Irish working-class population
in the East End.

At the same time, she was deeply involved in intellectual pursuits. A
devotee of the theater who had translated two of Ibsen's plays into English,[523] learning Norwegian to do so, she had considered a career on the
stage. John Stokes considers that she "found in . . . [Shakespeare's] hero-
ines—from Juliet to Lady Macbeth—evidence of a passionate commitment
that she was anxious to emulate," and perhaps it was so.[524] Whether it was
speaking on platforms in all weathers, standing up to police batons, organizing trade union branches, translating letters, or doing the "drudgery"
of clerical work, Eleanor Marx everywhere gave evidence of her burning
commitment to the cause of labor. No doubt to the "respectable" opinion of the day she was not only a bluestocking but as Lyn Pykett has
observed, "a wild woman as politician and social insurgent."[525] The prominent Fabian Beatrice Webb, née Potter, would not have minded Marx
being a bluestocking, but her "wildness" upset Webb's petit-bourgeois
prejudices. Webb has left us an interesting if snide diary portrait of Marx
as a twenty-eight-year-old:

> Gains her livelihood by teaching "literature" etc … and corresponding
> for Socialist newspapers. In person she is comely, dressed in a slovenly
> picturesque way with curly black hair, flying about in all directions.
> Fine eyes, full of life and sympathy, otherwise ugly features and expres-
> sion and complexion showing signs of unhealthy excited life kept up
> with stimulants and tempered by narcotics. Lives alone . . . evidently
> peculiar views on love etc, and should think she has somewhat natural
> relations with men! Should fear the chances of her remaining long
> within the pale of respectable society.[526]

Webb's calumny of Marx as a tart and drug addict says more about its
author than it does about its subject. One suspects that Marx's real offense

in Webb's eyes was to be a socialist feminist intellectual who believed that the working class had to emancipate itself and not meekly accept whatever charity and advice the middle classes condescended to dole out to them. Eleanor's contemporary, Marion Comyn, provides a more objective picture of a passionate personality:

> Willful indeed she was, but also an unusually brilliant creature, with a clear logical brain, a shrewd knowledge of men and a wonderful memory. . . . She either passionately admired or desperately scorned. She loved fervently or she hated with vehemence. Middle courses never commended themselves to her. She had amazing vitality, extraordinary receptivity, and she was the gayest creature in the world—when she was not the most miserable.[527]

Stephen Sanders—who later gravitated toward Fabianism, but was of a fairer cast of mind than Webb—recalls Eleanor Marx as "an attractive woman who had inherited a goodly portion of her father's brain-power and combative qualities which she placed unreservedly at the service of the masses."[528]

Marx "harangued, organized, and led the unskilled workers" at Silvertown, writes Chuschichi Tsuzuki.[529] She was the founding secretary of the Silvertown women's branch of the NUG&GL and earned the respect and gratitude of both the men and women of the district. Nor did she walk away after the strike ended, but served on the National Executive of the NUG&GL for many years, where she was known as "our mother," despite her relative youth.[530] She taught Will Thorne to read and write, and despite her gender and her middle-class background, she gained the undying respect and affection of that gruff son of the people, who, it must be said, was something of a male chauvinist. At Eleanor Marx's funeral in 1898, Thorne broke down and "'cried like a child' and his voice became almost inaudible as he tried to speak of the close friendship he had enjoyed with the deceased and the devoted work she had done on behalf of his union."[531] Eleanor would have been mourned, too, in Silvertown. She died, tragically, by her own hand after suffering great personal unhappiness. Perhaps, as E. P. Thompson has mused, she might not have made the decision had she known how much she was loved and respected in the movement.[532] Her death was an enormous loss, and over a century later, a Labour Party member in Silvertown spoke of her contribution to the local workers' lives.[533]

The Starvation Game

Apart from the arrival of Eleanor Marx on 6 October, it had been an eventful week in other respects. Silver's remained intransigent, and Matthew Gray must have been delighted to see the unions fighting with each other as the internecine dispute between the laborers and the ASE festered. At the Silver's board meeting on Thursday, 10 October, letters from Major Barnes, the Liberal MP for West Ham, and Mr. Curtis, the mayor, were read, "both offering mediation." A letter from Mr. H. Girling and twenty others on behalf of the Strike Committee, "forwarding new terms asked for by the Silvertown hands now out" was also read.[534] All such approaches proved a waste of time. According to the minutes of the ASE Executive Council, an article in the *Star* on 13 October announced that Silver's "rudely rebuffed" the overtures, and commented that it was clear that the company's "game" was to starve the strikers back to work on the old terms and conditions.[535] A letter from William Tyler had been read aloud at the Strike Committee in which Tyler advised that he "was instructed to inform you" that "after careful inquiry they [the directors] find that they have been paying higher wages than any other firm in our trade, and they cannot pay more than heretofore." The committee resolved to continue the strike and a mass meeting later the same day unanimously endorsed their decision. Eleanor Marx had no truck with arguments about "ability to pay" and insisted that the workers had the right to a living wage.[536] It was well within the company's means to grant the increases demanded.

In the same week, Marx had presided over the first meeting of a Silvertown women's branch of the NUG&GL, with women from the nearby Keiller's jam factory joining their sisters from Silver's. Local shopkeepers also met and decided to organize a relief fund for the benefit of the strikers' families, separate from the general fund run by the union. The strikers also received welcome support from workers at Woolwich Arsenal across the river, who had appointed a collection committee to raise funds for the Silvertown struggle.[537] One can imagine the hand of Pete Curran, Will Thorne's Scottish friend, behind the collection, for he was employed as a steam-hammer man at the arsenal.

Ben Tillett: "Tough and Dauntless"

The strike was now in its fourth week, noted the SDF's *Justice*. Over 1,800 workers were on strike, the paper noted (surely an underestimate) and "there was no prospect of an immediate settlement."[538] Early on Monday, 14 October, the management had thrown open the factory gates for any worker who cared to return under the old conditions, but none sneaked through the thick fog to take up the offer.[539] The previous Saturday, the strikers and their families and supporters had staged another huge rally, with 10,000 people marching along the North Woolwich Road to Victoria Park. Brass bands enlivened the great parade and the marchers heard speeches from the Strike Committee leaders, along with Michael Henry and Ben Tillett, who declared that a defeat for the Silvertown workers would be a defeat for the entire London working class.

The theatrical Irishman Michael Henry of the Coal Porters' Union has been long forgotten, but Tillett's name lives on as a central leader of the London dockers. Tom Mann recalled him as "short in stature, but tough; pallid, but dauntless; affected with a stammer . . . but the real orator" of the group that led the dock strike.[540] Like many of the New Union leaders, the half-Irish Tillett had been born in grinding poverty. His early life was a struggle to survive in a brutal world. He later wrote of himself in the third person as "a puny little fellow—a circus boy with limbs and body racked to effect an unnatural contortion; as a tired penniless little tramp, and homeless little waif; as a sailor, docker, agitator, a fanatical evangelist of Labour."[541] A formidable orator and organizer, he combined a tough intelligence with deep sensitivity, and later recalled that "the infernal, terrible degradation of London's slums . . . revolted my soul."[542] He saw the industrial battles of his fellow workers as a struggle for human dignity and resented middle-class reformers who did not "minister to the self-respect of the casual worker or produce a sympathetic appreciation of his qualities in the minds of other classes in the community."[543] Most of Silver's workers were in more or less permanent employment, but they were nevertheless only a rung or two above their immiserated casual brothers and sisters in the district, with no union contract to cushion them from arbitrary dismissal. Tillett rallied to their support with the same passion for justice that he had thrown into the struggle to build his own union on the docks.

Strike Funds Critically Low

Eleanor Marx also mounted the speakers' platform. By this time she had gained the workers' respect and confidence—and perhaps their love— through her diligent organizing efforts. They cheered on yet another rousing speech. John Stokes considers that it "was perhaps only through her involvement with the Silvertown strike . . . that [she] discovered her full vocal resources."[544] She exhorted the strikers to continue the struggle, but sounded a warning in the midst of all the enthusiasm of the great crowd on that cool autumn day. If hot-blooded, she was also firmly practical: the next three days, she said, would be critical. If more funds did not come in, the strikers would face starvation. The strike was dragging on and funds were dwindling. She also drew attention to the engineers who were still working in the factory, declaring that if they came out, the strike would soon be at an end. She must have known, however, that the ASE EC had no intention of calling them out. At the conclusion of the speeches, strike relief pay was distributed: 4 shillings, two-and sixpence, and two shillings, for men, women, and juniors, respectively.[545] Equivalent to roughly £17.20, £10.80, and £8.60 today, it was little enough, and as Marx predicted, harder times were looming.

At this stage the NUG&GL also deputized Edward Aveling to travel to France. A future auditor of the union, he was fluent in French, conversant with the situation at Silvertown, and thus was well equipped to act as an emissary to Silver's French workers at Persan.[546] Aveling's memory is tainted in the labor movement because of his sordid treatment of Eleanor Marx, and he was disliked by many who met him even before that. Personally, he was unprepossessing. George Bernard Shaw was of the opinion that "he had no physical charm except a voice like a euphonium," and Henry Hyndman quipped that "nobody can be so bad as Aveling looks."[547] Olive Schreiner believed that he was "a real criminal type," and others regarded him as a "serial sponger," always on the lookout for a loan.[548] Margaret Harkness disliked him so intensely that she refused to enter Engels's house when Aveling was there.[549] Originally a supporter of Herbert Spencer's Social Darwinist theories, he came to Marxism via the radical secularism of Charles Bradhaugh.[550] Yet despite all of this, he was an intelligent, well-educated man with a doctorate in the natural sciences who put his talents at the service of the labor movement, albeit, as Belfort Bax put it, "in a rather mechanical way."[551] This was particularly the case regarding the NUG&GL, and he was later to prove an effective organizer and propagandist for the legislated Eight Hour Day campaign. He also threw himself into support for the Silvertown strikers. Had he not treated Eleanor Marx so odiously he would no doubt be remembered more positively.

Striking Soldiers and Hobbledehoys

The marches and rallies continued. The following day saw 3,000 people assemble on Clerkenwell Green at a rally organized by the Finsbury Radical Club. Mr. Poole, the secretary of the Patriotic Club, a Radical workmen's circle at Clerkenwell Green, was in the chair, and Fred Harrison moved a resolution of support for the Silvertown strikers. Seconding the motion, Ben Tillett compared the firm's treatment of its laborers unfavorably with the care given to its horses and a resolution pledging moral and financial support was carried unanimously.[552]

The large turnouts at the strike rallies highlighted the broader wave of revolt that was breaking over the East End and nearby. A few weeks previously, according to the SDF's *Justice*, soldier-drivers at the Woolwich Arsenal had gone on strike against "sweating," only to be court-martialed and sent to the "glasshouse" (military prison) as punishment.[553] (It is entirely possible that the soldiers had been influenced by the ideas espoused by the NUG&GL's Pete Curran, who was a civilian worker in the arsenal.) Perhaps even more extraordinary was the news of a rash of strikes by schoolchildren in the East End. At the Old Canning Town School, just west of Silvertown, they had "emulated pupils in Scotland" and gone on strike. Mr. Puttick, the headmaster, complained that a "mob of hobbledehoys . . . armed with sticks and stones, had visited his school and drawn away thirty of the children." He alleged that they had threatened the caretaker with violence before marching off to South Hallsville School to call other children out on strike.[554] Schoolchildren in East Ham also struck, demanding, among other things, lower fees and shorter hours. One hundred of them marched on Barking to persuade others to join them.[555] Children in Beckton schools also walked out in protest against draconian discipline. The ringleader, a boy named Kirkpatrick, was "flogged" for chalking the words "ON STRIKE" on the school walls.[556] It was heady stuff, but there were disturbing developments for Silver's strikers in the following week.

Dispiriting News from France

On Wednesday, 16 October, distant thunder rumbled in the southwest and lightning flickered in the sky. The unsettled weather suited the occasion: Edward Aveling had returned from his mission to France with dispiriting news for the Strike Committee. The workers at Silver's Persan plant had refused his appeal for assistance. His friend, the French socialist Jules

Guesde, had been pessimistic from the outset, explaining that the Persan workers were relatively well paid and content. And so it proved.[557] If Silver's had got wind of Aveling's mission, and there is no reason to believe that they had not, they must have been delighted by his failure to get the French workers' support.

The management, indeed, appeared to have been completely unruffled by the continuing strike and the agitation in the streets. On 17 October, a week after rebuffing the offers of mediation by Major Barnes and Mayor Curtis, the board of directors held its regular weekly meeting in Cannon Street. The strike was Item 6 on the agenda and before reaching it, the board agreed to sell 1,950 shares in the West India & Panama Telegraph Company, each worth about £2/5/-. The minutes do not say why Silver's decided to unload the £2,437 in shares, but perhaps it was to use the money as a contingency fund for unforeseen expenses during the strike. The matter of the strike itself was swiftly dealt with. A second letter had been received from H. Girling on behalf of the Strike Committee, asking for a meeting with the directors. The only recorded response was that the board decided to send a further letter to the press, restating the company's position.[558] However, the company did agree to receive a strikers' deputation—perhaps only as an exercise in "spin" to mollify public opinion as it had no intention of seriously negotiating with the union.

The strike was now approaching its fifth week. The socialist *Commonweal* reported that "the men are as yet unconquered, though the last few weeks have been terrible for them to struggle through."[559] On Saturday, 19 October, strike pay was once again doled out, 6 shillings for men and 4 shillings for women and boys—more than the previous week—and this must have raised spirits somewhat. The Cannon Brewery, on the appeal of Elizabeth Cundy, the landlady of the Railway Tavern, had contributed £10/10/- of this. The Salvation Army was also "rendering generous help" noted the *Stratford Express*.[560] Nevertheless, the gulf between the huge financial resources enjoyed by the company and the meager reserves of the strikers yawned ever wider. The strike pay would not stretch far when it is recalled that a large loaf of bread cost fivepence and the strikers had many hungry mouths to feed.

Boots Worn Out Collecting Funds

There were still impressive turnouts at union meetings. On Sunday, 20 October, 3,000 strikers and their families rallied outside the East India

Dock gates in Blackwall. Speakers exhorted supporters to contribute gen-
erously to the relief fund to prevent Silver's from starving the strikers back
to work. The rain held off, but sheet lightning heralded its appearance the
following day, when a heavy downpour caused the adjournment of yet
another rally at Silver's factory gates.[561] The days were shortening, winter
was approaching, and the memories of heady days of the Indian summer
must have been fading fast. So too was any hope of a quick settlement of
the dispute. The strikers met again on Tuesday morning, with Eleanor
Marx calling for the workers' movement to unite to publish a labor press
to counteract the propaganda of the bosses. One incident at the meeting
highlights the courage and determination of the strikers, the females in
particular. Collection of funds for strike relief was a wearisome task, with
strikers tramping the streets knocking on doors and buttonholing passersby in working-class neighborhoods for donations. The most assiduous
collectors were young women strikers, a number of whom had completely
worn out their shoes as a result. Their contribution to the struggle was
recognized when a collection was made to buy new boots for them.[562] The
Stevedores' Union handed over an additional £50 to the strike fund, and
the meeting also heard speeches from H. Phillips of the Stevedores and
Thomas Walsh of the Seamen and Firemen, who were standing as independent workers' candidates in the West Ham Council elections.[563]

During this period, workers in the outer East End were beginning to
elect independent working-class representatives to local government. In
the same week, for instance, W. Wilkinson of the SDF topped the poll
in Barking ward in the East Ham Council elections, winning 2,157 votes
against 295 for Thomas Young, a landlord, 550 for Sam Glenry, a captain
of volunteers, and 932 for a Tory vicar called Henson.[564] Though it is
doubtless true that East End workers laughed when music hall comedians
caricatured ardent socialists, the agitators' words must have given strikers pause for thought, especially in the West Ham heavy industrial belt.
Eleanor Marx, Will Thorne, Tom Mann, and others did not stridently
proselytize for socialism in the abstract, but their actions spoke louder
than words, and the idea that workers had to organize politically as well
as industrially was a potent one. Nor were the socialist union leaders wild-
eyed and impractical. On the same day Walsh and Phillips spoke outside
Silver's gates, Tom Mann addressed the Strike Committee in session at
Cundy's and drew attention to a weakness of the workers' movement. The
strike, he believed, had exposed the huge problem of the lack of working-
class unity. Encouraged by their own union officials, the engineers and
other tradesmen at Silver's had refused to join the stoppage, and money

for the strike fund was not coming in quickly enough. What was necessary, he argued, was to "hasten on a Federation of the Trades" capable of
tackling the employers as a solid front.[565] It was a bold idea that was to
bear fruit in coming years, but it was not an immediate prospect.

Fruitless Meeting with Directors

Shortly afterward, a twenty-strong delegation from the Strike Committee
met with Silver's directors at Cannon Street. Any hopes of a settlement
were quickly dashed,[566] with Gray promising only a few minor concessions. "They [the delegation] were informed," the company minutes state,
"that the Board adhered to the decision not to pay higher wages . . . & that
the hands could resume work on the old terms if they wished to do so."
Gray said that "when work was resumed individual cases would be looked
into, & increased pay given if deserved; also that any grievances, such as
loss of pay through accidental omission to hang up their tickets, should be
remedied."[567] Yvonne Kapp also mentions that the company promised to
consider providing an employees' dining room.[568] It was a paltry conces-
sion, but in any case it took Silver's seven years to build it.[569] Such terms
were not acceptable to the delegation. Fred Ling "replied that they were
pledged not to go in on the old terms" and the meeting broke up.[570] The
same day, in bright autumn sunshine, a 250-strong procession of strikers
paraded with banners around the streets of West Ham behind a fife-and-
drum band, collecting money from onlookers as they went.[571]

The strikers were also investigating other ways to advance their cause.
Although the militant union leaders were committed to building new
unions of the previously unorganized, they did not dismiss the idea of
working with, in, and through "old" union bodies when this was possible. A few hours after the Strike Committee had left Cannon Street, Tom
Mann made his way to his first delegate meeting of the London Trades
Council at a pub in the City, the White Swan Tavern in Temple Street.
He had been elected to represent the Battersea branch of the ASE.[572]
The Trades Council, to which a number of the London branches of craft
unions were affiliated, was led by George Shipton, a conservative craft
unionist from the Painters' Union. Shipton had acted as a mediator during
the match girls' strike at Bryant and May's in Bow in 1888, but working-
class struggle and solidarity was not his style. The council had not played
any kind of role during the recent dock strike, and indeed Shipton had
fobbed off the dockers when they asked for his help. The council minutes

of 18 April 1889 reveal that Tillett wrote to the council for some assistance but did not receive any, because he "did not state the nature of the help he desired."[573] This did not stop Shipton and his cronies from asserting that "it was impossible to interfere [in the dock strike] without the consent of" the strike leaders.[574] Shipton also pretended not to know that a check for £50 sent to the council by the United Furniture Trades Union in Melbourne, Australia, was meant for the dock strike fund, and proposed to write—not telegraph—for clarification,[575] a procedure that would have wasted months of precious time. In this instance, bureaucratic obfuscation verged on treachery.

Most likely Ben Tillett had George Shipton in mind when he later lampooned labor aristocrats who "looked like respectable City gentlemen, wore very good coats, large watch-chains and high hats; and in many cases were of such splendid build and proportion that they presented aldermanic, not to say magisterial, form and dignity."[576] Not all of the council delegates were of the same ilk. Delegates Parnell and Davis of the Cabinet Makers' and Coopers' unions moved the following motion at a delegate meeting almost two months after the end of the dock strike:

That this meeting of Delegates considers the EC [Executive Council of the LTC] very much to blame for not offering the assistance of the Council to the leaders of the Dock Strike during that struggle and for not calling a delegate meeting to consider the matter when requested to do so by Messrs Cooper and Steadman.[577]

The motion was lost, twenty-five votes to fifteen, but Shipton's opponents won a majority of the votes for five vacant EC seats at elections on the same night. Tom Mann received thirty-four votes and Cooper of the Bargebuilders' Union, who had been an ally of the dockers, was also elected.[578] However, though the more responsive current on the council was greatly encouraged by the result, the situation regarding relief funds for Silvertown was becoming desperate. Mann and his allies were to poke and prod at the Old Guard, but Shipton was reluctant to do anything and was never in a hurry when he was instructed to act. Nevertheless, the council's deputations to Silvertown did, as we have seen, present the facts of the strike to many people living outside of the suburb.

The Mercurial Tom Mann

Tom Mann was one of the most influential workers' leaders to emerge during the birth of the New Unionism. Like Will Thorne, he spoke with a flat West Midlands accent, having been born in 1856 in a coal-mining village near Coventry. Like Ben Tillett, he had suffered unspeakable agonies as a child laborer. He went down the pit when he was nine years old, and was put to work dragging heavy boxes full of mullock in the darkness by a belt and chain attached round his waist. Many times, he tells us, "did I actually lie down groaning as a consequence of the heavy strain on the loins, especially when the road was wet and 'clayey' causing much resistance to the load being dragged."[579] When the mine closed after a fire in 1870, the family moved to Birmingham where young Mann was fortunate to be apprenticed to a toolmaking firm. In 1876, having served his seven-year apprenticeship, he quit the firm and moved to London, where he became active in the ASE and joined the fledgling Social Democratic Federation.

Mann realized instinctively the value of both industrial and independent political organization. Such views brought him into contact with other working-class SDF members such as Tillett, Burns, and Thorne, and earned the approval of the "General," Frederick Engels, who was not a federation member but had tremendous moral authority. These ideas also brought him into sharp collision with H. H. Hyndman, the SDF's autocratic leader and founder. Hyndman had started political life as a "Red Tory," and Mann recalls him as being of "essentially bourgeois appearance—tall hat, the frock coat, and the long beard." He believed that Hyndman's "bourgeois mentality made it impossible for him to estimate the worth of industrial organisation."[580] Hyndman argued that the unions detracted from the need for revolution, and he reserved his most withering scorn for Mann's advocacy of a campaign for the eight-hour day.[581] The dispute was to flare again toward the end of the Silvertown strike. By the time of the strike, Mann had matured into a charismatic speaker, an inspired organizer, and a talented journalist. Ben Tillett remembered that he "combined the qualities of whirlwind and volcano."[582] Although Engels noted Mann's susceptibility to flattery, Tillett insists that "he has never deserted the flag, even if he has sometimes attempted to plant it in impossible places," including overseas. Mann was a wanderer and was to spend several years in Australia before the outbreak of the Great War. In Melbourne, he worked with Frank Anstey in the Victorian Socialist Party. As Mann informs us, Anstey, who later became prominent as a left-wing

Federal Labor MP in Australia, was born in Silvertown. He had stowed away on a deep-water square-rigger in 1876 when he was eleven years old and later became an activist in the Australian Seamen's Union. No doubt his early experience of the poverty of Silvertown helped set him on the road to socialism. [583]

Hyndman's suspicion of the unions did not prevent other SDF members from joining Mann to mobilize support of the Silvertown strikers. The political council of the Wandsworth branch of the federation, for example, organized a mass meeting on Wandsworth Common on the Sunday afternoon of 27 October "to express sympathy with the strikers" and heard Will Thorne, Harry Hobart, and other socialists deliver fiery speeches from the platform. Supporters marched from Battersea behind the SDF brass band in bright sunshine, raising money for the strike fund as they went.[584]

Alexander Sloper, F.O.M.

The strikers marched and picketed almost daily, but bad weather prevented a scheduled parade on Monday, 28 October.[585] Flashes of humor showed the strikers were still resilient and full of Cockney cheek despite the looming winter and half-full bellies; the wage slaves might have agreed with Shakespeare's words, "The robbed that smiles steals something from the thief."[586] The next day, bystanders in West Ham would have laughed to see the well-known London "wide boy" (or grifter) Ally Sloper leading a procession of Silver's strikers through the streets to the strains of a fife-and-drum band.[587] A character in a well-known comic series, Alexander "Ally" Sloper supposedly lived in Mildew Court, was fond of a drink, and sported a bulbous red nose as a result. His nickname was a pun on his habit of sloping off down alleys to dodge rent collectors. The "Old Rumfoozler" was also known to attend Hyde Park rallies carrying a banner emblazoned with the words "ALLY SLOPER THE FRIEND OF MAN."[588] However, the "Alexander Sloper" who paraded the chilly streets of West Ham this autumn day appeared to be a union member as he sported a NUG&GL ticket in the band of his tall hat. He would have been outraged to hear Eleanor Marx's news that day that a local clergyman had been going around to houses in Silvertown, advising the strikers' wives to persuade their menfolk to go back to work on the old terms.[589]

Meanwhile, Silver's board, which held a special meeting the same day, wasted no time on the strike, preferring instead to deal with a tender for the construction of a new submarine telegraph cable between Cuba and the Canary Islands.[590] The subsequent weekly meeting on 31 October discussed a further tender for another new cable from Charlestown to Porto Plata, and the company also decided to sell off almost £2,000 in shares in the Panama Telegraph Company.[591] Business was still booming despite the strike, probably as a result of the sale and laying of stockpiled cables, and increased production at Persan. The board was also preparing to crank up the pressure on the strikers. Rumors persisted that Silver's was contracting out work to the Abbot and Anderson firm at Dodd Street, Burdett, and these appear to have been true.

Eleanor Marx's warnings about dwindling strike funds had caused a small surge in donations from worried supporters. Redoubled efforts to raise money had meant the Strike Committee could pay out its highest benefits to date: 7 shillings for men, 5 shillings for women, and 4 shillings for girls and boys.[592] Yet after seven weeks on strike and with no reserves to fall back on, the workers were feeling the pinch: the 2 November edition of *Commonweal* reported that "many women and children were suffering bitterly from hunger."[593] Winter was setting in. Steady rain on a number of days, with falling temperatures and dwindling supplies of coal, must have made the strikers' homes cold and cheerless places. On Sunday, 3 November, heavy rain forced the cancellation of a meeting in Hyde Park, and with it a collection for the strike fund.[594] The sight of truckloads of dismantled machinery leaving the plant in the rain, evidently for shipment to France, must have been dispiriting for the strikers.[595] There was no end in sight for what had become a cruelly bruising dispute for the strikers and their families.

VIII.
The Workers Disunited:
Skilled versus Unskilled at Silvertown

> The artisan creed with regard to the labourers is that
> the latter are an inferior class and that they should be
> made to know and kept in their place.[596]
> —THOMAS WRIGHT, 1873

THE SLOGAN "The workers, united, will never be defeated!" contains within it a great truth. Though there can never be any guarantees that a strike will be successful, the chances of victory are always improved when the workers make common cause. The great 1889 strike at Silvertown was undermined from the start by a lack of unity between skilled tradesmen and the so-called unskilled laborers. Britain's oldest and wealthiest union, the Amalgamated Society of Engineers, refused all entreaties to call out its Silvertown members in solidarity with the NUG&GL. The ASE's fitters,[597] along with members of the carpenters' union and the electrical instrument makers' association, rejected all pleas to join the strike. The men's refusal had the blessing of the Amalgamated Society of Engineers' (ASE's) ruling Executive Council and the officials of the other tradesmen's unions. Some craftsmen did make common cause with the laborers: Silver's unionized turners and smiths struck in sympathy with the laborers, or were suspended during the strike and received dispute benefit from the ASE.[598] Had the other tradesmen joined them, the chances of a union victory would have improved and the interests of British workers as a whole advanced.

The ASE men who remained on the job were mainly employed as fitters—skilled metal mechanics—on the refurbishment, installation, maintenance, and dismantling of the factory's machinery. The NUG&GL decried the fact that the fitters were working without the assistance of their laborers, dismantling machinery that was sent to Silver's factory at Persan in France, and repairing machinery at Silvertown operated by scab labor. The ASE retorted that their members were only working on light machinery that could be removed, installed, or worked on in situ without the assistance of laborers. The strikers believed that if the ASE men were to strike, Silver's would be forced to negotiate to end the stoppage, but the ASE argued that a withdrawal would have little impact, and indeed would jeopardize their own jobs, which could be taken by non-unionists. A substantial number of the engineering tradesmen at Silver's were non-unionists, and this helps explain the ASE's stance during the strike. The dispute generated great bitterness in Silvertown and highlighted the stark division that existed at that time between the "labor aristocracy" and the rest of the British working class.

Britain's Wealthiest Union

Founded in 1851 as the result of the amalgamation of a number of smaller, more specialized local artisans' associations, and some regionally based metal tradesmen's unions,[599] the ASE boasted a membership of some 55,000 by the end of the 1880s.[600] Members were drawn from twenty-six different trades.[601] The union had grown from an initial membership of around 12,000 under the leadership of its first General Secretary, William Newton. By 1889, the union's ruling body, the Executive Council, was meeting on a daily and sometimes twice daily basis under the direction of Newton's successor, Robert Austin.[602] The ASE was Britain and Ireland's wealthiest union. Between 1851 and 1884, its yearly income rose from £22,107 to £156,208,[603] huge sums for the time. Financial members were entitled to generous sickness, pension, and death benefits funds on a sliding scale depending on how much they paid in.[604] Although the union had engaged in some protracted disputes, most of its funds were disbursed as "friendly society" benefits. This was the case with most of the "old" unions at the time. Robert Knight, the General Secretary of the Boilermakers' Union, for example, estimated that 96 percent of his association's annual expenditures were for "benevolent purposes," and less than 4 percent went on labor disputes.[605] This emphasis on friendly society benefits reinforced the clannish, inward-looking philosophy of the craft unions. The ASE's Rule XVI reads like the prospectus of a cheeseparing capitalist insurance firm:

> No person shall be admitted a member who is deaf and dumb, or has lost a limb, or is subject to fits; or who is through imperfect vision obliged to use glasses at his work; but persons who have lost one eye may, if the remaining one be good, be admitted up to the age of thirty years, but must produce a medical certificate in proof of the soundness of the remaining eye. No person shall be admitted who has lost two fingers from one hand, or who is ruptured, unless it can be positively proven to the satisfaction of the local council that such is not detrimental to his capacity as a workman.[606]

Few of the ASE's industrial struggles were straightforward disputes over pay and conditions. Many were demarcation disputes designed to maintain a monopoly over certain types of skilled work. As Helen Merrell Lynd writes, citing Boilermakers' Union supremo Robert Knight, a "major purpose of the old unions was 'to wage merciless war upon intruders into the craft, whether general labourers or other craftsmen.'"[607] In particular, the union was determined to exclude non-"time-served" men from the industry. The preface to the ASE's 1885 rulebook stipulated that workers who had "not earned a right by probationary servitude," that is, apprenticeship, could never aspire to bona fide tradesmen and that any "such encroachments are productive of evil." The artisan, it stated, had a "vested interest" like the "physician who holds a diploma" in guarding against intruders.[608]

The craft unions' leaders were also for the most part opposed to independent working-class political action, preferring to support the Liberal Party in elections. Some even supported the Tories. John Burnett, who served as ASE General Secretary between 1875 and 1886, boasted that "no stronger barriers to social revolution exist than those which have been erected by the unions" and added that "the disbursement of their funds for friendly purposes . . . has rendered their members the most peaceful and contented portion of the toiling population."[609] Such sentiments confirm William Morris's contention that the craft unions "no longer represent the whole class of workers . . . but rather are charged with the office of keeping the human part of the capitalists' machinery in good working order and freeing it from any grit of discontent."[610]

The Aristocracy of Labor

The rift between unskilled and skilled workers had existed since at least
the early Industrial Revolution, a time when there was little distinction
between engineering artisans and those later known as "professional engineers." James Watt, the inventor of the radically improved steam engine,
was an instrument maker by trade. The celebrated engineer George Stephenson was a colliery enginewright, and John Rennie, James Brindley,
and William Fairbairn were millwrights.[611] In the eighteenth and early
nineteenth centuries, all engineers, along with smiths, patternmakers, and
the like, were regarded as artisans. Together, these skilled trades consti-
tuted an aristocracy of labor, which regarded itself as separate from and
superior to the working class. Some of these artisans, writes R. Angus
Buchanan, "rose to a higher position by designing, rather than building,
public works and large machines."[612] By the mid-nineteenth century, they
were recognized as professional engineers and members of the middle
class, white-collar specialists as opposed to blue-collar men. However,
in the words of the American social historian Dale Porter, the engineer-
mechanics, who continued to work with their hands, "remained proud
'aristocrats of labour'" and "were the most technically advanced of all the
trades." It followed that unions such as the ASE aimed to secure a "vested
interest in society, on the same order as doctors, brewers, or authors, rather
than the representation of the workers as a general class."[613] Though artisans are entitled to be proud of their skill, such pride came at a cost to
others and to the overall welfare of the working class. The labor aristocrats viewed other workers with suspicion as real or potential enemies
rather than friends. This was particularly the case with regard to so-called
unskilled workers, whom the craft unions wished to exclude from training
for skilled work and union membership at all costs.

To be fair, at the time the ASE was founded, support for socialist
theories and the idea of a united working-class movement was confined to
tiny circles of workers and intellectuals. Britain's first avowedly Marxist
organization, the Social Democratic Federation, was only created in 1884,
and Karl Marx was a little-known German refugee. Volume one of *Capital*
had been published in German in 1867, but the first English translation
only appeared in 1886. The mass upsurge of Chartism lay over half a
century in the past. The skilled toolmaker and ASE member Tom Mann
recalls in his *Memoirs* that as a youth he only gradually became aware of
socialist ideas distinct from the radicalism of MPs such as John Bright
and the secularism of activists such as Charles Bradhaugh. When Mann

was an apprentice, he found it difficult to make contact with the union.[614] When he found it, he soon discovered that he had broader social horizons than the narrow confines of craft.

Attempts to set up general and/or industrial unions had not been successful, apart from the Miners' Federation, itself formed in 1888 only as a loose amalgamation of regional bodies, and the Lancashire textile workers. The Grand National Consolidated Trades Union had vanished without a trace shortly after its creation in 1833, and similar bodies later came to naught. Some socialists, the SDF founder Henry Mayers Hyndman in particular, were suspicious of unions, seeing them as at best a distraction from making propaganda for socialism, and at worst as enemies that reconciled the workers with capitalism. In the case of the "old" unions, he had ample justification.

Keeping Labor Artificially Scarce

In essence, the existing unions before 1889 were concerned with narrow, sectional, occupational interests. The ASE was a bastion of such craft unionism, dedicated to keeping skilled labor "artificially scarce"[615] and "keeping up standards and keeping out interlopers."[616] Its rules were extremely restrictive. Members could be expelled if they were not of "good moral character,"[617] and in at least one sad instance a man who developed epilepsy was denied membership—and thus his livelihood—by the Executive Council.[618] Women were barred from membership; engineering was seen, strictly, as "men's work."[619] Nor could "unskilled" or "semiskilled" engineering workers join: membership was open only to tradesmen who had "served their time" as indentured apprentices during their teenage years. Though very little industrial work can be classified as completely unskilled, and many "semiskilled" workers were in fact highly skilled, they were permanently excluded from the craft brotherhood and paid much lower wages accordingly. In 1890, Mann and Tillett estimated that there were some 300,000 laborers and semiskilled workers in Britain's engineering industry.[620] However, the ASE and the other craft unions did not try to organize them, and indeed were often hostile to their unionization. The tradesmen's helpers at Silver's were a case in point.

Hard, Barren, Hopeless Lives

People often view the working class as monolithic, but it was, and still
is, often divided along fault lines of gender, ethnicity, and skill. Among
the labor aristocrats of the ASE and other engineering unions, there was
little idea of class solidarity. Robert Knight of the Boilermakers' Union
seemed almost to regard the laborers and semiskilled workers as biologi-
cally inferior beings who must "keep to their place" in the hierarchy of
labor. Laborers could never become tradesmen, no matter how skilled they
were. For Knight, it was a matter of innate ability, not the luck of being
able to secure an apprenticeship during one's youth.[621] At its worst, this
ideology bred what Eric Hobsbawm calls a system of "co-exploitation"
in the shipyards, building sites, and factories of Britain. Tradesmen's
assistants were paid around 50 percent of the wages of craftsmen[622] and
although "nominally fellow-workmen," the relationship between them
was sometimes more akin to that between "taskmaster and serf."[623] In this
cruel system, fitters' helpers might spend their entire working lives denied
the prospect of advancement to skilled work because they had missed
the opportunity of an apprenticeship in their youth. Many a gray-haired
laborer worked alongside a boy fresh out of apprenticeship, fetching his
spanners and even his dinner, and slopping out the "bogs" (the can in
U.S. slang), well capable of doing a tradesman's work yet forever barred
from doing so. This was an inhuman caste system based on accidents of
birth and location—and often on who rather than what you knew. Skilled
work was often passed down from father to son in what amounted to a
system of industrial nepotism. An American laborer has written movingly
of what it meant to be condemned to unskilled work:

> And being what we are, the dregs of the labor-market, and having no
> certainty of permanent employment, and no organization among our-
> selves, we must expect to work under the watchful eye of a gang-boss,
> and be driven, like the wage slaves we are, through our tasks. All this
> is to tell us, in effect, that our lives are hard, barren, hopeless lives.[624]

It was an enormous waste of human talent and potential. Yet, in spite of
everything, many thousands of laborers did manage to acquire craftsman-
level skills, particularly if they worked in non-union shops. Regardless,
they could never be eligible for a union ticket. In essence, craft unionism was a racket. So craft-proud were the officials of the ASE that in
1889 they refused membership to electricians, arguing that these new

tradesmen created by the Electrical Revolution were not skilled enough to join their ranks. The ASE's EC snootily advised them to form their own association, although they did deign to supply them with "a set of books belonging to the Society" to act as a model for their rules.[625]

Even outside the factory gates, the social division between tradesman and laborer was maintained. The East Ender Walter Southgate recalled in his autobiography that a "labourer in corduroy trousers, cap and red handkerchief around his neck, would have been given his marching orders had he dared to step into the saloon bar and order a drink." Laborers were confined to the public house bar, with the saloon strictly reserved for tradesmen, clerks, and other such worthies.[626] There is little wonder, therefore, that the majority of tradesmen at Silver's, imbued with a sense of caste superiority, refused to join in the laborers' strike. There were also other reasons—based on fear—for their actions.

Threats to the Craft Unions' Power

By 1889, the ASE's monopoly power was under threat from rising unemployment, increasing numbers of non-unionists in the trade, and technological change. Mann and Tillett estimated that there were three times the number of skilled engineers outside of the ASE as in it.[627] Some of these were time-served men who could not or would not join the union, as was the case at Silver's. Charles Sturton, the secretary of the Victoria Dock branch of the ASE, reported to the EC that 50 percent of the fitters who remained at work at during the NUG&GL strike at Silver's were non-union men.[628] The union feared, with good reason, that non-unionists were an increasing threat to its monopoly on skilled jobs and that employers would naturally favor them over its members. Since the early 1870s, British industry had fallen into a long slump, with steeply rising unemployment affecting the unskilled and even the "super aristocrats" of the metal trades. According to Mann and Tillett, 13 percent of the ASE's national membership was unemployed in 1877. Twelve years later, despite a recent, brief economic upturn, the proportion must have been larger.[629] It was increasingly difficult for the ASE to keep its labor artificially scarce, and it was unable to do so in the 1890s depression. It also could not afford to pay unemployment benefits to an expanded membership.[630]

A further threat to the craft unions' power came from the development of mass production techniques in industry, and from the introduction of new metalworking machines at the end of the 1880s.[631] The machines were introduced by the employers in an attempt to boost their declining rates of profit and, intentionally or not, the new division of labor encroached on the autonomy of the craftsmen, and hence their control over important aspects of their work. Semiskilled operatives on the new shaping machines, capstan lathes, semiautomatic screw cutters, and similar equipment could now perform their work more cheaply and quickly. This was probably already the case at Silver's by 1889, as we know that the firm had begun to employ toolsetters by that time.[632] In 1897 the threat of the new machinery and associated de-skilling was a key factor in triggering national industrial action by the engineering unions, during which time Silver's engineers struck for six months.[633]

"Giants' Work in the Emancipation of Labour"

In 1889, these matters of new technology weighed heavily on the minds of the ASE's executive councilors. For a brief period, however, these cautious and conservative men were intoxicated by the spirit of the New Unionism. On 16 September, they praised the despised dock laborers and their socialist leaders:

> The Executive Council of the Amalgamated Society of Engineers, on behalf of its members tenders the warmest congratulations to the whole of those who took part in the Dock Strike for the brilliant & unparalleled victory they have achieved in the cause of labour.... We further wish to express our extreme gratification and thanks to the whole of the Leaders of this great movement for the great ability they have shown in conducting the same, and also the wise moderation they have shown in pressing the men's demands, and we feel sure that when the history of this movement is written they will be recorded as men who have done giants' work in the emancipation of labour.[634]

They were brave words, but the councilors soon repented of them. Faced with the cold everyday facts of industrial life, the EC soon reverted to its customary craft union form, and nowhere was this more the case than at Silvertown.

Silver's non-tradesmen employees were denied membership in the craft unions, even if they worked directly with artisans and regardless of the level of skill they had achieved or were capable of acquiring. When their strike began, they joined Will Thorne's NUG&GL, which he had founded shortly before at the nearby Beckton gasworks. From the beginning, Thorne was insistent that his new union should not restrict membership to the relatively skilled stokers, who charged boilers and coke ovens in industrial plants, but that it should accept all other classifications of general laborers and semiskilled workers, regardless of ethnicity, age, job, or gender. For Thorne and his fellow socialists, the organization of the unorganized was a moral imperative and they believed that unions should be class, not sectional organizations. In a stinging polemic against Shipton, the Trades Council secretary who had dismissed the New Unions as "'mushroom societies' likely to die an early death," Thorne's comrades Mann and Tillett called for an organizing drive to recruit the 700,000 London workers who were outside of the unions.[635] Although the new general unions were battered by the depression and employers' offensive of the 1890s, they were to undergo "near vertical" growth after 1914.[636]

Although general labor unions did exist in some other countries—the Australian Workers' Union (AWU) is a good example—such associations were to play a significantly greater role in Britain than elsewhere. By the late 1960s, fully one-quarter of the total British union membership was to be found in the Transport and General Workers' Union and the General and Municipal Workers' Union,[637] which had descended from Tillett's Dockers' Union and Thorne's NUG&GL respectively. The new general unions recruited anyone who would join from across the industrial spectrum. The NUG&GL branches tended to be strongest in large workplaces[638] where they took on the role of industrial unions without, however, recruiting artisans, who remained in their respective craft unions.

"Call Out the Engineers, Sir!"

To the Silvertown strikers and their supporters, the craftsmen who remained on the job were no better than blacklegs who were prolonging the dispute. When the Trades Council's George Shipton came rather belatedly to Silvertown to address the strikers, one of them loudly advised him to "call out the engineers, sir, and the whole thing will be ended!"[639] Engels, Eleanor Marx, and John Burns agreed with this point of view. Michael Henry ferociously attacked the engineers at rallies and wrote a series of indignant letters to the ASE's EC demanding that they call their members out. There seemed to be plenty of evidence for his complaints. The *Stratford Express* reported somewhat hyperbolically that engineers, working without laborers, had dismantled "the greater part of the machinery" for shipment to France.[640] According to Will Thorne, the company had planned some time before to remove old machines and replace them with more up-to-date equipment. Thorne did, however, believe in the early days of the strike that the ASE would shortly call its members out.[641] He was mistaken.

Stung by the bitter criticism, almost three weeks after the strike began, the EC on 2 October asked Charles Sturton, the secretary of the Victoria Dock branch, to report on the Silver's dispute. The EC minutes record the substance of his report:

> Mr. Sturton said we had 20 members at Silvertown Works engaged at present on repairs *not one* of which was doing Labourers work.
>
> There are 17 non-members and 10 Turners also in the works. Any labouring work that is done is done by the Foremen some of whom are Shareholders. The company have a works in France and some of the machines have been sent there. 40 of which have been ordered in Manchester and never unpacked. Those who have been at work at Silvertown are of such small Dimensions that any one man can remove them without the aid of a Labourer.
>
> Mr. Sturton reported that a Non Society man had been doing some packing that the Labourers had done previously.[642]

The *Labour Elector* later revealed that the firm's carpenters—most or all of whom were union members—were employed during the strike making crates for the removal of machinery earmarked for shipment to France.[643] The carpenters announced that if the engineers went out, they would follow. Surely, this was bad faith or cowardice whichever way one looks at it, and nothing the ASE's EC said convinced the strikers. The EC reasoned that there were twenty-seven fitters still at work at Silver's, fifteen of whom were non-Society men. The four foremen fitters were all members of the Society. The ASE's turners and smiths either had been locked out or had quit work in sympathy with the strikers. All of those men were in receipt of strike benefits from the union.

The EC resolved to write to Will Thorne, with a copy to Michael Henry, stating that "the Council having considered the whole Question of the dispute at the Silvertown India Rubber and Gutta Percha Co sees no reason to withdraw our members from the aforesaid Works. But under no conditions are our Members to do any work that has been previously done by the Labourers."[644] On the contrary, the EC insisted, there was a case where two ASE members had refused to help a non-union fitter who asked for laboring assistance. The EC also resolved that should any ASE men be victimized for refusing to do laborers' work "then all of them must leave at once." Worried about the bad publicity, the EC further decided to write to the newspapers explaining their position, and to instruct the ASE's Woolwich No. 2 branch to send a check for £25 to Arthur Hillier, the secretary of the Silvertown Strike Committee.[645] When EC members visited Silvertown on a number of occasions, they substantiated Sturton's account. They also ridiculed Michael Henry's claims, declaring that he was unable to provide any proof to back his allegations of ASE men black-legging and reiterated that their members would strike if the company victimized anyone for refusing to do laborers' work.[646] The situation never arose. Silver's probably reckoned that it was best to keep the ASE men on the job, gainfully employed in repairing or removing old engines and installing new machinery while large sections of the factory were shut down. Provoking an escalation of the dispute would only strengthen the NUG&GL's hand.

"The Engineers Are Traitors"

The council strongly objected to John Burns's reported remarks at a mass rally in Victoria Park. Burns, who had until recently been a member of the ASE's EC, was widely quoted in the press as saying that the "chief enemies" of the strikers "were the men who remained at work," and that "the engineers are traitors if they do not ignore the counsel . . . of the Amalgamated Society." Their duty, Burns said, was "to help as the Stevedores had done."[647] Burns responded in a letter which, along with another from Michael Henry of the Coal Porters' Union, was read at the 11 October EC meeting, but not, alas, minuted or preserved. The EC majority, however, appears to have been embarrassed by the whole affair since a motion to "severely censure" Burns was lost by three votes and a motion to "ignore him" was carried by four votes.[648] After further hostile letters were sent by Mann's Battersea branch of the ASE, Michael Henry and others, the EC resolved on a motion by George Barnes to send a deputation to Silvertown to meet with the strike committee and the ASE members at Silver's to discuss what had become an ugly dispute.[649] The same Monday afternoon, 14 October, the deputation met with the Strike Committee at the Railway Tavern. They reported that they had heard no new evidence that would lead them to change their opinion. "Mr. Michael Henry"—"Author," the quotes and capital A in the minutes sniffed—"had the fullest opportunity afforded him for proving his statements that our members were doing labouring work but in this he signally failed." Henry had claimed to have "absolute proof" that at least one ASE fitter had "been seen at it," doing laborer's work.[650] He also alleged that a foreman fitter, a member of the ASE, had unloaded coal trucks.[651] For their part, the ASE men in the factory declared that they would cease work if directed to do so by the council, but they had no desire to because "it would not be of any benefit to those on strike." The EC again endorsed the deputation's findings.[652] Their strenuous public denials of wrongdoing did not, however, blunt the continuing harsh criticism of the union.

"Silvertown Blacklegs"

On 19 October, the *Labour Elector* reported that "the action of the Executive Council of the Amalgamated Society of Engineers is being very severely criticized in not calling out their members who are at work and therefore fighting against the strikers." The paper named and shamed a number of "Silvertown blacklegs" including:

Alfred Kernow, John Patterson, Benjamin Parker, Alfred Gibbs, J. Wilkinson—came out as a turner and went in as a fitter, C. Ball, Walter Valentine, Harry MacDonald, Daniel Hart, W. Ketley, W. Cadman, J. Gammall, W. Russell, R. Ritchie, M. Stables, Hugh Livingstone, George Morgan, A. Alford, Harry Brackley, Tom Wolf, screwer, and several recent importations from Scotland.[653]

Relations between the ASE and the strikers could now hardly be worse, and the EC majority's attitude hardened. A letter from Arthur Hillier on behalf of the Strike Committee asking for the ASE to participate in a solidarity parade was read but a motion proposed by George Barnes to "courteously answer" it was lost.[654]

The EC must have been relieved when an apology to the ASE men at Silver's was published in the 26 October edition of the *Labour Elector,* perhaps as a result of great pressure from the union and other sections of the labor movement. It is also possible that there were disagreements on the editorial board between Tom Mann and John Burns, both of whom were prominent ASE members. Perhaps Mann got the upper hand and counseled moderation, for Burns remained implacably hostile to the EC.

"As a result of a very careful investigation," explained the paper, the allegations of scabbing were "decidedly unfair to those men. We know that the Council of the Amalgamated Engineers have given definite instructions that none of their men must do any labouring work, nor are they doing any. An impression has been given that if these Engineers come out, the strike would terminate as a matter of course." The writer continued, "The Engineers do nothing but repair the machinery of the place, they make nothing new, and are now simply taking wages, certainly they are not helping the firm." The article estimated that there were twenty-seven ASE engineers working alongside fifteen non-Society men, twenty carpenters (mostly unionists), and twelve union instrument makers. Besides these craftsmen, there were some two hundred others working in the factory, including two forewomen, employed doing the "ordinary work of the factory," plus white-collar employees. Production was down, but some orders were being filled.[655] However, contrary to the *Elector*'s claim that the ASE men were "not helping the firm," two truckloads of machinery were taken out of the plant through the picket lines on 3 November.[656] It had been dismantled by union and non-union fitters and placed in crates made by union carpenters and was probably bound for France. The available sources do not mention whether the carters were unionists or not.

Taking the Bread from the Strikers' Mouths

It is unlikely that the strikers or their supporters were impressed by the *Labour Elector*'s change of heart, and the newspaper was soon forced to have a re-think. For its part, the EC majority refused to deviate from its course and harbored a mulish resentment against the strike leaders. This was shown at the EC meeting on 18 November, when a motion by James Watson and George Barnes (of the Marylebone and Chelsea branches) to donate £50 to the Silvertown strike fund was lost by two votes.[657] Nagging doubts and the need for self-justification continued. The following day the EC voted to send another delegation to Silvertown to investigate the rumor that French blacklegs were working in the factory.[658] The mission concluded, however, that "not one single Frenchman could be found or heard tell of as having been imported into the works."[659] The EC did not explain why French scabs should be any worse than British blacklegs (who *had* been imported). An NUG&GL organizer called Ward had expressed his union's attitude at a mass meeting the month before at Upton Park. The Silvertown workers, he said, "could not blame foreigners for coming and taking the bread out of their mouths when their mates, the men with whom they once made mud pies, did it."[660] The ASE EC was impervious to such strong words. On Monday, 25 November, they wrote to Will Thorne reiterating their belief that calling out the engineers would not affect the outcome of the strike.[661] The following day they approved the recruitment of ASE toolsetters for the "Silvertown Gutta Works," although they cautioned Charles Sturton that he should "not be in a hurry to do so"[662] and did not broadcast the decision.

The Dispute Intensifies

From this point, the inter-union dispute worsened. When an anonymous ASE man wrote to the *Star* to express his disgust with the refusal to call out the engineers, the EC petulantly instructed its lawyers to write to the editor to demand the author's name.[663] The paper sensibly ignored them. Nevertheless, in response to a circular from the London Trades Council, the EC voted unanimously to send a further donation of £25 to the Strike Committee.[664]

They also admitted William M. Thompson and B. T. L. Thompson, the Radical parliamentary candidates for Limehouse and Stepney respectively, to the meeting of 4 December. Thompson was a barrister who defended strikers pro bono during the dispute. He also later acted for ASE members in the 1897 strike at Silver's. A Protestant Irishman born into a family of "intensely Orange and anti-nationalist sympathies" in Derry, the thirty-two-year-old Thompson had become a Home Ruler, a strong democrat, and a supporter of the trade unions. He was also a powerful speaker and writer,[665] but his doubtless eloquent appeal for assistance to the strikers was ignored.[666] By this stage, the strike was dying and nothing that the EC decided would have had much effect and one suspects that they looked forward to the end with relief.

Inspector Vedy a Liar

Despite the £25 donation, the actions of the EC and its Silvertown members had come perilously close to sabotage of the strike. On Saturday, 23 November, James Rogers, a forty-year-old striker, appeared in the West Ham Police Court charged with "using force to compel" a fitter named Joseph Gemmell to cease work. St. John Wontner, prosecuting, said that when Gemmell had left the Works to go home for his lunch, a large party of pickets accosted him in Winchester Street. Wontner claimed that the strikers had blocked Gemmell's path and that he was "jostled, kicked about the legs and struck on the head with a stick by Rogers." Magistrate Ernest Baggally found the charges proven and sentenced Rogers to one month's imprisonment.[667] In the same week, the police arrested an ASE member from Canning Town named William Henderson when he went to Silvertown, supposedly to try to persuade the engineers to come out. A report in the *Labour Elector* did not give details of the charges against him, but expressed surprise that "the two chief witnesses against him were Hugh Walsh and another member of the ASE." The report suggested that Henderson's ASE branch should make representations to Walsh's branch "with regard to his action in getting a fellow member three months imprisonment."[668] According to another report, however, Henderson claimed that his presence in Silvertown had nothing to do with the strike and that Inspector Vedy and others were liars to claim otherwise. He had, he claimed, appeared outside the works to challenge an ASE man called Walsh, who had got him sacked from Silver's five months previously. Nevertheless, Inspector Parsons corroborated Vedy's evidence and Magistrate Baggally sentenced the prisoner to three months' hard labor for intimidation. Again, Wontner prosecuted and Matthew Gray watched proceedings from the public gallery.[669]

By this stage, Tom Mann had again changed his view about the engineers continuing to work at Silver's. This became clear when Fred Ling and another Strike Committee delegate called Parker addressed the London Trades Council in late November, and asked for support in getting the engineers out. Ling insisted that if they did so, "the firm would be obliged to give way, as they could not do anything if the machinery was stopped." After Ling and Parker left, Mann spoke in support of their appeal. Although he still believed that there was no proof that ASE men (as opposed to non-union fitters) were doing laboring work, he argued that "*it was undoubtedly the fact that, by enabling the firm to run the machinery*"—and thus produce finished goods—"*they were prolonging the strike.*"[670] One week later, the *Labour Elector*, in an article probably written by Mann, called on the ASE Council to send Matthew Gray an ultimatum: unless steps are taken to come to terms with the strikers, the ASE men should "leave in a body."[671] The ASE ignored the appeal.

Claims and Counterclaims: An Evaluation

Reading between the lines, it seems that a minority of councilors, including the future general secretary George Barnes, were uneasy about their colleagues' behavior. Though it was not proven that ASE men had done laborers' work, they had remained on the job alongside blacklegs who were most certainly doing the work of strikers. "This," considered the *Labour Elector*, "certainly deserves the strongest censure," because "unionists ought to refuse to work under such conditions."[672] Furthermore, the fitters had remained at work even after the ASE turners and smiths struck in solidarity with the laborers.[673] Their work helped keep the plant running, even if at reduced capacity, and they had dismantled machinery that was sent to Persan. Although the paper had earlier softened its hostile tone and apologized to those it had branded by name as blacklegs, it is clear that something was rotten and that no amount of obfuscation by the EC could hide it.

The ASE General Council seems to have been motivated in part by the desire to maintain its own sectional interests vis-à-vis those of the laborers, and also by a well-grounded fear that their members' jobs might be taken by non-unionists if they went on strike. As the *Labour Elector* admitted, if the ASE men came out, the union would perhaps be excluded from the works and scabs would take their places—and there were already seventeen of them in the factory.[674] Nevertheless, the ASE men at Silver's were bound by their own union's craft exclusivity, which had rebounded upon them and was fast becoming obsolete. The strikers' claim that the dispute would have ended quickly if the ASE men had come out is a moot point, but working alongside blacklegs was scarcely to the ASE's credit. Although it does not seem that ASE men did laborers' work, they did keep the plant running at reduced capacity. Had the machinery broken down and not been repaired, it would have been difficult for the scab machine minders to maintain production. A delegation from the London Trades Council found that "50 per cent of ... [the engineers] were engaged in productive work, viz, the manufacture of dies in which to run the rubber."[675] The ASE men and carpenters also assisted the company and prolonged the strike by dismantling and packing machinery for shipment to Persan in France. While the ASE turners and smiths stood out as principled trade unionists, the same cannot be said of the union fitters or their officials. The smiths and turners do not appear to have lost their jobs in the aftermath of the strike. If they had been sacked, it most certainly would have been mentioned in the EC minutes. The low point came in late November when the ASE man, Henderson was arrested and jailed on the testimony of his fellow union members, a matter on which the EC minutes are mute. Further, while the fitters told the Trades Council delegation that they would cease work if their union executive called on them to do so,[676] they certainly did not insist on it.

Scathing Attacks by New Unionists

The New Unionists and their supporters were scathing about the ASE's behavior. When the strike collapsed, the socialist *Commonweal* blamed the executive of "the richest trade union in England—the Engineers" who, by refusing to call their members out, had "lent their aid to one of the worst sweating firms in London."[677] In the aftermath of the strike, the *Labour Elector* opined that "among those directly responsible for the temporary defeat are the whole of the mechanics—not the engineers only—and especially from the fact that they did not bring the pressure of their voices to bear on the masters."[678] They might have added that Britain's richest union donated a paltry sum to the strike fund: £50 out of an annual income in excess of £150,000. The high-flown rhetoric with which the EC had celebrated the dockers' victory twelve weeks earlier had proved to be so much hot air. Frederick Engels, the grand old man of the socialist movement, was appalled. Although he believed, probably wrongly, that the ASE fitters had done laborers' work, his private assessment lays bare the reasons for the Society's behavior:

> At the Silvertown Rubber Works . . . where there was a twelve-weeks' strike, the strike was broken by the engineers. . . . And why? These fools, in order to keep the supply of workers low, have a rule that nobody who has not been through the correct period of apprenticeship may be admitted to their union. By this means they have created an army of rivals, so-called blacklegs, who are just as skilled as they are themselves and who would gladly come into the union, but who are forced to remain blacklegs because they are kept outside by this pedantry which has no sense at all nowadays. And because they knew that both in the Commercial Dock and in Silvertown these blacklegs would immediately have stepped into their place, they stayed in and so became blacklegs themselves against the strikers. There you see the difference: the new unions hold together; in the present gas strike, sailors (steamer) and firemen, lightermen and coal carters are all together, but of course not the engineers again, they are still working![679]

Though it would be wrong to place the whole of the blame for the strikers' defeat on the ASE, the union did virtually nothing to help the laborers, and much to hinder them. Though it is probably too strong to label the ASE's fitters as blacklegs, they perhaps fit the lesser category of miscreants known to Australian trade unionists as "grubs."[680] The one great lesson to come out of the Silvertown defeat was that the old slogan "united we stand, divided we fall" is indubitably true, as is its converse.

IX.
"There Is No Justice, Mercy or Compassion in the Plutocracy"

The law was made for one thing alone, for the exploitation of those who don't understand it, or are prevented by naked misery from obeying it. And anyone who wants a crumb of this exploitation for himself must obey the law strictly.[681]
—BERTOLT BRECHT

The freedom of contract is maintained by the truncheon. There is no justice, mercy or compassion in the Plutocracy.[682]
—CARDINAL MANNING, 1889

UNTIL EARLY NOVEMBER, the police had kept a low profile in Silvertown. Afterward, they began regularly turning up in force. There had been reports in the press of strikers roughing up blacklegs, and Matthew Gray was not at all happy about it. Nor was he any happier when pickets peacefully dissuaded would-be scabs or dupes from entering his premises to take their jobs. He was also irritated by what he regarded as a lamentable lack of enthusiasm by the police in restraining the pickets outside of his factory. In this, he was echoing the indignation of the dock moguls, who had railed at what they saw as police inaction during the earlier dock strike. The dock companies had been annoyed by the widespread cross-class sympathy for the dockers who, as Frederick Engels noted, "even have bourgeois opinion on their side," adding, "the merchants who suffer from this interruption of traffic do not blame the workmen, but the obstinate Dock companies."[683] However, as John Saville noted, a

change in the temper of public opinion towards New Unionism is noticeable already in the closing stages of the 1889 Dock Strike from a reading of the editorial columns of *The Times*. Prior to 28 August the leader writers had been fairly sympathetic to the dock laborers; but on that day, in a tough-minded editorial, *The Times* warned that "evidence is accumulating that intimidation is playing an appreciable, if not important, part in this strike."[684]

By the time the Silvertown strike broke out, the press was frequently complaining about the harassment of blacklegs. In one instance, up to a thousand pickets allegedly chased a few hundred blacklegs around the waterfront and in another case scabs narrowly escaped being run over by a "dock engine." The same report claimed that "many of the blacklegs have been so terrified by the menacing attitude of the strikers that they have abandoned work."[685] By the end of the year, notes Saville, "the 'sympathy' of *The Times* had been thoroughly dissipated" and the paper was in the forefront of those calling for the formation of a corps of strikebreakers under police protection.[686] Silvertown was to become a laboratory in which such strikebreaking methods were tested.

The employers did not initially get things all their own way. Many ordinary police officers regarded themselves as working class, were paid accordingly, and sympathized with the New Unionists. The police themselves were in dispute with the government over pensions during this period, and this would have further inclined the rank-and-file bobby to show leniency to the strikers. At the top, James Monro, the Metropolitan Police Commissioner, was reluctant to concede to the employers' demands for a violent crackdown. His initial attitude was that if strikers were found in commission of a crime, the police would arrest and prosecute, otherwise they would avoid robust methods.[687] A middle-aged and irascible Scot of strange religious opinions, Monro had served for almost thirty years in India as a high-ranking civil servant, judge, and Inspector-General of Police, and was used to getting his own way. Well liked by his men— he was to resign in 1890 because the Police Pensions Bill did not grant them what he believed they were entitled to—he was a reserved man of independent temper who did not suffer fools gladly and disliked being told what to do by interfering politicians and businessmen. A graduate of Edinburgh and Berlin universities, he was perhaps the closest thing in Britain's police force to an intellectual, and was a pioneer of modern detective methods (albeit unsuccessful in his hunt for Jack the Ripper in 1888).[688] However, middle-class sympathy for strikers was ebbing, and industrialists, MPs, and the press were outraged by the New Unions. Monro was going to have to bow to the establishment's wishes and crack down hard at Silvertown whether he liked it or not. Police truncheons, as the Catholic Lord Archbishop of Westminster, Cardinal Henry Manning, observed, would enforce "freedom of contract." Police discipline would prevail over any residual class solidarity and in Silvertown their actions would confirm Frederick Engels's *bon mot* that the state was in essence "prisons and bodies of armed men."

"Reign of Terror"

Police action played a big part in breaking the strike. When the strike was over, Sam Silver told shareholders that the "reign of terror" of the Silvertown pickets "might be traced to the inaction of the police," but that "the strike collapsed when the police were firm."[689] Any independence that Monro had earlier shown evaporated at Silvertown. On 6 December 1889, he wrote to the Home Office, apropos of a new strike at the South London gasworks, to offer "to extend to the masters and their employees the fullest protection which they can claim from any illegal intimidation on the part of the strikers."[690] Silvertown had proved to be a turning point in the way the employing class and the authorities handled the New Unionism and strikes. A few years later, dockers in Hull would be confronted with bayonets and gunboats, and the 1890s would be remembered as a period of intense class war in Britain.

Picketing was a grey area of the law, and there can be little doubt that many would-be blacklegs had been deterred from entering Silver's works by the pickets hooting and jeering outside the gates. Some scabs repented and had their trainfares home paid by the Strike Committee. With production greatly reduced through lack of steam and hands to work the machinery, Matthew Gray took action to reduce the effectiveness of the picket lines and to prosecute those responsible for what he claimed was intimidation. At the regular Thursday board meeting on 31 October, a company clerk named Vidler reported that a woman named Emily Verralls and some other scabs had been subjected to "molestation, assault, & damage to their houses at the hands of the Company's workpeople now on strike." This was the first time such matters had been raised at the Silver's board level—or at least recorded in the minutes, which suggests that until that time the strike had been relatively peaceful. This impression is reinforced by scrutiny of press reports at the time. The board placed the matter in the hands of Mr. Hutchins, the company solicitor, to determine whether summonses ought to be obtained against those responsible for the alleged offenses. The board also instructed the secretary, William Tyler, to draft a letter to Police Commissioner James Monro to call "attention [to] the organised intimidation practised at Silvertown."[691] After that, the board did not meet for a fortnight, evidently considering the matter was well in hand, although it is highly likely that some intense lobbying of political figures took place behind the scenes. As we have seen, Silver's was well connected and many MPs and other influential people were shareholders in the firm.

Picketing: "Calculated to Produce Intimidation"

Since the dock strike, the police and government had been under intense pressure from employers and their friends in Parliament to act firmly against strikers. The shipping and dock companies were in the forefront of this lobby, and Silver's joined the clamor. In mid-September, stung by criticism of alleged police inactivity during the dock strike, Commissioner Monro had sent a testy note to C. M. Norwood, the Deputy Chairman of the London and India Docks Joint Committee, objecting to "undeserved reproach."[692] Norwood's criticism concerned the handling of pickets, who had effectively closed down the docks during the strike along a sixteen-mile front. The dock companies insisted that picketing was illegal. Monro was tight-lipped, but was clearly of two minds about this and tilting toward the employers' point of view. He informed the Home Office in September 1889 that "when it leads to open intimidation, whether by threats, or violence, or reasonable apprehension of violence, the police will act in cases which come under their personal notice or in which complaint is made and substantiated to their satisfaction." He then cancelled any implied caveats by endorsing the employers' view that picketing "*does covertly aim at, and is calculated to produce intimidation.*" Not surprisingly, he also "favour[ed] a copy of the opinion by Messrs. Wontner as to the state of the law on this point."[693]

Wontner & Sons was an aggressively anti-union legal firm that operated out of chambers on Ludgate Hill (and which has premises in The Strand in Westminster today). The principal partner in the firm, the forty-seven-year-old St. John Wontner, had begun practicing law under his father's guidance almost a quarter-century earlier and the firm had acted as solicitors for the Metropolitan Police, the Home Office, and the Treasury for over sixty years. St. John Wontner's grandfather had been appointed Governor of Newgate Prison in 1822 and afterward served as Marshal of Her Majesty's Gaols (Jails). The family, therefore, had earned a good living by interpreting the law, prosecuting felons, and locking them up.[694] Wontner's curious name harks back to the Middle Ages when they earned their living by hunting moles—"wants" in medieval English—for their hardwearing skins. By 1889, Wontners was hunting trade unionists instead, figuratively speaking. Unsurprisingly, the firm advised that picketing did breach the Conspiracy and Protection Act of 1875 in the "sense of putting undue pressure upon workmen or employers."[695] As Wontner's advice to Monro would boost the firm's business, their legal opinion on picketing was scarcely disinterested, but there can be little doubt that they were also ideologically committed to the anti-labor cause. The Silvertown strike was shaping up as a test case and when during its dying days NUG&GL stokers picketed at the South London gasworks, Monro was confident that the law backed muscular policing. In a letter to the Home Office, he promised that he could "extend to the masters and their employés the fullest protection which they can claim from any illegal intimidation on the part of the strikers."[696]

Any Pretense of Neutrality Abandoned

At Silvertown, after a sluggish start, the police abandoned any pretense of neutrality. Commissioner Monro replied promptly to Silver's letter[697] and shortly afterward sent reinforcements to Silvertown. On Tuesday, 5 November, the fiftieth day of the strike, large numbers of pickets turned up at the factory gates to prevent or dissuade blacklegs from entering. The previous Saturday, a striker had entered the factory disguised as a sailor. He had witnessed one man working in the telegraph shop and another in the cutting shop. He also saw fitters doing laboring work in the fitting shop, but was recognized shortly afterward and ejected from the premises.[698] It was blacklegging on a relatively small scale, but it appears to have incensed the strikers, who turned out in force on that Tuesday morning in bright sunshine to watch the scabs creeping to work. This time the pickets were confronted by a large contingent of Metropolitan Police, who escorted the blacklegs through the gates.[699] From now on, the police were a constant presence in the Silvertown streets. Satisfied, Silver's board of directors decided not to send Monro a further letter demanding action.[700]

Until November, the strike had been relatively peaceful, but the company's stepped-up efforts to bring in strikebreakers, combined with hunger and bitterness over the return to work by a few of the original strikers, had inflamed the situation. Gray had prevailed upon Commissioner Monro to provide a greater police presence, and he was determined to press charges against strikers he accused of assault or intimidation of blacklegs. On Friday, 8 November, the West Ham police magistrate found a number of strikers guilty of intimidation—perhaps of Emily Verralls—and bound each of them over with a £5 fine to keep the peace.[701] For poor working people, during a protracted strike, this was a huge sum of money.[702] A further summons, for assault, had also been served on one of the strikers, company solicitor Hutchins reported.[703] Around the same time, sensational articles appeared in some of the East End newspapers, alleging serious assaults on a local blackleg and her elderly mother. Two strikers, James Bone, a rubber mixer of 1 Emma Street, and his sister-in-law, Rose Morgan, of 3 Emma Street, were charged "on two informations" (*sic*) with assaulting and intimidating Margaret Dinsmore of Silvertown on 9 November. Dinsmore, who worked in the rubber-mixing shop with Morgan, was scorned by her neighbors as a blackleg. Her version of what happened was reported uncritically in the *East End News* in an article titled "Intimidation at Silvertown: a striker knocks down an old lady of 63 and brutally kicks her."[704] In this version, published before the matter had been resolved in court, but with Dinsmore's claims presented uncritically as fact, the blackleg said she had left her house in the evening to go shopping. When she returned she saw about thirty people she recognized as strikers milling around her door. The strikers, she testified, jeered and hooted at her as she went inside. Shortly afterward, she answered a knock on the door and was confronted by Rose Morgan, who allegedly said, "I'll slap your face, you blackleg." Dinsmore replied, "I'm doing no harm going to work," whereupon Morgan stepped up and slapped her face despite Morgan's sister's remonstration of "Don't, Rose, don't. You know what you'll get." Dinsmore claimed that at this stage James Bone assaulted her and then attacked her mother, Mrs. Miles, "an old lady of 63." According to Dinsmore, a doctor subsequently diagnosed a fracture to one of Miles's ribs. This, Dinsmore claimed, resulted from the assault. The first hearing of the case was adjourned.[705] It was all grist to the company's mill, and appeared to support Wontner's claims of a reign of terror in Silvertown. As we shall see, it was confected.

"Great Pluck and Determination"

From this time on, the West Ham Police Magistrate Baggally had to deal with a welter of charges, almost all "at the instance of Matthew Gray," reported *Lloyd's Weekly Newspaper*.[706] In one case in mid-November, the strikers William Mitchell, Samuel Hazelhurst, Emma Broadbridge, Minnie Skinner, Annie Doyle, Nellie Doyle, Emily Lacy, Mary Bacon, Lizzie Lowe, Nellie Stanley, Maggie Sullivan, Nora Cruthley, Alice Holmes, and Bessie Drury were jointly charged with intimidation and riotous behavior. On the day of the hearing, they marched to the court in West Ham from Silvertown with their supporters, their singing and cheering muffled by a thick fog. The prosecutor in this case was the ubiquitous St. John Wontner, who did his best to secure convictions. Magistrate Baggally, however, did not think that the incidents had been very serious. In all likelihood, the picketers had merely engaged in the usual hooting and jeering at the blacklegs going to work. *Lloyd's Weekly* reported Baggally's ruling that,

> he did not think the evidence showed that the girls took part in any act of violence, but he said he must caution the girls and their friends of the gravity of their conduct. If it was continued the offenders would be severely dealt with. They were perfectly entitled to go out on strike, but they had no right to threaten others who desired to go to work.[707]

Baggally bound the strikers over to keep the peace and fined them 5 shillings each. When they left the court, they were welcomed by a large crowd of cheering well-wishers and marched in a body back to Silvertown.[708] The *Labour Elector* wrote up the affair as "a great triumph over the masters," and lauded the girls for showing "great pluck and determination."[709] By this time, any doubts that women could not be good trade unionists must have been dispelled.

Although Wontner and Gray would have been displeased with the verdicts, Baggally's remarks cast doubt on the legality of picketing. He admitted that the strikers had not attacked or physically impeded the scabs, but he still fined them for merely saying things. Ernest Baggally was a reasonably independent-minded man, so the fines hint at the pressure that was building up to crush union power. The Tory establishment was determined to break the strike through legal means, and the *Labour Elector* warned that a defeat at Silvertown would "indirectly affect hundreds of other trades, by giving masters some hope that they may successfully withstand the demands of their men." Recognizing the way the tide was running, the paper appealed to the London Trades Council to stop "quarrelling about the past," to "take up the case, and send the Silvertown strikers men and money."[710]

"System of Intimidation and Terrorism"

By Wontner's own admission, picketing had been effective in turning back would-be blacklegs at the factory gates. On 17 November, *Lloyd's Weekly* quoted a courtroom speech by Wontner in which he alleged that a "system of intimidation and terrorism" existed in Silvertown. "Every day," he sputtered, "hundreds of strikers collected in the road at the top of the cul-de-sac [the works' gates] and hooted at the people as they came out." Though he could not point to instances of violence, Wontner was dismayed that "the hooting seemed to have a great effect even on the men employed at the works, but to the women it became a deterrent, and the result was that very shortly the women left their employ."[711] The unspoken aim of Wontner's court performance, however, was not just to persuade the magistrate to dish out stiff sentences against picketers, although he certainly hoped for that. He was also playing to the gallery—in this case "respectable" middle-class public opinion—which, he no doubt hoped, would prevail upon the Metropolitan Police to take even stronger action against the picketers. The strike had now entered its eighth week and was paralyzing one of the capital's greatest industries.

X.
November: Hunger and Cold
❖❖❖

> When crimes begin to pile up they become invisible.
> When sufferings become unendurable the cries are no
> longer heard. The cries, too, fall like rain in summer.[712]
> —BERTOLT BRECHT

> I have worked hard and long, enduring many sleepless
> nights. I have been hungry and thirsty and have often
> gone without food. I have shivered in the cold, without
> enough clothing to keep me warm.[713]
> —CORINTHIANS 11:27

ON 6 NOVEMBER 1889, the same day that the police first turned out in force in Silvertown, the strikers' brass band performed outside the works, playing a dead march dead slow before parading through the streets via West Silvertown to repeat the performance outside the company's head office in the distant City. Large "turn-outs" of both sexes and all ages stood bareheaded in the thin sunshine beside them,[714] noted the *Times*.[715] They had no chance of shaming the directors, if that was their aim in doffing their caps. One also suspects that by this time many of the middle-class passersby would have become indifferent or even hostile to East End strikers. The following morning, in near-freezing temperatures, Tom Mann gave a fiery speech at the factory gates. He might have warmed the strikers' hearts, but he could not fill their bellies nor could he clothe their shivering bodies. When strike pay was distributed at this meeting, it had dwindled to 4 shillings for men and 3 shillings for women.[716] That those who did not participate in the processions were docked a shilling testifies, perhaps, that some of the strikers were faltering in their resolve and needed extra "encouragement" to participate. This was hardly surprising given the privations they were experiencing, but it also suggests that some of the strikers may have been looking for alternative employment. By this time, the strikers and their families must have been subsisting on little more than bread, with the odd scraping of dripping perhaps, and they would have had no means of heating their rooms save for what coal slack they could scavenge or steal. Their children, routinely malnourished to start with, must have suffered cruelly, and it must have broken their parents' hearts to see it.

Hunger and Its Consequences

Persistent rumors had also been circulating that some of the women had turned to prostitution during the strike. The stories were not meant to gain sympathy for the strikers, and Eleanor Marx angrily denounced them as pernicious propaganda.[717] One wonders, however, whether there was not some substance to the tittle-tattle. There was a huge demand for the services of prostitutes in Victorian London. As many as 80,000 women serviced perhaps two million clients a week according to one estimate, or twenty-five per girl.[718] Although the middle-class stereotype saw prostitutes as "fallen women" and thousands of brothels existed in London, alongside thousands of other "disreputable houses,"[719] prostitution was sometimes a "transitional occupation" for ill-paid working-class women between the ages of eighteen and twenty-two.[720] Will Thorne recalls walking with visitors along the Connaught Road in Silvertown. "Near the station is the main entrance to the Albert Dock," he wrote, "and I showed them one of the familiar sights of this place at night time, a crowd of women who are always waiting to meet the sailors and firemen that work on the ships."[721] Some factory women went "on the game" part-time to supplement their meager incomes or plied the ancient trade in times of exceptional destitution. For middle-class moralists, the "girls" were the problem, not the social system that created prostitution or the men who availed themselves of it. Factory girls were in any case commonly regarded as women of easy virtue,[722] and primly middle-class Beatrice Webb had slandered Eleanor Marx herself as a drug-addicted harlot after their meeting in the British Museum tearooms. The Silvertown women had shown themselves to be courageous in the face of adversity, but they were only human and by this time many of them were close to starvation, so it is possible that some did succumb to the temptation to make some money by soliciting in the Royal Victoria Gardens. Two shillings strike-relief pay would buy them perhaps five loaves of bread to last them a week with nothing left over for other food, heating, rent, and sundries. On the other hand, one night with a young virgin might be worth as much as £25— more than a factory girl could make in a year of toil. In Bertolt Brecht's earthy words, *"Erst kam seine Fresse, dann die Moral,"* which freely translated means "Your gob comes first, then morality."

The strikers' families received assistance from the Salvation Army and sympathetic shopkeepers, but great hunger and cold were stalking the dreary streets of Silvertown. In mid-November, a slow trickle back to work began, and Matthew Gray was keen to speed it up by whatever means at his disposal. Fred Ling told the strikers that when Silver's gave three workers—Macmillan, Carter, and Christie—an ultimatum either to quit their company houses in Twyford and Winchester Streets or return to work, they had reluctantly gone back through the factory gates.[723] Ling did not seem bitter against the three men, but instead directed his anger against Gray for ordering the evictions. Around the same time, the company brought a few scabs over the river from Kent by boat. There were not many up to this point, but with many thousands of unemployed tramping the streets looking for work, the strikers must have been worried by the prospect of desperate men driven to scab. The plight of the Silvertown strikers was by this time only a few removes from the misery of the casual laborers thrown out of work. If such suffering concerned the members of Silver's board and the company's shareholders, they never said so publicly, nor did they care. Their behavior confirms Cardinal Manning's contention that "there is no justice, mercy or compassion in the plutocracy." (The Cardinal was the head of the Catholic Church in Britain and had helped broker a settlement of the recent London dock strike.) A kind of "compassion fatigue" combined with hostility to the New Unions also seems to have taken hold in the middle classes, some of whom had donated to the dockers' strike funds earlier that year.

The Silvertown workers' diet was scanty in the best of times, but after two months on strike, they could look forward each day to little more than dry bread. Meat, fish, fruit, and vegetables would have been beyond their means. This struggle between Capital and Labor was grossly unequal. Gray's residence in Lessness Park was only a few miles across the river as the rooks fly across the darkening autumn sky, but it might as well have been on another planet. Few of its denizens ever set foot in places such as Silvertown; any factory owners who once lived there had long since moved out. Their tables groaned with produce that the strikers could never imagine themselves eating, even in the best of times. One can imagine the servants waiting nervously at Gray's table on damp November evenings during the strike. As Mrs. Beeton insisted, "Dinner, being the grand solid meal of the day, is a matter of considerable importance; and a well-served table is a striking index of human ingenuity and resource."[724] Meals most certainly were a matter of great ingenuity over in Silvertown, where crammed in their cold terrace rows the Silvertown men and women ate their crusts, huddled together for warmth under what scraps of blanket and coats they owned, and perhaps praying for a miracle. By this stage, there would not have been even a scrape of dripping to spread on their bread and that would have been stale. One wonders what they might have made of Mrs. Beeton's blithe contention that "the nation which knows how to dine has learnt the leading lesson of progress."[725]

Yet there was solidarity and idealism in Silvertown that would have been incomprehensible to Isabella Beeton or the denizens of Abbey Wood. In Silvertown, the Reverend Stopford Brooke told his parishioners that half-starving single girls had given their strike pay to married workmates so that their children might be fed.[726] Though some people did on occasion do horrible things to each other in the East End—Jack the Ripper, for instance, was stalking and killing women in this period—solidarity was almost instinctive and without it life could not have been sustained. The East End writer Bill Fishman quotes a local doctor who believed that "if the poor were not so wonderfully generous to one another the result would be a generation of idiots."[727] Sadly, relentless hunger, cold, and illness can bleed altruism and principles from the most selfless hearts. Hope like love can turn into its opposite. One striker who returned to work around this time was a young woman who had given her all for her comrades, and had been given new boots by the Strike Committee after wearing out her old ones collecting money for the strike fund. Shortly afterward the poor wretch went back into the factory and the windows in her house were broken with stones,[728] perhaps by other women strikers with whom she had once tramped the streets with eyes ablaze with hope. Her reasons for abandoning the struggle have not been recorded, but it is entirely possible that she did so in order to be able to buy medicine, milk, or bread, for a sick child or parent, or for herself, with prostitution the only other way to end the agonies of hunger. This melancholy incident highlights the desperation that was beginning to settle over Silvertown.

The effects of the strike were also rippling out beyond the ranks of the strikers, and spelled "ruination" for the petty shopkeepers of West

Ham, lamented a small businessman called George Hay. Hay wrote to
Robert L. Curtis, the mayor of West Ham, asking him to intervene in the
dispute. Curtis promptly complied, but company secretary William Tyler,
no doubt acting on Matthew Gray's instructions, declared in a letter to
the press that "of course the directors cannot consent to such an interview."[729] They could have—*of course*—but Silver's was clearly determined
to force an end to the long strike on their terms, and was not concerned
about repercussions for the broader community. Tyler had earlier written
to Curtis informing him that as the workers were well paid and had been
led astray by "unscrupulous agitators," there was no need for interven-
tion.[730] Further offers of mediation by City financier J. Hume Webster and
West Ham Alderman Phillips in early November were also unceremoni-
ously rebuffed.[731]

The heavy police presence and prosecutions did not cow the most
militant of the strikers and their supporters at this stage. On Sunday,
17 November, the SDF combined with the Gasworkers' Union to march
through the streets of Tottenham, making a great din with cheering,
red flags, a contingent from the Sons of Phoenix, and two brass bands.
They collected £10 from passersby "after expenses" and followed up with
another mass meeting at Page Green on Seven Sisters Road, the following
weekend.[732] The same weekend, the strikers marched from Silvertown to
Victoria Park for another rally. At the first meeting, Fred Ling announced
to loud hooting and groans that Silver's had refused to meet Sidney
Buxton, the West Ham MP, with a view to mediation. It was then that
Ling declared angrily that if Matthew Gray ever went to hell, he "hoped
he'd be a stoker there to make things hot for him." Ben Tillett declared
that Gray was hoping that winter would combine with hunger to drive the
strikers back to work on his terms.[733]

Hope and pride still remained in the hearts of many of the strikers. A
correspondent of the *Daily News* was impressed by the large number of
women in the crowd at the gardens. Their presence, he wrote, "marks
a new and most important feature in the history of Trades Unionism.
Silvertown, near Woolwich, is so remote that it has escaped general attention. Yet here, some three thousand persons have been out on strike for
nearly ten weeks."[734] The correspondent also put his finger on an aspect
of the strike that did not bode well for the workers. Silvertown might lie
only five miles downstream from the City of London, but it was almost
another world, cut off by the river, the docks, and the marsh, and invisible to most Londoners. Many, too, chose not to see what was happening.
The days were shortening, winter was advancing, and the dark clouds

overhead mirrored ominous developments in the strike. Had Ling and Tillett known what lay ahead a couple of days later, their rhetoric would have been even stronger. There were also nagging rumors that French and British scabs would soon descend on Silvertown.[735] The rumor of French scabs proved untrue,[736] but British scabs were soon in evidence.

Scab-Herding in Rural Essex

That same weekend, a country solicitor and reserve army major named William Howard advertised for workers in the *Essex Standard*, a weekly newspaper circulating in rural Essex and Suffolk. Howard promised "permanent employment" for sixty laborers "near Colchester at $4\frac{3}{4}$d per hour (the work to consist of from 59 to 60 hours)." Interested persons were requested to meet him at the Colchester Reserve Army drill hall to apply for positions.[737] It was a tempting offer. Colchester is an ancient market town lying on the swampy River Colne near the Essex coast at the terminus of a railway from London. Too isolated to have been affected directly by the early Industrial Revolution, it began to catch up following the establishment of an army barracks there in the 1850s, which created a demand for goods and services. By the late 1880s, the town boasted breweries, engineering works, and processing factories, and its population had grown to around 30,000.[738] It promised to be a fruitful recruiting ground for blackleg labor given its isolation, close rural hinterland, late industrial development, stunted labor movement, and rising levels of unemployment.

Howard was acting on the instructions of Christian (Chris) Gray, one of Matthew Gray's five sons, who had traveled up from London to brief him.[739] It is possible Wontner and Sons recommended Howard as a reliable friend of the employing class, and Colchester would have appealed as a large country town untouched by Radical labor agitation. The depression had created a sizable "reserve army of labor" which Howard and Gray could tap into. The blacklegs could be conveyed directly to London by train. Wages, too, were considerably lower in Colchester than in London, and though $4\frac{3}{4}$d an hour was not especially high pay in the metropolis, particularly given Silvertown's astronomical rents, it was worth considerably more in rural districts.

The advertisement in the *Standard* did not reveal that the Colchester men were to be employed as blacklegs in Silvertown, so it is not surprising that 250 laborers milled around the drill hall at the appointed time clamoring for the sixty jobs. Some would have been unemployed or underemployed locals, and others might have been keen to leave dreary jobs in Colchester for the supposed excitement and high wages of the capital. Most were disappointed: Howard picked out sixty of the most likely looking fellows and dismissed the rest, doubtless consoling them with the promise that more volunteers would soon be required. The successful applicants entrained for Liverpool Street Station the same day[740] under the personal direction of Chris Gray.[741] Matthew Gray was putting into practice the ideas advocated by the *Times* for the mass recruitment of "free laborers" to take the jobs of strikers.

Patriotic Duty to Scab

It was the start of a trial of wills between the company and the strikers. When the first batch of Colchester men arrived at Silvertown via the District Line from Liverpool Street Station—doubtless a rare treat for country folk—they learned that they would be required to scab on the strikers. The money on offer seemed attractive, but by the right-wing *Essex Standard*'s own admission, the men were "reluctantly induced to turn out by the dissentients under the influence of the agitators of the Union";[742] in other words, many declined Silver's offer of employment when they realized they were required to scab. Many of them perhaps were strong and vigorous, and could afford to spurn employment under such conditions. Some perhaps resented being tricked into scabbing. Subsequent batches of Colchester men were not so principled, or were desperate for work at any cost, for they could not credibly claim not to know what they were getting into. Curiously, some other later arrivals appeared to believe it was their patriotic duty to scab; one group wrote to Major Howard testifying that "we, as British workmen, are only too glad to inform you that there was not one man absent on our arrival at Silvertown."[743] One can almost feel the tug of the collective forelock. Silver's was also moving to fine-tune the operation with the help of the Metropolitan Police, who were much more responsive following Gray's complaints to Commissioner Monro, and the strong likelihood that persons in high places had added their support from behind the scenes.

The Strike Committee redoubled its vigilance following the surprise arrival of the first contingent of rural blacklegs. The following week, chairman George Bateman and two other strikers went to Liverpool Street and Stratford stations to attempt to turn back fresh parties of Colchester scabs. The police were waiting on the platform and quickly herded the blacklegs aboard a District Line suburban train, "followed by Bateman on the lookout for a chance to talk to them," reported the *Labour Elector*. Realizing what he was up to, the police took the scabs in first-class carriages to Charing Cross—probably the only time in their lives these poor country folk would enjoy such luxury!—in an attempt to shake off the pickets. Bateman was persistent, however, and he managed to talk to the Colchester men on the platform at Charing Cross, "much to the disgust of the master, and his swell mob of five who were 'protecting' the blacklegs." Bateman does not seem to have convinced them to defect, however, for they were loaded aboard a steam launch at Charing Cross Pier and taken downriver to the company wharf at Silvertown. The boatman reportedly later told the blacklegs' minders that if he had "known their errand, he would not have brought the launch to the pier."[744]

The Entertainments at Colchester

The Strike Committee also decided to send a contingent to Colchester. Led by the volatile Irishman Michael Henry, a number of strikers took the train down and set about disrupting Major Howard's recruiting business. The Silvertown men seem to have contacted potential allies in the town beforehand as a "flaming red placard" appeared in the windows of the Liberal Club in the High Street. Another sign at the Radical Club denounced "BLACKLEGS." Entertainment was at a premium in provincial Colchester, and the theatrical Henry was the man to provide it for the townsfolk. He organized an impromptu meeting in the town center and launched into a diatribe against Silver's, Major Howard, the Marquess of Salisbury, the Duke of Bedford, and other establishment worthies. Soon, a large crowd had gathered, some merely curious bystanders, some sympathetic to the unions, others hostile. A number of the latter stood somewhat unsteadily after issuing forth from public houses and jeered at the union men. Henry was interrupted by hecklers shouting "We don't want you here," and a section of the crowd sang "Rule Britannia" in an attempt to drown him out, a vain task for Henry had a pair of leather lungs and was clearly enjoying himself into the bargain. The interjectors, he declared—and perhaps not without reason—were under the influence of drink, specifically the strong ale known as half-and-half. One wonders whether, in the fashion of elections since the time of Hogarth, these patriotic plebeians had not been provided with free refreshments. Henry hinted at the possibility. Certainly, the scene was reminiscent of the election campaign described in *The Ragged Trousered Philanthropists* in which mobs bribed by free beer paraded the streets bawling out "Good old Sweater (i.e. of labor)."[745] Mr. Sparling, the secretary of the Colchester Conservative (Tory) Club, mounted the steps near the Corn Exchange, saying that he could refute many of Henry's statements because he had shortly before been speaking with one of the Silvertown managers. Sparling staunchly defended William Howard, whom he claimed had "done more than most men for the welfare of working men and no one less deserved the violent abuse that had been heaped upon him by the speaker," Michael Henry. Two strikers, George Brown and E. White, replied, assuring the crowd that what Sparling had to say was not true, and appealing to local workers and unemployed to stay away from Silvertown. White also warned that $4\frac{3}{4}$d an hour in London was not worth much more than $2\frac{1}{2}$d in Colchester, given the higher cost of living and rents in particular. Chris Gray was also in the crowd. He told the man from the *Essex Standard* that he had thought of speaking but did not need to as Sparling had done such a good job. Afterward Henry and the strikers repaired to an alehouse to continue argument and discussion with the locals, well lubricated with the local strong ale, hinted the *Standard*.[746] Overall, the impromptu meeting had probably provided sleepy Colchester with more excitement than it had experienced since 1884 when an earthquake shook the town.[747] Although Henry's efforts might have convinced some would-be blacklegs not to apply for jobs at Silver's, back in Silvertown matters had taken a turn for the worse for the strikers.

Serious Collision with the Police

On Tuesday, 19 November, according to the *Stratford Express*, "a serious collision occurred between the police and the Silvertown strikers." Tempers had been frayed because of police interventions that blatantly exceeded any brief they may have had to keep the peace in Silvertown in a neutral way. Intentionally or otherwise, command of the police "on the ground" had been entrusted to a trio of reactionary, union-hating senior officers drafted from outside Silvertown, namely Inspectors Parsons, Vedy, and Bishop. When another party of Colchester men arrived at the factory gates ready to start work, the pickets persuaded a large number of them to go home. That might have been the end of it, but Inspector Parsons followed the defectors to the railway station, boarded their train, and escorted them back through the gates into the factory, clearly exceeding any brief to keep the peace. The pickets, no doubt, were incensed by such blatantly partisan behavior. Later that morning a greengrocer called Woolgar crossed the picket line with food for the blacklegs, who had been billeted aboard the company cable ship, the SS *Dacia*, which was tied up at the Thames wharf inside the factory grounds. It is possible that Woolgar was from outside of the district, because most of the local shopkeepers had boycotted Silver's. It is also possible that his mission was a deliberate provocation engineered by the company; it would have been much less bother, and more efficient, for them to ferry in supplies to the scabs by launch. According to the press, he was "roughly handled" by the strikers and the police moved in to protect him.

An hour or so later, serious violence broke out, started according to the strikers by the police who, under the command of Inspectors Vedy and Bishop, had been massing in Factory Road. According to the police, the strikers threw stones at them, whereupon on the inspectors' command they baton-charged the picket line. In the ensuing melee, which swirled around the factory gates and surrounding streets, a number of workers were seriously injured and taken to Poplar Hospital. Another bystander, a man named England, was badly injured when he came out of the Royal Arms pub to see what the commotion was about. England was hospitalized as a result of a heavy blow to the head, and rumors spread that he might die. An eighteen-year-old striker was also seized and beaten with fists and truncheons by a knot of seven officers before pickets managed to carry him off to safety. According to the *Stratford Express*, the police also attacked a number of women and children, including the wives of two strikers named Jarvis and Pincott. [748]

Silvertown Outraged by Myrmidons

Silvertown was furious. There was blood on the streets, unnecessarily so. Large crowds assembled in Factory Road, with thickets of police keeping watch from a safe distance farther up the road. Fred Ling and other speakers verbally lambasted Parsons and Bishop for their actions but charitably excused the constables as "acting under orders"—perhaps they wanted to avoid further violence, knowing it would tarnish their cause. The constables had indubitably acted under orders, but they had wielded their truncheons with relish. Any residual class solidarity had evaporated like mist off the marsh. Ling reported that although the Strike Committee had twice written to Scotland Yard asking for Bishop to be sent home to Plaistow, and Parsons to North Woolwich, their appeals were in vain. The inspectors were hard men who made no pretense of neutrality, and must have been the types Scotland Yard believed best able to assist Silver's in the dispute.[749] It was a hard lesson in the facts of life in a class society: the friendly bobby metamorphoses into an establishment myrmidon during strikes.

The following day, a large crowd of what the police described as "disorderly persons" congregated in the North Woolwich Road. A strong contingent of police, some mounted, charged the crowd, scattering them up the road. Among the strikers was a thirty-three-year-old rubber mixer, James Russell, who admitted in court to "shouting at the top of his voice" and throwing stones at the constables. Magistrate Baggally fined him 40 shillings, in default to fourteen days' hard labor. The same day, the police arrested John Smith, a forty-nine-year-old laborer, and charged him with being drunk and disorderly. The magistrate did not believe his protestations of sobriety and sentenced him to fourteen days' jail without the option of a fine. In both cases, Wontner and Sons prosecuted, with Matthew Gray watching proceedings from the public gallery.[750] At the same session, William Smith, thirty-two, a laborer of Canning Town, was sentenced to twenty-eight days for being drunk and disorderly and assaulting PCs Scott and Willett.[751]

For their part, Matthew Gray and the Silver's board did not directly mention the violence when they held their regular meeting at Cannon Street two days later, but they were clearly pleased with developments. They noted approvingly that a strike supporter named Henderson—no doubt the ASE man from Canning Town previously mentioned—had been sentenced to three months' imprisonment for intimidation in another case, and two other strikers had been given fourteen days' imprisonment and a £2 fine each. The minutes also note with some understatement that "a draft letter to Commissioner Monro was read & considered; but as it was reported that the Police had within the last few days shown more activity, it was decided to hold the letter over." Another delegation from the Strike Committee had been heard and sent away empty-handed.

Confected Charges

Gray also mentioned that the charges against James Bone and Rose Morgan, previously adjourned, were to be heard the following morning in the West Ham Police Court.[752] The case was again adjourned,[753] but when it was finally heard Gray must have been disappointed. He told the board that "in the case of Bone & Morgan the magistrate had dismissed the summonses, as well as the cross-summonses taken out by the defendants, ordering each side to pay its own costs."[754] Appearing for the strikers, William Thompson had given a very different version of events to that splashed across some of the newspapers. Miles and the blackleg Dinsmore, he argued, had been drunk and abusive. She and her daughter had gone to Bone's house, possibly to demand repayment of a loan. Dinsmore had called Bone's wife a "b____ striker" (censored in original article) and "a thing," Thompson said. Morgan had replied, "don't call my sister a thing," whereupon Dinsmore and her mother had attacked Bone, grabbing him around the neck and scratching his face. Bone and Morgan, Thompson stated, had only acted in self-defense. A further sixteen witnesses were called and the hearing lasted until after dark before Baggally dismissed the charges.[755] The claim, therefore, that an innocent Mrs. Miles had suffered broken ribs because of assault by strikers was confected; more likely the fractures were caused by Miles falling down when intoxicated. The *East End News* did not, however, retract its claims that the strikers had bashed the old woman and her daughter. Undoubtedly, some of the mud stuck and helped discredit the strikers in middle-class eyes.

The strikers did have some other successes during this period. Local traders denounced the seventy or so Colchester men who were billeted aboard the *Dacia* as blacklegs, and refused to supply them with meat and other foodstuffs. As a result, the company was forced to drive some bullocks and sheep into the works to provide for them.[756] Though a rubber factory would not have made the most hygienic slaughterhouse, and indeed might have been illegal even under the lax public health laws of the time, those were laws the police were not interested in upholding. It would also seem that the *Dacia*'s crew did not appreciate sharing their floating home with blacklegs, for it was reported that they became union men during the strike and remained so afterward.[757] From late November, however, the strikers were to have less and less to celebrate. The observation of West Ham Magistrate Baggally that "as a rule the strike had been remarkable for the great moderation of conduct" on the part of the strikers[758] failed to cut through the perception, fostered by the company and its allies, that a wave of violence had been unleashed in the East End. The police maintained a large contingent in Silvertown, strike funds dwindled, hunger increased, and the trickle back to work swelled into a brimming rivulet.

XI.
The Great Strike Collapses

> One can be right and still be beaten . . . force can
> vanquish spirit . . . there are times when courage is
> not its own reward.[759]
> —ALBERT CAMUS

WEDNESDAY, 27 NOVEMBER, dawned dark and bitterly cold. The temperature struggled to rise above freezing and the first snow of winter fell on Silvertown. When daylight came, it revealed a monochrome world: the whiteness of the fresh snow in startling contrast to the dark mud, the chimneys of brick and iron, the latticework of the dockside cranes, the immense stacks of coal, and the smoke-blackened walls of the factory hulking into the sky above the workers' terraces. To the chagrin of the pickets shivering in their thin clothes, a stream of workers had made their way through the factory gates in the predawn murk. The trickle back to work had become a flood. The hissing of steam, billowing smokestacks, and the rhythmic throbbing of machinery indicated that production was almost back to normal. A scant five miles distant, yet a world away, Matthew Gray, warm and well-fed in his office in Cannon Street, may have toasted "General Winter" for his contribution to the victory. The strikers were cold and hungry, their dwellings not much warmer than the frigid air outside, their boots and clothing worn thin. Their children were in distress. Force was confident that it was about to vanquish spirit.

"Where There's Life, There's Hope"

A reporter from the *Stratford Express* estimated that an extra 150 "hands" had trudged through the sharp white frost to start work. It would, he observed, make it difficult for the others to stay out.[760] The *Times* claimed that double that number returned.[761] Either way, it was ominous news for the strikers. A striker said, "Where there's life, there's hope" and noted that the NUG&GL planned a mass meeting for the following Sunday at Blackheath, south of Greenwich, but he must have been filled with foreboding. The *Times* declared confidently that "the strike was rapidly breaking up" and claimed that "fully one-third of the strikers have given in and gone back to work" at the old rate.[762]

Meanwhile, Tom Mann and Fred Ling were working feverishly to salvage what they could. On 27 November, Ling and another strike leader called Parker addressed a session of the London Trades Council. In response, the council resolved to send another delegation to Silvertown on Saturday, 30 November. George Shipton also reported that Matthew Gray had rejected a further offer for the council to mediate in the dispute.[763] Mann endorsed Ling's call for the council to prevail upon the ASE to call out the engineers who were "enabling the firm to run the machinery" and thus "prolonging the strike."[764] There was little chance of success; the ASE's EC was more concerned in finding out the identity of an ASE member who had criticized their behavior in a letter to the press than with the looming defeat at Silvertown.[765] The following day, the five-man LTC delegation met with men and women strikers in Cundy's at Silvertown and gathered a great deal of information about working conditions and wages in the plant.[766] Though the information forms a valuable historical record, it did not spur the council to undertake any concrete action in solidarity with the strikers. A report in the *York Herald* that the council had "decided to ask all workmen in competing firms throughout the country to come out in support of the Silvertown strikers, should the directors decline to renew negotiations" was wildly inaccurate.[767] According to Yvonne Kapp, there was now a "stampede" back to work, and the demoralized pickets were no longer "molesting" blacklegs.[768] Perhaps they no longer even hooted at those who so lately had been their comrades. Matthew Gray's report to the Silver's board meeting of 28 November that many strikers had returned to work since that previous week's meeting, bringing the total to 650 including "new hands," was probably accurate, given that it was not issued for public consumption.[769] Gray must have been convinced of victory, because a special board meeting held the following day did not discuss the strike at all.[770] Tom Mann told strikers that he had been invited to have lunch with the Lord Mayor of London the following Tuesday, 3 December, and that he would put it to him to write to "Brisbane and the colonies" to raise money for the strike fund, as had been done during the dock strike.[771] Realistically, such a *deus ex machina* was a forlorn hope at this stage of the strike.

An Army of Occupation

The police had maintained a conspicuous presence on the streets since their savage attack of the previous week, and the workers must have regarded them as an army of occupation. Indeed, the officers were by now routinely contemptuous of the workers' rights. On Thursday, 28 November, the seventy-fourth day of the strike, Princess Beatrice opened a church fundraiser at the Tate Institute in Silvertown. She entered the suburb through the local railway station, which had been "gaily decorated" for the occasion. The festive mood soured when the police snatched a union banner, which some strikers had been peacefully holding aloft in the crowd outside the institute. The strikers had broken no law, and although the police later returned the banner, they had managed to damage it, intentionally or otherwise.[772] Two days later, William Tyler wrote a triumphal letter to the *Times*. He was "glad to say" that the firm had lately taken on a few calendar operators and could now generate enough steam to reemploy 350 of the "old hands." The latter were working alongside over two hundred imported blacklegs—many of them from Colchester—bringing the total to 795, with a wages bill for the week of £1350. He also claimed, probably not without foundation, that many of the original strikers and those who stood down because of industrial action had found employment elsewhere.[773]

"A Tie of the Most Revolutionary Red"

The hard-core strikers were still determined to fight on. Indeed, those most active during the dispute would have had little choice given the certainty of victimizations. They had some loyal friends. The first Sunday in December saw what the *Labour Elector* reported as a "good meeting" in Victoria Park. On the same day, in Bloomsbury Congregational Chapel, the Reverend Brooke delivered a hard-hitting sermon supporting the strikers, and collected over £61 for the strike fund from the congregation.[774]

Augustus Stopford Brooke was an unconventional clergyman. Born in Donegal in Ireland to a well-to-do Protestant loyalist family, he seemed destined for a career as an Anglican priest. Educated at Trinity College in Dublin, he was ordained in London in 1857, and started work as a curate in Marylebone. The district was a poor one, and the suffering he saw there seems to have precipitated his break with "the Tory Party at prayer," even though he had become prominent enough to become a chaplain to Queen Victoria. In a sermon titled "Salt without Saviour," preached in Bedford Square Chapel, Brooke announced that he could no longer believe in the miracle of the Incarnation, and that he "had become disillusioned with the conservative social and political attitudes of an essentially aristocratic church." He sought links with the Unitarians but never formally joined them, preferring to maintain his independence.[775] Brooke had become what future generations would call a liberation theologian. A journalist observed that "in addition to being an Irishman and a strong Home Ruler . . . [Brooke] is also a bit of a Socialist and a keen sympathiser with the sufferings of the poor." Fittingly, it is said that he delivered his pro-striker sermons "wearing a tie of the most revolutionary red."[776] It is likely that the Christian socialist clergyman in George Bernard Shaw's play *Candida*, James Mavor Morell, is modeled on Brooke.[777] Had more of the nation's clergy followed this remarkable man's lead the strikers might have triumphed; more often than not, they were indifferent or hostile to the New Unions. Some, as we have seen, owned shares in Silver's, while others worked actively to weaken the strikers' resolve. These "reverend sweaters" would not passively "render unto Caesar that which is Caesar's," but would ensure it—and enrich themselves at the same time.

Almost a Thousand at Work

Meanwhile, temperatures at Silvertown had plummeted to around 20 degrees overnight and the thermometer hovered below freezing during the day. On Wednesday, 4 December, strike relief was doled out: 5 shillings to the men, 3 shillings to the women, and 2 shillings for girls and boys, the smallest amount to date.[778] It was painfully inadequate to provide food and warmth in a bitter winter, but Fred Ling remained hopeful, claiming fancifully that money was coming in "more liberally than ever."[779] Even if this was the case, many of the strikers were no longer listening to the militants. According to the minutes of the next day's board meeting, about 990 workers were now on the job, including about 250 imported scabs.

Not surprisingly, Gray spurned another offer of mediation by the London Trades Council, and confident that victory was within its grasp the Silver's board agreed to write a letter of thanks to Mr. Howard, thanking him "for his co-operation with Mr. Christian Gray in obtaining labourers" from Colchester.[780] In the face of such intransigence, the Trades Council majority simply gave up. They rejected a resolution that described Gray's conduct as "most unjust and despotic" for refusing to negotiate, and voted down another motion that called for a full delegate meeting to consider action and financial support for the strikers. Instead, they agreed to leave the matter in the hands of the secretary, George Shipton, and adjourned for a fortnight.[781] The next time they met, the strike was over, as they must have foreseen—and even hoped.

"An Air of Complete Dejection Prevailed"

A second LTC deputation did visit Silvertown on Saturday, 7 December, but it "found the men discouraged for protracting the Strike as a sufficiently large number had gone in to work as to practically put the whole factory in full working order."[782] The *Stratford Express*, which had been reasonably sympathetic to the strikers, reported that it was difficult to stop the drift back to work, particularly by those who had been stood down because of the strike action.[783] According to Yvonne Kapp, Tom Mann advised the strikers to go back to work, as they could no longer hope to win.[784] The following Monday, 9 December, a general meeting of the strikers recognized the inevitable and declared the strike officially over. The *Times* reported that "in the dismal room above a coffee tavern in which the committee sat an air of complete dejection prevailed."[785] Earlier, on the morning of that dull winter's day, the Strike Committee's chairman, George Bateman, had presided over a smaller meeting of eighteen men of the committee in the Hack Road Hall. Significantly, no women attended, despite their earlier enthusiasm for the strike. It was impossible to win, said Bateman, and a motion to call off the strike was carried with one dissenting die-hard vote.

Such tiny meetings were in stark contrast to the huge gatherings early in the strike, and Bateman and his comrades must have been uncomfortably aware that the overwhelming mass of the workers had voted with their feet. In fact, some 350 more went back that very day. Out of the 3,000-strong workforce, only 450 were still out on strike,[786] and some of these had probably found employment elsewhere. There was no question of a negotiated settlement; it was a case of every man for himself, and return to work on the old terms. The Strike Committee made the news public in a handbill distributed the following day.[787] Samuel Silver's palace of industry was back in full production, its lights blazing out over the fog-bound river and the frozen marsh, squatting in Silvertown's mean streets like some colonial fortress among the huts of a conquered people.

"Impossible to Deny Some Sympathy for the Labourers"

The Great Silvertown Strike had been crushed, and the New Union upsurge blocked. The *Times* found the defeat gave "no cause for real regret," and saw the failure as a warning to others, though it did admit that it was "impossible to deny some sympathy for the Silvertown labourers." Some would suffer much more than the majority. The paper recognized that "several hundreds" of the strikers would be victimized and would have to "face the coming winter with such courage as belongs to men who have no immediate prospect of employment."[788] Tom Mann told the Trades Council that the strike relief fund would continue to provide for those blacklisted, though it seems unlikely that the appeal was sustained for long.[789] For their part, the strike diehards faced their coming ordeal philosophically. They passed a resolution at the conclusion of the strike that reads in part: "The committee look upon their defeat as a victory, and upon the struggle of the last twelve weeks as an earnest of future demands on the part of underpaid labour, and of the granting of them by overpaid capital."[790]

Management rejoiced, and no doubt bourgeois "public opinion" along with them. The regular Silver's shareholders' meeting in February 1890 unanimously passed a long-winded resolution, moved by the prominent Oxford mathematician Professor Bartholomew "Bat" Price, which gloated over the workers' defeat. "This meeting," the motion read in part,

> declares and hereby places on record its sense of the great and valuable services rendered to the Company during the recent Strike at the Silvertown works, in the firm, prudent and just action of Mr. Matthew Gray, the Managing Director, and tenders to him its acknowledgements and thanks for these services.[791]

The resolution takes up several pages of the company minutes book, perhaps hardly surprising given the Bat's reputation as an indefatigably garrulous board and Oxford committeeman. A biographer notes that

Price's "omniscience in university business was hinted at in Lewis Carroll's lines, 'Twinkle, twinkle little bat / How I wonder what you're at.'"[792] The motion also praised the managerial and supervisory staff and "those workmen and workwomen who remained steadfast at their employment."

Ten Shillings a Share, Tax-free

At the same meeting, Silver's declared a half-yearly dividend of 5 percent, or 10 shillings a share, tax-free.[793] Congratulations for holding the line against the New Unions flowed in, among them one from the well-known rubber firm of Charles Macintosh in Manchester.[794] The *India-Rubber Journal* realized the significance of the victory for Capital as a whole in an editorial that reads in part:

> We rejoice to see the long struggle is coming to an end. ... The directors have felt it right all along to take a firm stand. ... They felt that if they gave way in this matter it would lead to further strikes throughout the rubber trade, and of this agitation the natural result would be that prices would be increased. In consequence, there would be a loss to British trade, because other countries paying a lesser wage rate would be able to compete on unfair terms with the British manufacturer in the markets of the world.[795]

Class Justice

Silver's board of directors gloated that Fred Ling, "one of the foremost strikers at Silvertown," had appeared in the West Ham Police Court on 11 December, and had been convicted of "using language leading to a breach of the peace."[796] Once again, St. John Wontner prosecuted and the Radical barrister William Thompson appeared for the defense. According to Inspector Parsons and two other prosecution witnesses, Ling had declared in a speech delivered outside the factory gates on 2 December that a Colchester blackleg called Palmer, who had received "a jolly good hiding," had deserved what he got.[797] The *Essex Standard* reported that "Matthew Hamilton Gray, an engineer at Silvertown," had "deposed that the defendant was one of the men who went out on strike," which was surely stating the obvious and was itself scarcely a crime. The magistrate fined Ling £2, "the maximum penalty under the Act," and ordered him to pay 19/6d court costs, plus Wontner's £2 costs,[798] in total an amount worth something like £257 in today's values.[799] It was a harsh penalty for a destitute man. Ling was one of the 250 strike activists denied reemployment.[800] Though Ling might well have uttered the offending words, the policemen who testified against him had conspicuously sided with the company during the dispute and could scarcely be described as neutral or independent witnesses. It was class justice. The strike had been surprisingly peaceful until the police appeared in force on the Silvertown streets, as Magistrate Baggally had noted. Inspector Parsons, it should be recalled, had vastly exceeded whatever legal authority he had when he escorted blacklegs off a train after they had tried to return to Colchester. His fellow inspectors had also ordered a baton charge outside the factory, which had seriously injured a number of strikers and their families, along with at least one innocent bystander.

The Fates of the Victimized

The "payback" continued after Christmas, when George MacDonald, a striker domiciled at 2 Jubilee Terrace, Silvertown, was convicted of intimidation and assault against a man named Charles Dessent outside the factory on 11 December. Dessent had brought blacklegs from Colchester during the strike, and MacDonald was also alleged to have knocked one of them down. The magistrate bound him over to keep the peace for six months and fined him £10 with a £10 surety.[801] Whether he managed to find such a huge sum after a long strike, and with slim prospects of finding another job, is not recorded, so the chances are that he went to prison by default. We have no way of knowing the fates of those victimized after the Great Strike; they are shades on a forgotten canvas. Unless they managed to scrape together the fare for a passage aboard an emigrant ship to North America or Australasia, they would have paid a high price for their activism.

Many would have shared the fate of Dan Cullen, an East Ender who had played a leading role in the 1889 Dock Strike. An autodidact well read in sociology and history, with a passion for Shakespeare's works and an admiration for Engels and Michael Davitt, Cullen had dreamed of a better world. Since outright victimization would have drawn the wrath of the union upon the foremen's heads, Cullen was "disciplined" or "drilled" with dribs and drabs of work. "Ten years of it broke his heart," writes Jack London, "and broken-hearted men cannot live." He died alone with his cheap prints of Engels and Garibaldi on the walls of his dreary room.[802]

The lives of those victimized at Silvertown would not have been much different after their strike. Industry was falling into a terrible slump. They had little chance of employment and they were destitute save for the remnants of the strike fund. The wealthy old unions were indifferent to their fate and the new ones would soon be battling for survival.

Splendid Temper and Courage

On the workers' side of the class divide, there was bitterness, sorrow, and despair. No one could blame the Silvertown workers for going back to work. They had little choice, as the SDF's *Justice* put it, because "for nearly three months men, women and children literally starved, till human nature could hold out no longer, and they had to give in."[803] The *East London Advertiser* agreed, noting that during the strike "there were about 3,000 persons dependent upon the charity of the public" and that "many families were very near starvation, and this is undoubtedly the cause of its non-success."[804] There had been tremendous solidarity. Some of the single women had given their rations to fellow workers with children, but there was a limit to how much their debilitated bodies could stand. The Reverend Stopford Brooke attacked the firm for treating the workers like machines, and praised the

> splendid temper of the true gentlemen—a sacrifice of the private good for that of their fellows. They had made the cause of the women their own; they were remarkable for independence, honesty, and temperance, showing a striking contrast to the selfishness, the slavery to money as money, the want of justice and pity displayed by the employers.[805]

Silver's solicitors wrote to Brooke demanding an apology for alleged slanders and inaccuracies,[806] but he refused to comply, stating that he had every reason to trust the word of the "company's former workpeople, friends of mine." "You appear to think," he riposted, "that the managers of your company have no responsibility to outside opinion" despite their refusal of all offers of arbitration. He finished by advising Silver's that his solicitors would "attend to any communication you may send them."[807] He refused to retract his allegations and offered to submit all of them to independent arbitration. Should they prove false, he would publicly apologize.[808] He heard no more from the firm. Nor did the craft unions escape censure in the NUG&GL's strike postmortems. The Strike

Committee denounced the ASE's EC as "in a large measure the cause of the present failure."[809]

The Spirit of the Women

On the other hand, the Strike Committee did not forget the organizations that had given them support. These included the NUG&GL, the Coal Porters' Union, "and especially the East Finsbury Radical Club and the Salvation Army."[810] Toward the end of the strike, when circumstances were most dire, the "Sallies" had contributed £100, originally collected for the relief of dockworkers' families.[811] The *Labour Elector* also noted another important and indeed groundbreaking aspect of the strike:

> In closing this chapter of labour history, we are inevitably prompted to place on record the magnificent courage, patience, and perseverance of the women who were engaged in the struggle. There will probably be no brighter record than theirs . . . and Trade Unionism owes them its thanks. Had all the strikers and those who came out with them been imbued with the spirit of the women, the battle would probably have been won.[812]

Do as Australia Did for the Dockers

The NUG&GL believed that had all the London unions pulled together, the strikers could have ridden out the bitter cold and hunger. Had the unions "contributed fairly towards the Silvertown Strike Fund," argued a Gasworkers' official, "their women and girls would not have gone without food and clothes as they had done. It was their duty to respond as Australia had done for the dockers."[813] In that, the established unions signally failed. The reactionary attitude of many of the older union leaders is summed up in the remarks of Trades Union Congress secretary Henry Broadhurst during the 1889 upsurge. Regarding the New Union leaders, he warned that "their emissaries enter our camp in the guise of friends in order that they may better sow the seeds of disruption. Let the workers beware of them."[814]

Silver's operated in a competitive market, especially for telegraph and electrical cables. A mile or so downstream at North Woolwich was W. T. Henley's, a competitor who would have been eager to gobble up some of Silver's market share. Though Gray had been quick to transfer some production to Persan in France, the company's factory there was relatively small, employing only three hundred workers, and could not have coped with much larger production. Had the wealthy established unions thrown their support behind the strike, Silver's would have started to hurt. Those unions, however, had been indifferent. The *Labour Elector*, which, after an initial hostile article, had been surprisingly moderate regarding the ASE, noted:

> Among those directly responsible for the temporary defeat are the whole of the mechanics—not the engineers only—and especially from the fact that they did not bring the pressure of their voices to bear on the masters. No unionist has a right to come out on strike against the wishes of his executive. But they had a perfect right to make representations . . . [which] would have been effective.[815]

Even more culpable, the paper stated, were those appointed to the Strike Committee who "proved to be cowards and deserted them without a word. Among these the two who deserve the most censure are Messrs Atkins and Scrine. These two men . . . were among the first to go in. What wonder the strikers grew faint-hearted."[816] Scrine, it may be recalled, was the committee's first chairman and he must have played an active role in bringing the workers out on strike before he deserted them. It is even possible that he was an agent provocateur.[817] As we have seen, the *Labour Elector* speculated that Gray had intrigued to prolong the strike to advance his own pecuniary interests and, uncharacteristically, he did not pursue legal action.[818] One way of prolonging and sabotaging the strike would have been to plant his creatures in the Strike Committee. On the other hand, perhaps Atkins and Scrine were merely fair weather trade unionists, "all mouth and trousers" (in the vivid Cockney vernacular) during the heady days of Indian summer, but devoid of principle and courage when the going got tough.

A Grim Christmas . . .

Silvertown was a grim place even in the best of times, part of what Jack London later saw as the "huge man-killing machine" of the Abyss. Now, with the bitterness of defeat in their souls and with bodies starved of food and warmth, the winter of 1889–90 must have been one of terrible physical and emotional hardship for the workers. Christmas must have been especially cheerless in the bleak slum terraces crouched around the great factories smoking and stinking in the frigid winter air. On Christmas Day, the thermometer plummeted to freezing after a few mild days and frost sparkled on the ground. Coal cost around one shilling and sixpence per hundredweight. It was cheaper to buy it by the ton, but the working poor seldom had the cash to purchase the larger amount.[819] After the strike, they would not have been able to buy it at all.

And with the Christmas frost and chilblains came the public benefactors who ignored the East End poor for the other 364 days of the year. It had almost become traditional that such "great public shows of beneficence were fully reported in the local press," writes William Fishman.[820] Thus, in 1889, the poorest children of Silvertown were given a Christmas treat in the large hall at the Tate Institute opposite the sugar refinery. One thousand children— doubtless most of them barefoot and ill-clad despite the frost—were given bags containing "a huge piece of really good cake, with an apple and an orange." Assembled under a "giant" Christmas tree, the children were entertained by the Ye Chips Minstrel Troupe from Woolwich. One of those supervising the ceremony was a Mr. Gray[821]—the name is surely not coincidental.

Afterward, the gentlefolk would have traveled back to their residences for family Christmases that would have been the stuff of fairy tales to the Silvertown children. The daughters of these well-to-do personages would perhaps have perused the 1889 Christmas Supplement to the *Young Ladies' Journal*, with the latest "triple Paris fashion plates."[822] As for the women of the East End, they would "seldom get new clothes; boots they are often entirely without" as they had "no need to appear in the light of day." As a result, many appeared to be in the "dull middle of middle age" when in fact they were young.[823] Their prettiness, Jack London observed, was "no more than a promise with no grip on time and doomed to fade quickly like the colour from a sunset sky."[824] Part of the reason was chronic malnutrition. In contrast, Mrs. Beeton has left us with a typical Christmas menu for an affluent family such as Matthew Gray's:

A noble dish is a turkey, roast or boiled. A Christmas dinner with the middle classes of this empire, would scarcely be a Christmas dinner without its turkey; and we can hardly imagine an object of greater envy than is presented by a respected portly pater-familias carving, at the season devoted to good cheer and genial charity, his own fat turkey, and carving it well.[825]

The turkey would have been one of at least five courses and it would have been "a board to tempt even ghosts," as Lord Byron once wrote of an aristocratic family feast.[826] There were perhaps many ghosts in Silvertown, but they would have been tempted by a stale crust of bread, and even a small turkey was unaffordable for the Silvertown workers that Christmas. A large one cost about twenty-five shillings in pre–Great War London.[827] Were there babies across the Thames in leafy Abbey Wood, their families might have simpered over Emily Huntington Miller's Victorian ditty:

Hang up the baby's stocking
Be sure you don't forget!
The dear little dimpled darling,
She never saw Christmas yet.[828]

In contrast, almost one in five babies born in Silvertown would never see their first Christmas. Many of the remaining infants would never see more than four of them. The others would grow up stunted by malnutrition. As Mrs. Pember Reeves wrote of the children of the London poor, "The outstanding fact about the children was not their stupidity nor their lack of beauty—they were neither stupid not ugly—it was their puny size and damaged health."[829] With poor food and unhealthy housing, it could not be otherwise. The Abyss took healthy young life and by the second and third generations had crippled it even before birth.

. . . And a Miserable New Year

New Year's Eve must have been equally melancholy for the vanquished strikers, and they can have had little to look forward to in the coming year. The thermometer fell to below 24 degrees F (around minus 5 Celsius) overnight, and a dense, freezing fog blanketed the city. Although New Year's Day had been observed as a Bank Holiday since 1871 in Britain, it seems unlikely that Silver's would have given their employees the day off with pay. The workers would have made their way to the factory gates in the bone-chilling predawn cold, feeling their way with their hands along the walls, blinded by the fog, toward the blazing lights of Samuel Silver's great cathedral of industry. There would be no respite from lives of toil and poverty.

Self-Sacrifice, Courage, and Perseverance

Armchair generals will be quick to insist that Silver's workers went on strike prematurely without adequate preparation. Life, however, is usually messier than such theorists would have us believe. Silver's was a sweat-shop, and the tyrannical and arbitrary methods of management meant that the factory was waiting for a spark to ignite an industrial conflagra-tion. The victory of the dock strikers provided the spark. Although it is indubitably true that strikes need careful preparation and, preferably, the building up of a war chest, Silver's laborers had not had a union, or been allowed to join a union. Indeed, the NUG&GL was only months old when the strike began, and it lacked the resources of the older unions. The Sil-vertown workers had to build their own organization as they went. In the end, they were unsuccessful, but it was not for lack of courage on their part, and had all the existing unions rallied behind them, they could have won. This fact was noted by some columnists in the mainstream press at the time, one of whom lamented, "I can't help feeling a melancholy interest in the Silvertown strike—now at an end" and which "has been somewhat neglected by the labour leaders."[830]

The middle classes, too, had rallied to some degree to support the dockers, but they had largely turned against upstart workers accused of intimidating "free laborers." Over the next decade, the middle classes would become hysterical in their opposition to the New Unions, John Saville noted.[831] This was evident in the way "public opinion" responded to the strike that broke out at the South Metropolitan Gasworks almost immediately after the collapse of the Silvertown strike. In the *Penny Illus-trated Paper*, a columnist wrote:

> It is sincerely hoped that the threatened gas strike will not come off. Very keen must be the sympathy with all struggles for higher wages on the part of the men concerned with the manufacture of gas. The life really is an awful one. The immense furnaces are calculated to suggest to the casual visitor no possible comparison but that of life in the infernal regions. The men are stripped to waist, and perspire profusely. But the public takes little heed of all this, and their sympa-thies will not be with the men. Moreover, the practical failure of the Silvertown strike is a serious warning. Very sordid and hard is the life of the people of Silvertown. . . . Their attempts to get better wages have ended in failure.[832]

Though there was little love lost among London merchants for the monopolistic dock companies, Silver's was a different case. It was a go-ahead, innovative firm at the very forefront of the Electrical Revolution, an exemplar of modernity. It also seems to have been chosen, or to have chosen for itself, the task of damming the tide of wage demands unleashed by the dock, Beckton, and Bryant & May strikers. For this it received the fulsome praise of the ruling class. Faced with the choice of supporting either the big capitalists or the workers, the middle classes plumped for the former, particularly when strike action threatened their creature comforts. Horrible though the working conditions might be at Silver's or the South London gasworks, the middle classes could ignore, downplay, or even deny them when it was in the interests of "public opinion" to do so. As Eric Hobsbawm has shown, there are plenty of "revisionist" historians today willing to deny the undeniable horrors of working-class life in the Victorian Age,[833] and in this they continue along a well-worn path.

The firm, too, had connections through board member Henry Marsham with the levers of political power at the highest levels in the land. This doubtless had helped Silver's to persuade the police to take strong action against the strikers. To the ruling class, Matthew Gray was "firm" in his resistance to the workers. His opponents would have preferred the adjective "ruthless." The socialist weekly *Commonweal* denounced him as a "Napoleon of Capitalism" who would brook no arbitration.[834] Not to be outdone, Hyndman's rival newspaper *Justice* declared after the strike that "Gray and Tyler [the company secretary] would have disgraced a Turkish pasha and we are afraid that the lot of the strikers will now be ten times worse than it was before."[835] We must leave the task of reconstituting the post-strike atmosphere in Silver's factory, with its overbearing managers, vindictive supervisors, and tyrannical rules, to the reader's imagination. The triumphalist rhetoric of the shareholders' meetings, however, does, supply some broad hints about what the defeated strikers had to endure.

Another factor in the workers' defeat was the relative remoteness of Silvertown, which, although only a few miles down the Thames from the City of London, was strangely isolated in the middle of the long artificial peninsula between the Victoria and Albert docks and the River Thames. To Jack London's affluent friends, everything that lay just east of the city was a mystery. Silvertown was even more mysterious, cut off as it was by a thick belt of slum streets, factories, marshland, and docks, a region that few West Enders ever entered.

Though the fledgling NUG&GL had no official representation at Silver's before the strike, it is possible there was a nucleus of members in the factory. Fred Ling is recorded shortly after strike action began as being the secretary of the Silvertown branch of the union, and he clearly had some knowledge of the methods of the New Unionism. Whatever the case, when anger boiled up across the factory, militants such as Ling were there to encourage and channel it. We also know that Walter Drummond of the Stevedores' Union was familiar with the faces of a number of Silvertown workers from the dockworkers' rallies that they had attended out of solidarity. Ling was to prove a lifelong labor activist, and he was in his element. His message was simple: Gray had gone back on his word; the factory hands worked long hours for paltry wages, often in tiring, unpleasant and even unhealthy conditions. They should resist the man they soon characterized as a tyrant. The word "strike" had flamed around the echoing shops of the great factory and its siren call was irresistible to the overworked and underpaid men and women of Silvertown. Even before the end of the strike, Frederick Engels had written to Jules Guesde:

> For the past four months the workers of London's East End have not only given themselves to the movement body and soul; they have also provided, for their comrades in all countries, an example of discipline, self-sacrifice, courage and perseverance equalled only by the Parisians when under siege from the Prussians.[836]

The men and women at the rubber and telegraph works had played a tremendous role in that historical drama. For twelve long weeks, 3,000 previously unorganized Silvertown workers and their families picketed, marched, sang, laughed, and suffered terribly through a protracted dispute. "For nearly three months," concluded the SDF's *Justice*, "men, women and children literally starved, until human nature could hold out no longer, and . . . they had to give in."[837] The boldest strikers were victimized and left jobless in the depths of a bitter winter. To date, their story has been little known. In his autobiography, Will Thorne merely tells us that "the strike fizzled out,"[838] but with all due respect to a grand old man of labor, the Silvertown struggle deserves a better epitaph than that. Had the Silvertown strikers received the same kind of financial support as the dockers enjoyed—£30,000 from Australia alone[839]—the chances are that they would have forced Matthew Gray to the negotiating table and won most of their modest demands. There can be little doubt either that the employer's victory at Silvertown stiffened the resolve of the capitalist class as a whole to face down the New Unions. Using the methods tested at Silvertown, the employers were to launch a decade-long offensive against the unions that fully merits the description of class war waged under the banner of "freedom of contract." Much of what came later was a refinement of the "Silvertown Formula." Employers would not negotiate with their workers or recognize their unions. They would repudiate all offers of outside arbitration. They would replace the ad hoc recruitment of scabs with the mass enrolment of blacklegs in country districts. They would billet the scabs inside the factory or other worksite and would mobilize large numbers of police—and later soldiers and gunboats—to protect them. The idea of the sit-down strike or factory occupation as a countermeasure does not seem to have occurred to the Silvertown strikers. This is not surprising, given that they were raw recruits to trade unionism and their union itself was in its infancy.

The employers would also make full use of the courts to prosecute and punish strikers and to criminalize picketing. Finally, they would make use of the already willing press to depict the strikers as thugs depriving "free laborers" of their right to work. It was a recipe for class war, and Silvertown was the first New Union defeat.

XII.
Epilogue
—◆◆—

> The "New Unionism" . . . changed the whole face of the
> British Trade Union Movement that had mainly con-
> sisted of reformist, liberal-minded craftsmen and skilled
> unionists. . . . It rejuvenated the industrial trade union
> movement. It established on a firm footing the political
> Labour Movement. . . . It was this spirit of the "New
> Unionism" that made international working-class soli-
> darity a reality, and, strange to say, the historians hardly
> notice the revolution we created . . . Still, we did not
> fight for history, praise, or to secure kudos. It was the
> lives of our people and their bread and butter we were
> thinking of. We were struggling to lift ourselves out of
> the slime of poverty into the fresh air of freedom.[840]
> —WILL THORNE

EIGHT YEARS AFTER the defeat of the Silvertown laborers' strike, the
factory was again hit by industrial action. Surprisingly, given the dubious
role of the firm's skilled artisans in the 1889 strike, the second wave of
strikers were members of the fitters' union, the Amalgamated Society of
Engineers. The strike, which was part of a national confrontation between
the Employers' Federation of Engineering Associations and the ASE and
other metal unions, was to last six months. By this time, the spirit of the
New Unionism had spread widely, even into the hitherto conservative
craft unions. The engineers' strike was part of the savage class war that
had engulfed Britain since the Silvertown workers' defeat of 1889 and
the onset of deep economic slump. The appeal of the new radical general

labor unions was highlighted by the phenomenal success of the first
London May Day rally, held on Sunday, 1 May 1890, in Hyde Park. The
rally, which was called on the initiative of Eleanor Marx's Bloomsbury
Socialist Society and Will Thorne's NUG&GL, drew more than 500,000
people to demand the introduction of a legislated Eight-Hour Day.[841] It
is highly likely that Fred Ling and other Silvertown workers were in
the crowd. In contrast, a mere sprinkling of people attended a rival rally
called by George Shipton to support a vague call for "shortening" the
workday without any idea of how to achieve it, save perhaps to appeal to
the employers' "better nature."[842] In the same year, the Eight-Hour Day
was adopted as official policy by the TUC by 193 votes to 155 over the
strenuous opposition of its reactionary secretary, Henry Broadhurst, who
resigned shortly afterward.[843] Shipton was to lose the position of LTC
secretary to the socialist James MacDonald in 1896, and by the end of
the decade control of the ASE fell into the hands of a militant tendency
inspired by the New Unionism. By the turn of the century, despite bruising battles with the employers and their allies in the courts, police forces,
and on the parliamentary benches, the unions were growing steadily and
had launched the Labour Party as an independent working-class political force. Silvertown, despite the 1889 defeat, was to become a bastion of
industrial and political labor.

The 1890s, however, were not a time of plain sailing for the labor
movement. Some branches of the New Unions perished, the victims of
mounting unemployment and the employers' counteroffensive. All grap-
pled with great financial strain. In his report of November 1889, the
NUG&GL's national treasurer, William Byford, noted that the heavy
expenditure on strike relief was "almost unprecedented in the annals of
trade unionism" in Britain.[844] Politically, West Ham, of which Silvertown
was an important part, was in the forefront of the movement for independent working-class political representation. Paradoxically, the Silvertown
branch of the NUG&GL had almost perished by the end of the decade.
Everything the workers' movement was to achieve came only after a protracted period of class war.

In the aftermath of the Silvertown strike, the British economy plunged
into the depths of a terrible depression. Unemployment and underemploy-
ment, ever-present evils in Victorian London even in the best of times,
grew to alarming proportions. This gave the employers the whip hand.
By the early years of the twentieth century, the Silvertown NUG&GL
branch, like many others, was fighting for survival. The Silvertown wom-
en's branch had collapsed, and even the London Dockers' Union struggled

to survive, in part, Frederick Engels considered, because of the "stupidity" of its leaders.[845] In late 1889, the South London gasworks was the scene of a crushing defeat for the NUG&GL. By the end of the decade, the employers had brought a series of court actions that virtually outlawed picketing and seemed, on the face of it, to leave the unions defenseless against the use of "free labor" to break strikes. Silver's remained one of the most irascible of employers, despite the fact that it was cushioned from the worst effects of the depression by virtue of its position on the cutting edge of the new electrical technology. The six-month strike of ASE members at Silver's in 1897 ended in defeat, as did the nationwide metal unions' struggle of which it was a part.

Dog Days in Silvertown

The 1889 strike had seriously weakened the NUG&GL in Silvertown, but Fred Ling and his comrades were determined fighters. The union even won some small battles in the strike's aftermath, such as when it fought off an attempt by the chemical manure works to reduce wages by 10 percent. The women's branch continued under the leadership of Eleanor Marx, who also sat on the NUG&GL's General Executive. In 1891, a Silvertown soapworks branch was founded, with a local man, H. Pryke, as secretary.[846] But any gains were small and the union had to fight for its very survival. The soapworks branch seems to have merged with Ling's branch soon afterward, or else it disappeared. In 1893, the depression had bitten hard across the country. A number of NUG&GL branches collapsed and the union struggled to maintain a foothold in Silvertown. Ling's Silvertown branch yearly remittances to the central union amounted to £42/5/10½d and the women's branch to £4/12/9d in total.[847] As the union's first national conference had set individual dues at tuppence per week,[848] or slightly more than 8/6d per year per member, the main Silvertown branch at that time must have had only slightly more than one hundred members and the women's branch around a dozen. Even with high rates of unemployment, there were still many thousands of workers in the suburb's factories, so it was a very low rate of unionization. The following year, 1894, was a real trial for the union. The Silvertown women's branch disappeared, but a women's branch emerged in nearby Canning Town and sent £19/4/2½d to the central office (indicating a membership slightly below fifty), so it is possible that this branch came about as an amalgamation with the Silvertown women's organization.[849] Will Thorne admitted at the 1895 National Conference that it had been another "very trying" year for the union movement. The Silvertown branch's remittances were down to £22/9/4d,[850] indicating a membership of between fifty and sixty. In 1898, remittances fell still further,[851] but remittances of slightly less than £10 for the final quarter of 1900 suggest that membership increased to around 160. Thereafter, the branch fell on evil times. Only 15 shillings were collected in the final quarter of 1905 and 8 shillings in the second quarter of 1906, suggesting a membership of around half a dozen.[852] Shortly afterward, Fred Ling's name ceased to appear in the quarterly reports. Whether he died, retired, or moved elsewhere was not recorded. Perhaps he was tired and ill and lacked the energy he had displayed in previous years. Surviving union documents give no clues about the fate of an activist who had given so much to the movement through the dark years of depression and repression.

The Engineers' Strike of 1897

There is no record of the laborers at Silver's engaging in any industrial action of any consequence after the failure of the 1889 strike. The number of NUG&GL members in the plant had dwindled and the management would have been quick to sack "troublemakers" at a time when laborers could be replaced many times over by the hungry men and women standing at the factory gates desperate for employment. In the latter half of 1897, however, a bitter dispute broke out in an unexpected quarter: the engineers'. It is impossible to say what the attitude of Silver's laborers was to the tradesmen's strike. No reference to the ASE strike at Silver's appears in the surviving NUG&GL files, nor do the ASE files provide any clues. Arthur Field mentions in passing that Eleanor Marx was involved in the strike but does not say whether this was on behalf of the NUG&GL. In any case, several hundred of the most active NUG&GL members inside the plant had been victimized after the 1889 strike and the Silvertown branch was in the doldrums.

Silver's had tolerated the ASE and the other craft unions so long as they proved themselves "moderate" and respectful. The ASE, however, had changed in the near decade since the laborers' strike. Militant leaders had replaced the conservative old guard, and at the same time, skilled engineers across the country were facing grave threats to their job security and wages that gave them little option but to fight. The ASE strike at Silver's was part of a nationwide confrontation between the engineering unions and the Employers' Federation of Engineering Associations, which had been formed in 1896 with the declared aim "to protect and defend the interests of employers against combinations of workmen."[853] Many thousands of tradesmen were locked out across the country by employers ably led by Colonel H. Dyer, a pugnacious ideologue who doubled as the chairman of the Armstrong heavy engineering works at Elswick on Tyneside in northern England.[854] The "granite face" presented by the federation in 1897–98 to the unions is a clear illustration of Daniel Guérin's thesis that heavy industry was forced into confrontation with labor because of the narrow limits within which production is profitable. At a time when competition dictated the massive injection of yet more fixed capital, the imperative to claw back wages and emasculate the unions was pressing. The federation was determined to assert the employers' control over work processes, which to some degree had been the prerogative of the craftsmen. Since the late 1880s, the employers had been trying to replace older technology with new American-style labor-saving, semiautomatic machine tools such as capstan lathes and milling, slotting, planing, and shaping machines. These greatly speeded up, cheapened, and simplified the work, as much of it could be carried out by semiskilled operatives after the machines were set up for production runs by skilled toolsetters. As a result, a huge number of tradesmen faced redundancy or downgrading. This was particularly the case with turners, slotters, screwers, borers, and other tradesmen who had utilized traditional, labor-intensive metalworking methods to repair machine parts and produce commodities for sale. Sounding the tocsin for an inevitable confrontation, the *Amalgamated Engineers' Monthly Journal* warned that "modern machinery has revolutionised our trade" and "the methods of ten years ago are obsolete today."[855] The changes hit at the privileges of the labor aristocrats of the metal trades. At Silver's and some other factories they went on strike. A much greater number were locked out across the country.

Obsolete Rules

One of the central aims of the ASE and other craft unions had been to keep their labor scarce and dear, in part by allowing only their members to carry out relevant types of skilled work. The ASE's rules barred membership to those who had acquired tradesmen-level skills by other than the traditional route of an apprenticeship. By the end of the 1880s, this had rebounded on the union, much as Marxist critics such as Engels and Tom

Mann had predicted. At the beginning of the 1890s depression, there were at least three times as many skilled engineering tradesmen outside of the ASE as in it. The new metalworking machines added a fresh threat, with semi-skilled operatives able to perform simplified tasks as efficiently as tradesmen, with increased output, with much less training, and for a fraction of a traditional craftsman's wage. The machines were a necessary element of the American-style mass production methods that Dyer was determined to introduce into Britain. His opponents were equally determined that those who carried out the work should be paid the old ASE rates: a lathe operator, for example, should be paid the same rate as a union turner. Conflict arose because, as the union put it, they wished to "level up" wages, whereas the employers wanted to level them down.[856] The union also wished to have some say over when and where the new machine tools were introduced so as to shield their members from the alarming effects of their wholesale introduction. In such a climate, the union also resolved to restart the campaign for the eight-hour day without loss of pay in order to share around the available work.

"Freedom to Manage"

The advantages of the new technology for the employers were clear; wages bills would be cut, output increased, and the rate of profit bolstered as a result. Colonel Dyer insisted that the employers were "determined to obtain the freedom to manage their own affairs which has proved to be so beneficial to the American manufacturers as to enable them to compete."[857] Dyer's model was American industry, which was far in advance of Britain's in regard to mass production and—as a direct consequence, de-skilling of the engineering workforce.[858] His words were an ominous threat for the engineers, and hinted at still greater exploitation of semi-skilled labor. As Karl Marx earlier observed, "The more the division of labour and the application of machinery extend, the more does competition extend among the workers, and their wages shrink together."[859] The new technology and further division of labor was forced upon the individual capitalist by the dictates of the capitalist system as a whole. As Marx explains it:

> The capitalist continually seeks to get the best of competition by restlessly introducing further subdivision of labour and new machines, which, though more expensive, enable him to produce more cheaply,

instead of waiting until the new machines shall have been rendered obsolete by competition.[860]

As a result, the niche skills of the engineering tradesmen, which gave them considerable control over industrial processes, would be undermined. De-skilling had arrived among the "super-aristocrats" of the engineering trades, many decades after the start of the Industrial Revolution when other traditional trades such as sewing pin-makers had disappeared under a wave of technological change and new divisions of labor.

The time had come when the exclusion of unskilled and semiskilled engineering workers from the union made no sense at all. Engineers were also facing a massive erosion of their status. As Eric Hobsbawm has noted, there was a growing gap between "shop and top," separated by a layer of white-collar employees from which the managerial levels could recruit.[861] The world had changed; fitters and millwrights could no longer pretend that they were anything other than proletarians, or that their industrial interests did not dovetail with those of organized labor as a whole. The stage was set for a massive confrontation, and Silver's, as one of Britain's most aggressive employers of engineers, was to be in the front line of the struggle. Silver's had maintained its market share in part by virtue of its place at the forefront of technological change. Competition for the expanding market for telegraphic and electrical goods demanded the introduction of mass production techniques, and the firm was determined to introduce these in its plants. Not to do so meant it would perish.

Changing of the Guard in the ASE

The previous decade had seen a power struggle inside the ASE in which the old guard, led by Robert Austin, had lost ground to a more militant tendency strongly influenced by the New Unionism. In 1892, Tom Mann came close to winning the election for General Secretary and in 1896 George Barnes won it outright.[862] Mann had been a key ally of the NUG&GL strikers at Silvertown in 1889, and Barnes had been sympathetic. Barnes and Mann were keenly aware that the union had to get rid of its restrictive membership practices, and to operate as part of the broader working-class movement if it was to survive; unity was a pressing practical imperative, not a luxury or an idealistic dream. Unity of engineering workers in particular was pressing. The ASE, Mann argued, was weakened because it did not "belong to any real federation of unions of all trades connected with a particular profession," and it suffered from "sectional isolation which frequently lands it in a position of active hostility with the other unions in the engineering trades." In particular, it was bedeviled with demarcation disputes.[863] Though the ASE's membership was to grow by 20,000 in the next few years,[864] Mann estimated that there were still some 100,000 tradesmen outside of the union. It was "a positive disgrace," he claimed, that in some large factories in London the union had no more than 5 percent membership.[865] Some of the weakest branches were in London's East End, which has a bearing on the outcome of the engineers' strike at Silver's.

"War Is Declared"

Nevertheless, with a membership of 90,000 in 1897, the ASE was a formidable organization. In alliance with other engineering unions, it was even more powerful. With annual membership receipts of £750,000, it was able to amass a huge war chest for the looming industrial dispute. In the June edition of the *Monthly Journal*, Tom Mann announced that "war is declared between the Employers' Federation ... and the ASE over the question of wage rates on machines." He forecast that the employers' aim would be to deplete the union of its funds, but added, optimistically, that he doubted they would be able to sustain a completely united front in the event of a mass lockout given the diverse nature of the trade. "The employers," he added, "have sought the quarrel, let them have it; everything favours the men, the state of trade, the prospect for next year; the union's finances, and the opinions of the members. Therefore, my voice and action goes in favour of the standard wage-rate for machine-workers, and the 48-hour working week."[866]

The union had recently balloted its London area members on the question of the eight-hour day and found a large majority in favor of a campaign to achieve it.[867] In sum, the union's list of demands boiled down, in addition to a 48-hour week of six eight-hour days, to the following: collective bargaining across the industry; a ceiling of eighteen hours overtime in any four-week period except in unavoidable cases of ship breakdown, sea trial trips, and repairs to vessels; and piecework rates to be fixed by mutual agreement, but at no less than day work rates. Further, though the union agreed to recognize the employers' right to decide what new appliances would be used, it demanded that "the recognised class of operatives working machinery to be paid the standard rate of wages."[868]

The union pressed its claims and also built a united front with the other engineering unions. By mid-1897, a good number of London engineering firms had granted the 48-hour week without loss of pay, ninety-five by July, including the London and West India Dock Company.[869] It might have seemed that the unions would win their demands after a short struggle, but Colonel Dyer was determined to compel the companies that had granted shorter hours to renege on their agreements and to block any further capitulation. Silver's, along with the other hardline firms in the Employers' Federation, was determined to keep the 56-hour week, which was standard for engineering artisans.

Silver's position on shorter hours was summed up in the *India Rubber Journal*, which considered that a 48-hour week meant "a rise in wages all-round, without any surplus profits to warrant this great change," adding that "56 hours per week is the lowest engineers ought to work, and many in the rubber trade to our knowledge have worked 65 and 70 hours per week, and were glad to do it."[870] As far as Silver's went, this was patent nonsense. The firm had ridden out the slump with its profits virtually intact, and had expanded its Silvertown workforce to around 4,000 by the time of the dispute. In 1897, the firm made a record profit of £72,810.[871] Its net profit for 1897, despite the ASE strike, amounted to not less than £41,044/14/9d and it was able to pay shareholders the usual 10 percent dividend, and still carry forward £13,173/1/1d.[872]

In mid-June, an employers' council of war met in Carlisle and flatly rejected the demand for shorter hours.[873] A month later, the *Belfast News-letter* forecast that a "universal lock-out was imminent"[874] and by August, many firms had locked out their engineering workers. As late as the following month some 218 London firms were working shorter hours,[875] but this was the high tide of the unions' advance. Afterward, the advantage slipped inexorably to the employers. The Executive Council of the Engineering Employers' Federation met again at Leeds on 5 October and resolved to reject any suggestion of arbitration.[876] By this stage, the Silvertown engineers had been on strike for over three months and thousands of other workers were locked out across London.

Although the strike was largely ignored in the minutes of Silver's board and general meetings, the firm was one of the most intransigent in the land. Early on in the strike, Matthew Gray arranged for the bulk of cable production to be switched to the Persan factory in France,[877] a measure he had previously used in the 1889 strike. It seems likely that there were stand-downs of non-trade employees at Silvertown as a result, although there is no mention of this in extant NUG&GL files. The firm was perhaps also aware that though the ASE was a formidable force nationally, it was weak in the East End. According to the *Monthly Journal*, the union began the year with only 275 full members in the local Victoria Dock branch, which covered Silver's, and less than 1,500 in the East End as a whole.[878] Silver's likely continued to employ a large number of non-union engineers despite the ASE's recent rule changes and, when the strike broke out, the firm was quick to call in the services of well-organized strikebreakers. The organization Silver's turned to was National Free Labour Association (NFLA). The watchword was "freedom of labor."

Streamlined Scabbing Operation

According to the London *Times*, the New Unions were exerting a "tyranny" over workers who wished to make their own individual contractual arrangements with their employers. Such views were part of respectable "public opinion" and endorsed by many eminent people. Herbert Spencer, for example, the most influential philosopher of the Victorian Age, railed against union coercion and defended "freedom of contract" in his 1891 introduction to a collection of essays titled *A Plea for Liberty*.[879] His individualistic ideology was shared, broadly, by conservative union leaders such as George Shipton and Henry Broadhurst to whom the idea of the closed shop was anathema. John Saville considers that the middle and upper classes regarded the activities of the New Unions with a "horror" that is "difficult to appreciate fully."[880] For well-heeled Victorian citizens, "freedom of contract" was a cornerstone of laissez-faire doctrine, and the phrase became a battle cry that found concrete organizational expression in the Silvertown Formula. Those who mouth the slogan might well believe that they are championing the broader cause of liberty. For the working class, however, laissez-faire—the anarchy of the market—depends on what Marx called "despotism in the workshop," which they can only resist by collective action.

Organized Recruitment of Blacklegs

A key element of the Silvertown formula had been the large-scale recruitment of scabs, who were escorted across picket lines under heavy police protection and billeted inside the factory, a kind of reversal of the sit-down strike.[881] These measures were taken up and refined by employers in subsequent disputes throughout the following decade. Moreover, they did not shrink from using strong-arm methods against strikers, using either official or unofficial bodies of armed men. Underworld "firms" such as the Kelly-Peters Gang and the Deptford "Eye-Ball Buster Gang"[882] were employed as bruisers in the battle to smash the unions, and operated with the covert knowledge and encouragement of the rich and the powerful, up to and including the prime minister, Robert Cecil.[883] In 1889, Silver's had put together on short notice an impromptu scab recruitment agency at Colchester under the direction of Chris Gray and the local solicitor Major Howard, whose efforts had contributed to the union's defeat. In 1897, Silver's utilized a ready-made national blackleg recruitment agency, the National Free Labour Association (NFLA), which had been created by a cabal of the most fanatical union haters and laissez-faire ideologues in the land.

The Scabs at Silvertown

Although it is probable, as Gareth Stedman Jones claims, that blackleg labor was "statistically . . . insignificant"[884] on a national scale, the NFLA was able to mobilize considerable numbers of non-unionists during the ASE strike at Silver's. As Jones understood, large-scale scabbing or the threat of it was also a potent tool with which to demoralize strikers.[885] Significantly, the scabs used at Silver's were, or claimed to be, skilled workers, which must have had a considerable psychological effect on the strikers: unskilled country yokels and urban lumpenproletarians were one thing, but a horde of scab tradesmen was the stuff of nightmares for craft unionists. On 13 July, according to the *Times,* a large contingent of scabs, comprising around two hundred fitters, turners, smiths, and so on, "were sent from Fenchurch Street Station by the 10.35 a.m. train, in special first-class carriages, to the india-rubber and gutta-percha telegraph works at Silvertown."[886] They had been dispatched from the NFLA offices nearby, and the fact that they were given free first-class railway tickets to dodge roving pickets indicates that they were managed by an organization with considerable funds at its disposal. The ASE had mobilized its own forces on the same day, when a 5,000-strong crowd of engineering workers demonstrated outside the NFLA's headquarters. The scabs, however, were whisked away safely by police and the NFLA's own strong-arm squads. Although pickets persuaded a number of the blacklegs not to enter the plant, and others left the works at dinner time and did not return, the

NFLA immediately sent thirty replacements. Silver's management—
again as during the 1889 strike—billeted the blacklegs inside the plant,
providing them with beds and meals, and paid them the full pre-strike
union rate. Things took a very curious turn when an NFLA squad turned
up to picket the pickets outside the factory gates.[887]

"Dogmatic Pressure Group"

As informed ASE members were aware, the NFLA was the creature of
a club of hardline employers, landowners, right-wing politicians, and
sundry intellectuals known as the Liberty and Property Defence League.
Sometimes known as "Wemyss and Company" after its leading light, the
league was inspired by the individualistic doctrines of the Social Darwinist Herbert Spencer. It was, as one historian puts it, "a thoroughly
dogmatic pressure group for extreme laissez-faire."[888] Set up in 1882 as
the State Resistance League,[889] its ideological descendants were to be
writers such as Ayn Rand, Milton Friedman, and Friedrich von Hayek,
and today's well-funded neoliberal and neoconservative lobby groups
and think-tanks. The league's driving force was Francis Charteris, a.k.a
the 10th Earl of Wemyss, a Scottish aristocrat, landowner, industrial-
ist, and MP. He remained an indefatigable opponent of trade unions and
socialism throughout his long life.[890] Other prominent members of the
league included George Livesey, who had inflicted a stinging defeat on
NUG&GL stokers at the South London gasworks in late 1889; the ultra-
right-wing Italian economist and sociologist Vilfredo Pareto; the officers
of the Master Builders' Association; the engineering federation's arch-
"Americanizer," Colonel Dyer; G. A. Laws of the Shipping Federation, a
ruthless opponent of the maritime unions; Alexander Siemens of the well-
known engineering firm; and the union-hating Sir William Lewis, the
first Baron Merthyr, a South Wales pit-owner and founder of a colliery-
owners' federation. It would be interesting to know if Matthew Gray and
his fellow board members were members of the league, but even if they
weren't, they shared its aims and ideology.

The ASE's assessment of the NFLA's creation by this vested interest
group was accurate, although the NFLA's office holders were at pains
to appear independent.[891] The association was perhaps the most highly
organized scabbing operation in British labor history, and it scored some
notable successes in its thirty-five years of existence. In some ways it was
the equivalent of union-busting and spying outfits such as Pinkerton in

America, but it also mimicked the organization of the bona fide trade unions. Eric Hobsbawm estimates that it had 2,500 members nationally and that it was active in organizing blacklegs against the rail strike that led to the Taff Vale judgment.[892] The NFLA itself boasted of a membership of 200,000 in June 1898,[893] although this appears to be a gross exaggeration. The association held regular congresses, but these were stage-managed affairs with bogus "delegates" who included "Jimmy Wall's eyeball busters" and other unsavory elements.[894]

Free-Labour Bill & Co.

The public face of the NFLA was the Stepney-born policeman's son William Collison. Thirty-two years old in 1897, Collison liked to be known as "Free Labour Bill," although his critics had earthier sobriquets for him. Geoffrey Alderman describes him as "an accomplished self-publicist," and although he stressed his East End origins, he cut a flamboyant figure and mixed with powerful people.[895] According to his own account, he was instrumental in setting up an omnibus workers' union, which he placed under the patronage of Archibald Primrose (a.k.a. Lord Rosebery), a strong imperialist and anti-socialist. Soon afterward, the members rejected the "primrose path" and Collison was replaced by people he branded as "political adventurers and Socialistic notoriety hunters."[896] This seems to have been the root cause of his virulent antagonism against independent workers' associations and socialism, and it was reinforced when he was prevented from finding work on the docks for lack of a union card.[897]

According to Collison, the organization was set up in 1893 to "emancipate labour from the industrial despotism of the unions," which had carried out a "reign of terror"[898] against those who were "entitled to work for any wages [they] might think fit."[899] During the engineers' strike of 1897, this account continued, the NFLA's Fenchurch Street offices were "besieged" by men seeking work. Between July and August, 8,645 men were put on the NFLA's books and a "corps of 200 pensioned police" was formed to escort blacklegs to and from work.[900] Although some gullible people might have believed themselves to be part of an independent organization, the NFLA was a creature set up and funded by the major employer groups and Wemyss's Liberty and Property Defence League. Collison set up "Free Labour Exchanges"—probably modeled on similar bodies set up earlier by the Shipping Federation and often headed up by retired police inspectors. To register, workers had to sign a pledge to work with both unionists and non-unionists, in effect a promise to scab.[901] Membership dues amounted to 2/6d per year,[902] or less than a penny per week, but signing on with the association did not cost anything. These "dues," however, could scarcely cover the expensive overheads of running an organization that had been conjured up from nothing yet could afford to transport scabs by train in first-class, protected by a paid private police force. Collison himself received an annual salary of £300 in 1902,[903] rather more than quadruple the average earnings of a general laborer.[904] It is clear, writes Geoffrey Alderman, that "powerful people pulled the string which alone gave . . . [the association] life and vitality."[905] When the economy revived, and unemployment fell, union membership grew rapidly, the employers embraced collective bargaining, and the NFLA died.

"The Prince of Scabs and Blacklegs"

The NFLA's membership included numbers of strong-arm men, and Collison, himself, was not averse to using strong-arm methods personally. It appears that the regular police would turn a blind eye to it. In early August 1897, he was summoned to appear before Alderman Sir John Whittaker Ellis at Mansion House to answer charges of threatening bodily injury on an ASE member called William John Harris, a fitter who worked at Silver's. Harris, along with another picket, had been sent to Fenchurch Street to make sure that ASE men were not tricked by the NFLA into scabbing. Furious, Collison emerged from the Grapes public house in nearby Lime Street and was alleged to have said, "If you fellows don't clear out of this I will punch you on the nose and have you locked up into the bargain."[906] The pickets refused to move, and according to Collison's lawyer they jeered at him as "the prince of scabs and blacklegs." According to the ASE men, Collison further threatened Harris, declaring: "And you, you black ----, I will knock every ---- tooth out you have got." No doubt he was feeling cocky, for he had earlier escaped conviction on a charge of assaulting another picket.[907]

The prosecutor in the case, the veteran pro-union Radical William Marcus Thompson, used the opportunity to ask where the NFLA funds came from. Mr. Geoghegan, for the defense, objected. Thompson insisted that it was relevant, as the NFLA was a bogus organization, financed by the employers. Thompson had hit a raw nerve, for as Alderman observed, Collison was "always notably silent about one point: who were the financial backers who enabled him to keep the movement going?"[908] One backer, the Earl of Wemyss, was not coy about his involvement, telling two French researchers in 1902 that the NFLA was "an artificial association which receives all its funds from us [the Employers' Parliamentary Council], but we have tried to give it a life of its own so as to make an impression on the public mind."[909] Not surprisingly, Ellis ruled that the question had nothing to do with the case and dismissed the charges. The ASE men and Thompson had scant chance of securing a favorable ruling. Ellis, a former Lord Mayor of the City of London, was a Tory plutocrat whose reactionary politics had also led him to publish an anti-nationalist pamphlet on the Irish land question.[910] He was able to double as a magistrate because of his position as an alderman in a "rotten borough" that entrenched the interests of City businessmen and financiers and was not subject to democratic election or oversight.[911] Collison's acquittal was in sharp contrast to the convictions and stiff sentences meted out to union pickets by the police and courts. The September edition of the ASE's *Monthly Journal* noted a number of instances of pickets "hauled before the magistrates and fined—in some cases imprisoned—for very trifling offences."[912]

Employers Gain the Upper Hand

By November, the battle was raging with "a ferocity unparalleled in industrial warfare," commented the *Monthly Journal*. Many engineering firms had been compelled to rescind the eight-hour day by dint of threats by the Employers' Federation to cut off their raw materials and other supplies.[913] As Tom Mann had worried, the employers had dragged out the dispute for so long that the unions' finances were being rapidly depleted. The Employers' Federation, on the other hand, had an immense war chest and could count on the support of the state. By December, the ASE's strike funds were dwindling at a rate of £4,000 to £5,000 per week— perhaps anything up to £4 million in today's values—and in January the union was forced to levy its members at the rate of thruppence a week.[914] By mid-January, the number of lockouts had spiraled and although the new levy was yielding £3,000 per week, the union still had a weekly deficit of £6,000.[915] By the end of the dispute, the ASE alone had spent £250,000 in strike funds.[916] The unions met with the Employers' Federation and after a series of ballots, the struggle was called off.[917] The unions withdrew the central demand of the eight-hour day without loss of pay and were forced to make other concessions under the terms of the York

Agreement. There would be no closed shops or ceilings on overtime, and the question of who would operate the new machines would be at the employers' discretion. Workers would also be "rated" according to ability and paid accordingly. However, employers would recognize the unions, piecework would only be introduced if it did not undercut day labor rates, and a grievance procedure would be instituted.[918] Although the ASE had been severely bruised, it was not defeated. Its locked-out and striking members had returned to work in a disciplined manner, and the union's strength would recover as economic circumstances improved.

In Silvertown, for the second time in less than a decade, Silver's had "seen off" a revolt by its workers. The firm had suffered only minor inconvenience as a result of the strike and its shareholders enjoyed the full fruits of their investment. The *India Rubber Journal*, the mouthpiece of the rubber and electrical employers, gloated over Silver's victory. The magazine exulted that the engineers, "the great body" of whom were allegedly "incapable of thinking for themselves," had received a sound drubbing. Their distress, it added, was entirely due to the "ignorance and madness of the strike leaders" who had "plunged 80,000 men into extreme misery and plight deplorable" and concluded by exhorting the members to "send Messrs. Barnes, Burns, and Mann about their business."[919] Matthew Gray, who had stepped down at Silver's as Managing Director and taken over as Chairman, told a meeting of shareholders:

> In the recent strike in the engineering trades our Silvertown works were amongst the few selected for attack. On representation being made to us by the Unions we went carefully into the whole question of the eight-hour day, and we found that the real object of the agitation was not the declared object. The desire of the Union was to force an increase in wages of about 15 per cent, and to gain further control of the working of the shops. We informed a deputation of the affected workpeople employed by us that we could not agree to their demands. The Unions then called their members out on strike and picketed our works. The strike has, however, terminated, and the normal condition of things is restored.[920]

The firm's buoyant revenues, plus the transfer of production to Persan, had enabled Silver's to ride out the industrial storm. It is also probable that, despite the ASE's general claim that "the supply of blacklegs has been a failure,"[921] the NFLA's provision of skilled scabs had contributed to the firm's victory.

The Labor Movement Consolidates

In retrospect, the ASE strike was but one admittedly important battle in the overall class war. From 1914, the British unions' membership and power grew exponentially,[922] and outfits like the NFLA withered. The ASE's change of orientation allowed it to survive the setback, and its membership grew rapidly with the return of better economic conditions. It was the same with the general laborers' unions. In 1898, the engineering unions were forced to yield ground and sign the York Memorandum. They were not, however, crushed, as some of the more militant employers had wished. Indeed, as Wayne Lewchuk has noted in his study of the British vehicle industry, after 1898 and before 1914 the unions headed off further attempts by employers to cut wages and wring out further productivity.[923] In 1915, Will Thorne announced that the NUG&GL's income for the final quarter of the year amounted to over £35,000, "the largest reached in the history of the union." In today's terms this was worth anything between £2.19 and £12.9 million, depending on how it is calculated.[924] Total membership had climbed to 133,241, of whom 115,919 were financial.

The turnaround was visible in Silvertown, where under the energetic new NUG&GL Branch Secretary, J. H. Hollins, a stalwart of the Social Democratic Federation (SDF), the branch's remittances began to climb from the disastrous lows of Fred Ling's last years in office. The branch remitted £29/9/0 in the final quarter of 1915, which indicates a membership of around 300. Possibly, the union had once again begun to claw out a place at Silver's.[925]

The Rise of Political Labor

Despite the depression and the employers' anti-union offensive, the 1890s saw political labor go from strength to strength in West Ham and in its heavily industrialized southern districts in particular. Union reversals highlighted the need for a party of labor, and socialists had always seen the political and industrial labor movements as complementary. By the late nineteenth century, the dream had become an imperative. The ruling-class offensive had culminated in a series of court rulings that effectively outlawed picketing and in 1901 the Taff Vale judgment established that trade unions were liable for damages sustained by loss of trade during strikes.[926] Labor, it was clear, needed an independent voice in Parliament

in order to override such decisions and implement reforms that syndical-
ism alone could not win. The left wing of the workers' movement had
known this for many years. In 1889, for example, Will Thorne had argued
strongly at the NUG&GL's first national conference for an independent
working-class political organization, and his sentiments were echoed publicly by Silvertown Branch Secretary Fred Ling the following year in a
call for independent workers' representation in Parliament.[927] Four years
later, Thorne summed up as follows:

> During a strike there are no Tories or Liberals among the strikers, they
> are all workers. At Election times there are no workers, only Liberals
> and Tories. During an election there are no Tory and Liberal Capital-
> ists, and all of them are friends of the workers. During a strike there
> are no Tories and no Liberals among the employers. They are all capi-
> talists and enemies of the workers.[928]

In 1891, Thorne was elected to the West Ham Borough Council on
the SDF ticket. His was a lone socialist voice at the time, but the movement was gaining in strength. The following year saw the Scottish miner
Keir Hardie elected to Westminster, representing West Ham as the first
independent socialist MP in British political history. Although he lost the
seat at the 1895 election, the socialists won it back in 1906 and thereafter
built up an unbeatable lead over their Liberal and Tory opponents.[929] In
1894, the SDF joined together with the Independent Labour Party (ILP)
and the West Ham Trades Council to fight the September elections.[930]
Four years later, a coalition of socialists, Radicals, and Irish nationalists
won control of the West Ham Borough Council: the first time such a local
administration was formed in Britain. Although they lost their majority in 1898, they were returned a few years later and consolidated their
hold.[931] From the start, this was a profoundly working-class movement,
by, for, and of the workers. That it emerged some years before organized
labor took hold in the inner East End was due to the mushroom growth
of heavy industry in the outer or "other" East End. There was little space
in the vast new factories for the old patriarchal master-servant relation-
ships that were characteristic of the small workshops of the old East End.
Nor were the middle-class Fabians very influential in the southern parts
of West Ham, a fact Diana Banks-Conney puts down to the greater social
cohesion and class solidarity of the heavily industrialized regions.[932]

"Flatulent and Venomous Twaddle"

The strongest political tendency was the SDF. By the 1920s it dominated the southern wards of Custom House and Silvertown, and the unions were well established under the leadership of activists such as J. H. Hollins, Fred Ling's successor as Silvertown NUG&GL branch secretary. In the 1922 Westminster elections, the SDF's alderman, Jack Jones, won the West Ham south seat with a crushing majority over his Tory opponent. In 1924, he increased his vote to 12,777 as against the Tory's 2,948.[933] In 1902, a *Times* editorial sneered at the "presumptuous" and "uneducated" socialist aldermen in West Ham, one of whom, it sniffed, was "a baker's carman," and thus presumably congenitally incapable of doing tasks best left to those born to rule. Moreover, ranted the editor in what could be taken as a call to remove the upstarts, "it should be the business of states-manship to protect them from themselves, as well as to protect other people from their folly."[934] The article appears to have been one of what Edward Bristow described as a "long and abusive series on 'Municipal Socialism'" inserted into the *Times* by the indefatigable Earl of Wemyss.[935] Alderman Terrett replied eloquently, repudiating the "diatribe" as "five columns of flatulent and venomous twaddle." He argued with some reason that in fact "West Ham is one of the best and the most economically governed bor-oughs in the United Kingdom due to its Socialist majority."[936]

Collective Gains of the Working Class

The West Ham Council became a model for other labor and socialist councils that did so much to improve the quality of life for the British working class. Much more could have been done. Some of the leaders of the New Union movement had started out as socialist firebrands, only to move steadily to the right. This was especially true of Eleanor Marx's great friend Will Thorne, the founder of the NUG&GL, although unlike some, he never turned his back on the cause of labor. Marx herself was to die by her own hand in 1898. The tragic circumstances of her death were, in brief, that Marx and Edward Aveling had never formally married. In 1898 he married another woman behind her back. This did not stop him from returning to her when he was seriously ill after an operation for an undisclosed illness probably related to his alcoholism. After confessing, he prevailed on her to enter into a suicide pact with him. He brought the poison from a pharmacy and she drank it down. Aveling did not do so but returned to his legal wife, only to die shortly afterward. As a number of Eleanor Marx's friends observed, it would have been better if he had not survived his operation, for she would have lived and devoted her great talents to the cause of labor and socialism. She enjoyed enormous respect and affection among her comrades, and had she lived perhaps would have prevailed on others to hold fast to the Marxist vision of workers' emancipation. As Gareth Stedman Jones notes, the dreams of Engels, Marx, Mann, and others of a mass socialist labor party were to lead only to "the bureaucratic machine politics of Herbert Morrison's London Labour Party."[937] The end result was today's "Blairism," the neoliberal policies of recent party leader Tony Blair that chained a once independent working-class party to the interests of the City. Nevertheless, the process triggered in 1888/89 did transform the face of British life. It enabled working people to live more dignified and comfortable lives, to educate their children, care for their health, and ensure that they did not go through life chronically malnourished. Although we today might consider the vast outer London Council estates at Dagenham and Becontree to epitomize drab monotony, for the Cockney families who had lived in one verminous room at Silvertown or Stepney, they were palaces. Not only did the children have their own rooms, but there were baths and inside lavatories, and they might luxuriate in their gardens on summer evenings among the glorious splashes of color provided by the flowers they had grown. The New Unions, too, gave the laborers a sense of their worth and provided them with the weapon of collective action against the power of the employers. Engels considered that in 1889 the East End workers had set an example for the workers of the world, and so they had. The Silver's workers lost their battle, but their sacrifices contributed to better lives for the working class as a whole, including future generations up to today. The Silver's Strike Committee could not but recognize defeat, yet insisted that their struggle was an "earnest" for the future. It is a lesson that perhaps needs to be relearned in today's neoliberal age, with its recycled dogmas from the Earl of Wemyss's day. Above all, the Silvertown experience points to the need for working-class unity, something as pressing now as it was back then. It is, however, a beautiful historical irony—and a testament to the vision of the New Union pioneers—that Will Thorne's general labor union of the unskilled and semiskilled outcasts is today amalgamated with Robert Knight's Boilermakers in the General, Municipal and Boilermakers' Union, the GMB. Class unity can override narrow sectional interests.

Today, Silvertown is a shadow of its former industrial self. Nazi bombing, slum clearance, long-term decline, the closure of the docks,

Thatcherite de-industrialization, economic globalization, and technological change—all have contributed to make Silvertown almost a ghost town. Yet it has a vivid history, and the struggles and sacrifices of its laboring people helped build a movement that recast the face of Britain. Many of the gains of that movement are today under sustained attack, often by the direct biological—and certainly the ideological and social—descendants of those who sweated the "people of the machine and the Abyss." Those who today resist what is in effect the declaration of class war by a feral ruling class may find inspiration in the story of these forgotten laborers over 120 years ago. Their story epitomizes the message of the great American socialist and trade unionist Eugene V. Debs:

Ten thousand times has the labor movement stumbled and fallen and bruised itself, and risen again; been seized by the throat and choked and clubbed into insensibility; enjoined by courts, assaulted by thugs, charged by the militia, shot down by regulars, traduced by the press, frowned upon by public opinion, deceived by politicians, threatened by priests, repudiated by renegades, preyed upon by grafters, infested by spies, deserted by cowards, betrayed by traitors, bled by leeches, and sold out by leaders, but notwithstanding all this, and all these, it is today the most vital and potential power this planet has ever known.[938]

Abbreviations

—◆◆—

ASC	Aggregate Share Capital
ASE	Amalgamated Society of Engineers
EC	Executive Council (of the ASE)
ECH	Eastside Community Heritage
ETU	Electrical Trades Union
GDP	Gross Domestic Product
GMB	General, Municipal and Boilermakers' Union
ILP	Independent Labour Party
IRGP&TW	India-Rubber, Gutta-Percha & Telegraph Works
IRJ	*India-Rubber, Gutta-Percha and Electrical Trades Journal*; short form: *India-Rubber Journal*
LMA	London Metropolitan Archives
LTC	London Trades Council
MPHC	Metropolitan Police Historical Collection
MMG	Maritime Museum, Greenwich
MP	Member of Parliament
NA HO	National Archives Home Office (files)
NFLA	National Free Labour Association
NUG&GL	National Union of Gasworkers and General Labourers
SDF	Social Democratic Federation
TUC	Trades Union Congress
UW MRC	University of Warwick, Modern Records Centre, Coventry

Glossary

Note: In deference to the practice of my New York publisher, I have used U.S. spelling throughout, except when quoting British sources or when using proper nouns as appropriate. Thus, for example, I have referred to the labor movement in general, but to the (British) Labour Party.

Abyss	Jack London's atmospheric term for the East End of London.
"Arfur" (Arthur) Daley	Shady Cockney businessman in the long-running British TV series *Minder*.
beadle	Minor secular or religious official.
Black Country	Old industrial area in the West Midlands of England. So called because of the concentration of coalmines and smoky heavy industries. Includes the cities of Birmingham, Wolverhampton, and Coventry.
blackleg	Scab or strikebreaker.
Blitz	The Nazi aerial bombardment of Britain during the Second World War. From the German *blitzkrieg*, or "lightning war."
bobby	English slang, equivalent of U.S. beat cop.

Brummie	A person from the city of Birmingham in the English Midlands. *Brum* in the local dialect.
City of London	The City, uppercase C, refers to the ancient local government area of central London; the "square mile" undemocratically controlled by its financial and banking institutions. It is distinct from the city of London, with a lowercase c, which refers to the metropolis as a whole and which is largely governed by the Greater London Council.
coal porter	Docker or longshoreman engaged in loading or unloading coal from ships' holds.
Cockney	Strictly speaking, Cockneys were those born within earshot of "the sound of the Bow bells," that is, the bells of St. Mary-le-Bow church in Cheapside, just east of St. Paul's Cathedral. More broadly, it includes a person from the wider and newer East End of London, and is synonymous with East Ender. The term also refers to the colorful dialect spoken in the East End, a form of speech characterized by glottal stops, rhyming slang, and disdain for standard grammar.
constant capital	Investment in plant, machinery, raw materials, etc. Part of the "organic composition of capital." Also known as fixed capital. See also *variable capital*.
demarcation dispute	Conflict between unions over which should have coverage of the workers in a particular job. Called *jurisdictional disputes* in the United States.
diaspora	The scattering, dispersal, or mass emigration or expulsion of a population.
docker	British equivalent of a U.S. longshoreman.

East Ender

See Cockney.

ebonite

Form of hard rubber produced by heating raw rubber to high temperatures with sulfur. The invention is usually attributed to James Hancock, but there is some evidence of its independent discovery at Samuel Silver's works.

engineer

Distinct from the professional engineer, the British engineer in the sense most often used in this book is a skilled metalworker engaged in the installation, removal, and repair of machinery. The American equivalent is machinist. In Britain, fitter is a commonly used synonym. See also Turner.

Fabian

Originally an advocate of gradual change to socialism; an ultra-reformist as opposed to revolutionary socialist. Scorning agitation, they often placed their faith in the compilation of reports on socioeconomic conditions designed to influence official policy.

gaffer

Foreman, supervisor, or boss in general.

gutta-percha

The refined and solidified sap of a number of Southeast Asian rainforest trees. Once called "gum inelastic" and regarded as the poor cousin of rubber, or "gum elastic," gutta-percha's extraordinary qualities as an insulator made it a much-coveted commodity during the nineteenth century. It was used in particular for the insulation of submarine telegraph cables, as at Silvertown.

J.P.

Justice of the Peace, local judicial officer.

knees-up

Convivial time, party, or dance, in either a pub or private home, as in the Cockney song, "Knees-up, Muvver Brown."

labor aristocracy	Highly skilled and well-paid craftsmen who often saw themselves as distinct from and superior to the rest of the working class.
laissez-faire	Literally "let it go," or "let it be." Doctrine that property rights are sacrosanct and that the state should stay out of social and economic affairs except to guard against theft and working-class action. Today's neoliberalism.
leading or charge hand	Sub-supervisory employee who occupies a place between a shop floor worker and foreman. In closed shops they are usually union members.
lighterman	Worker employed in the loading, unloading, movement, and mooring of cargo barges alongside ships.
London Over the Border	The newer East End lying over the River Lea, comprising districts such as West Ham, Silvertown, Beckton, and Barking. During the late nineteenth century, these districts were outside the territory governed by the Greater London Council.
Lucknow	Indian city besieged by rebels during the Indian Mutiny of 1857.
MP	Member of Parliament.
Newham	Present-day name for the London Borough of West Ham, of which Silvertown forms a part, and which is now part of Greater London.
piecework	Payment by results as opposed to fixed hourly, daily, or weekly wages.
Podsnappery	Mr. Podsnap is a sanctimonious hypocrite in Charles Dickens's *Our Mutual Friend*, fond of quoting the Bible to justify the suffering of the poor.

Q.C.	Queen's Counsel, a jurist appointed by letters patent of the Queen as a person learned in law. Term is K.C. during the reign of a king.
Radical	Member or supporter of the left wing of the Liberal Party, some of whom were pro-labor.
Reformer's Tree	Tree in Hyde Park burned in 1866 during the occupation of 200,000 people demonstrating for manhood suffrage. The stump became a notice board and focal point for Radical demonstrations.
Scotland Yard	The London Metropolitan Police headquarters.
silvertail	Australian slang for a well-heeled person.
Social Darwinism	Doctrine associated with the Victorian philosopher Herbert Spencer. Spencer vociferously espoused laissez-faire dogma. He opposed socialism and the trade unions and any form of "socialistic" legislation aimed at improving the lives of the poor. Indeed, he believed that the poor should die out, as they were biologically unfit to live. Ironically, his grave is just across the path from that of Karl Marx in London's Highgate Cemetery.
stevedore	Highly skilled worker engaged in the loading and unloading of ships, including by the erection and use of lifting tackle at a time when dockside cranes were rare.
stoker	Semiskilled worker employed to charge furnaces as in gasworks and boiler rooms.
Stratford	Industrial suburb of outer East London; a different place than the better-known Stratford-on-Avon.

tanner	Sixpence.
toff	Cockney term for an upper-class person; from "toffee nosed."
toolmaker	Skilled engineer employed to make jigs, dies, molds, cutting tools, gauges, machine tools, and so forth.
toolsetter	A skilled engineer employed to set up semiautomatic machine tools operated by semiskilled workers.
Tory	A member or supporter of the Conservative Party. See also Whig.
turner	A skilled engineering worker employed to make and repair machine parts on a lathe and other metal-shaping machinery. Some workers were employed as fitters and turners. See Engineer above.
variable capital	That part of capital disbursed as wages. See also constant capital.
wen	A boil or abscess. Used figuratively by William Cobbett in the phrase "The Great Wen" to describe London.
Whig	A member or supporter of the old Liberal Party. See also Tory.
whip	Member of the caucus of a parliamentary political party charged with ensuring that MPs vote along party lines.
wide boy	London term for a spiv or wheeler-and-dealer who lives by his wits, often by defrauding the gullible.

Bibliography
—◆◆—

1. ARCHIVAL SOURCES

British Library, St. Pancras has some files of British Labor History ephemera relevant to the place and period studied.

British Library Newspaper Archives, Colindale, holds files of national and local newspapers with material relevant to Silvertown.

City of London Metropolitan Archives, Clerkenwell: The collection includes the files of the India-Rubber, Gutta-Percha and Telegraph Works Company. These include minutes of Board and General Meetings for the period between 1864 and 1918.

Eastside Community Heritage, Ilford, Essex, holds transcripts of interviews with elderly Silvertown and North Woolwich residents.

Essex Record Office, Cheltenham, has a small collection of historical ephemera and some theses relevant to Silvertown.

London Metropolitan University, TUC Library, North London; The Trades Union Congress Library has collections of rare pamphlets, including from the Amalgamated Society of Engineers and the National Union of Gasworkers and General Labourers. The library also has the London Trades Council's Minute Books for 1889, which include the minutes of Executive and Delegate meetings.

National Archives, Public Record Office, Kew, holds Home Office (HO) correspondence for 1889 relating to London trade unions.

National Meteorological Archives, Sowton, Exeter: Official weather records for London, 1889.

Stratford Library and Archives, Stratford, Essex, holds a great variety of photographs, documents and newspapers relating to West Ham and Silvertown.

University of Warwick, Modern Records Centre, Coventry: The Modern Records Centre holds a vast amount of material. Relevant documents include the Minutes of the Amalgamated Society of Engineers Executive Council for 1889, and the Half-Yearly and Quarterly Reports of the National Union of Gasworkers and General Labourers for the period 1889 to 1914. The centre also has files of the ASE *Monthly Journal* for the relevant periods.

2. Books, Pamphlets, and Journal Articles

Alderman, Geoffrey. "The National Free Labour Association: A Case-Study of Organised Strike-Breaking in the Late Nineteenth and Early Twentieth Centuries," *International Review of Social History* 21/3 (December 1976): 309–36.

Alexander, Cecil Frances. *Hymns for Little Children,* 5th ed. (London: Joseph Masters, 1852).

Amalgamated Society of Engineers. *Rules (Part 1),* as revised at the fourteenth delegate meeting, held at Manchester (London: Cooperative Printing Society, 1915).

———. *Rules,* revised at Nottingham, 25 May 1885 (Melbourne: Australasian-American Trading Company, 1890).

Aveling, Edward. "The Eight-Hour Working Day," pamphlet, ca. 1890. British Library, British Labour History Ephemera, 1880–1900.

Aveling, Edward, and Eleanor Marx-Aveling. "The Factory Hell" (London: Socialist League, 1885).

———. *The Woman Question* (London: Swan, Sonnenschein, Lowery, 1887).

Aveling, Marian, and Joy Damousi. *Stepping Out of History: Documents of Women at Work in Australia* (North Sydney: Allen & Unwin, 1991).

Ball, Michael, and David Sunderland. *An Economic History of London, 1800–1914* (London: Routledge, 2001).

Ballhatchet, Joan. "The Police and the Dock Strike of 1889," *History Workshop Journal* 32/1 (1991).

Barrett, Duncan, and Nuala Calvi. *The Sugar Girls: Tales of Hardship, Love and Happiness in Tate & Lyle's East End* (London: Collins, 2012).

Bax, E. Belfort. *Address to the Trades Unions* (London: Socialist League, 1885).

Bédarida, François. *Will Thorne: La voie anglaise du socialisme* (Paris: Fayard, 1987).

Blake, Lewis. *The Great Explosion: Silvertown 1917* (London: Park Hill Publications, 2001).

Booth, Janine. *Guilty and Proud of It! Poplar's Rebel Councillors and Guardians, 1919–25* (Pontypool: Merlin Press, 2009).

Borough of West Ham. *Book of West Ham* (London: Official Publications Bureau, 1923).

Brecht, Bertolt. *Bertolt Brecht Poems 1913–1956.* Ed. John Willett and Ralph Manheim with Erich Fried (New York: Methuen, 1976).

Brecht, Bertolt. *The Threepenny Opera* (Harmondsworth: Penguin Classics, 2007).

Briggs, Asa. *Victorian Cities* (Harmondsworth: Penguin, 1968).

British Weekly Commissioners. *Toilers in London; Or Inquiries Concerning Female Labour in the Metropolis* (London: Hodder and Stoughton, 1889).

Bristow, Edward. "The Liberty and Property Defence League and Individualism," *Historical Journal* 18/4 (1975): 761–89.

Buchanan, R. Angus. "Gentlemen Engineers: The Making of a Profession," *Victorian Studies* 26/4 (Summer 1983).

Camus, Albert. Preface to Georges Bataille, ed., *L'Espagne Libre* (Paris: Calmann-Lévy, 1946).

Charlton, John. *The Mass Movement and the New Unionism in Britain, 1889: "It just went like tinder"* (London: Redwords, 1999).

Crouch, Archer Philip. *Silvertown and Neighbourhood (including East and West Ham): A Retrospect* (London: Thomas Burleigh, 1900).

Eastside Community Heritage. *North Woolwich: Stories from the Riverside* (Stratford, Essex: Eastside Community Heritage, 2003).

Ellis, Havelock. "Eleanor Marx," Pts. 1 and 2, *The Adelphi* (London: September 1935).

Engels, Frederick, Paul Lafargue, and Laura Lafargue. *Correspondence*, vol. 2: 1887–1890 (Moscow: Foreign Languages Publishing House, 1959).

ETU. *The Story of the ETU: The Official History of the Electrical Trades Union.* Foreword by Walter C. Stevens (Hayes, Bromley, Kent: ETU, ca. 1953).

———. *Souvenir of Fifty Years of the Electrical Trades Union, 1889–1939* (Manchester: ETU, 1939).

Evans, Hilary. *The Oldest Profession: Illustrated History of Prostitution* (Newton Abbot: David and Charles, 1979).

Fido, Martin, and Keith Skinner. *The Official Encyclopaedia of Scotland Yard* (London: Virgin Publishing, 1999).

Field, Arthur. "Eleanor Marx," *Social Democrat* 2/9 (September 1898).

Fishman, William J. *East End 1888: A Year in a London Borough among the Labouring Poor* (Nottingham: Five Leaves, 2005).

———. *East End Jewish Radicals, 1875–1914* (London: Duckworth, 1975).

Florence, Ronald. *Marx's Daughters: Eleanor Marx, Rosa Luxemburg, Angelica Balabanoff* (New York: Dial Press, 1975).

Foakes, Grace. *Four Meals for Fourpence.* Ed. Joanna Goldsworthy (London: Virago, 2012).

Garfield, Judith. *Stories from Silvertown* (Stratford, Essex: Eastside Community Heritage, 2001).

Gifford, Denis. *Victorian Comics* (London: George Allen & Unwin, 1976).

Gissing, George. *The Nether World.* Ed. Stephen Gill (Oxford: Oxford University Press, 2008).

Gosling, Harry. *Up and Down Stream* (London: Methuen, 1927).

Guérin, Daniel. *Fascism and Big Business* (New York: Pathfinder Press, 1973).

Harkness, Margaret. *In Darkest London* (London: Black Apollo Press, 2003).

Harris, Christina Phelps. "The Persian Submarine Telegraph of 1864," *Geographical Journal* 135/2 (June 1969).

Headrick, Daniel R. *The Tentacles of Progress: Technology Transfer in the Age of Imperialism, 1850–1940* (Oxford: Oxford University Press, 1988).

Hill, Graham, and Howard Bloch. *The Silvertown Explosion: London 1917* (Stroud, Gloucestershire: Tempus, 2003).

Hobsbawm, Eric, ed. *Labour's Turning Point, 1880–1900: Extracts from Contemporary Sources*, 2nd ed.(Brighton: Harvester Press, 1974).

———. *Labouring Men: Studies in the History of Labour* (London: Weidenfeld and Nicolson, 1968).

Howarth, Edward G., and Mona Wilson. *West Ham: A Study in Social and Industrial Problems* (London: J. M. Dent, 1907).

Howell, David. *British Workers and the Independent Labour Party, 1888–1906* (Manchester: Manchester University Press, 1983).

Hyndman, Henry Mayers. *Further Reminiscences* (London: Macmillan, 1912).

— — —. *Reminiscences and Reflections* (London: Macmillan, 1912).

Johnson, George, ed. *The All-Red Line: The Annals and Aims of the Pacific Cable Project* (Ottawa: James Hope, 1903).

Kapp, Yvonne. *Eleanor Marx: The Crowded Years, 1884–1898* (London: Virago, 1979).

Leventhal, F. M., ed. *The World of Labour: English Workers, 1850–1890* (New York and London: Garland Publishers, 1984).

Lewchuk, Wayne. *American Technology and the British Vehicle Industry: A Century of Production in Britain* (Cambridge: Cambridge University Press, 1987).

Llewellyn Smith, Hubert. *The History of East London From the Earliest Times to the End of the Eighteenth Century* (London: Macmillan, 1939).

London Borough of Newham. *West Ham, 1886–1986* (Newham: Council of the London Borough of Newham, 1986).

London, Jack. *The People of the Abyss.* Introduction by Jack Lindsay (London: Journeyman Press, 1977).

Love, Steve, and David Giffels. *Wheels of Fortune: The Story of Rubber in Akron* (Akron, OH: University of Akron Press, 1999).

Lovell, John. *Stevedores and Dockers: A Study of Trade Unionism in the Port of London, 1870–1914* (London: Macmillan, 1969).

Lynd, Helen Merrell. *England in the Eighteen-Eighties: Toward a Social Basis for Freedom.* Introduction by Gerald M. Pomper (London: Oxford University Press, 1945).

Mann, Tom, and Ben Tillett. *The "New" Trades Unions: A Reply to Mr. George Shipton* (London: Green & McAllan, 1890).

Mann, Tom. *Tom Mann's Memoirs* (London: Labour Publishing, 1923).

Marriott, John. *Beyond the Tower: A History of East London* (New Haven and London: Yale University Press, 2011).

Marx, Karl, and Frederick Engels. *Manifesto of the Communist Party,* in Marx and Engels, *Selected Works,* vol. 1 (Moscow: Progress Publishers, 1969).

— — —.*Marx and Engels on the Trade Unions.* Ed. Kenneth Lapides (Moscow: Progress Publishers, 1971).

Marx, Karl. *Capital,* vol. 1 (London: Everyman, 1972).

Matthews, Derek. "1889 and All That: New Views on the New Unionism," *International Review of Social History* 36 (1991).

McDougall, Donald, ed. *Fifty Years a Borough, 1886–1936: The Story of West Ham* (West Ham, Essex: County Borough Council of West Ham, 1936).

McGrath, Melanie. *Silvertown: An East End Family Memoir* (London: Fourth Estate, 2003).

Meier, Olga. *The Daughters of Karl Marx: Family Correspondence, 1866–1898* (Harmondsworth: Penguin, 1984).

Morton, H. V. *The Heart of London* (London: Methuen, 1925).

— — —. *The Spell of London* (London: Methuen, 1935).

Newham History Workshop. *A Marsh and a Gasworks: One Hundred Years of Life in West Ham* (Plaistow, Essex: Parents' Centre Publications, 1986).

NFLA. *The National Free Labour Association: Its Foundation, History, and Work* (London: NFLA, 1898).

Pagenstecher, Dr. *History of West and East Ham* (Stratford, Essex: Wilson & Whitworth, 1908).

Partridge, Eric. *A Dictionary of Slang and Unconventional English.* Ed. Paul Beale (London: Routledge, 1984).

Pember Reeves, Mrs. *Around About a Pound a Week* (London: G. Bell and Sons, 1914).

Phillips, Tom. *A London Docklands Guide.* Ed. Peter Marcan (London: Peter Marcan Publications, 1986).

Porter, Dale H. *The Thames Embankment: Environment, Technology, and Society in Victorian London* (Akron, OH: University of Akron Press, 1998).

Porter, Roy. *London: A Social History* (Harmondsworth: Penguin, 2000).

Powell, W. Raymond. *Keir Hardie in West Ham: "A Constituency with a Past,"* Socialist History Occasional Papers, Series 19 (London: Socialist History Society, 2004).

Radice, Giles, and Lisanne Radice. *Will Thorne, Constructive Militant: A Study in the New Unionism and New Politics* (London: George Allen and Unwin, 1974).

Raw, Louise. *Striking a Light: The Bryant and May Matchwomen and Their Place in Labour History.* Foreword by Sheila Rowbottom (London: Continuum, 2009).

Ross, Ellen, ed. *Slum Travelers in London: Ladies and London Poverty, 1860–1920* (Berkeley: University of California Press, 2007).

Sanders, W. Stephen. *Early Socialist Days* (London: Hogarth Press, 1927).

Saville, John. "Trade Unions and Free Labour: The Background to the Taff Vale Decision," in *Essays in Labour History: In Memory of GDH Cole 25 September 1889–14 January 1959.* Ed. Asa Briggs and John Saville (London: Macmillan, 1960).

Schaffer, Gordon. *Light and Liberty: Sixty Years of the Electrical Trades Union.* Introduction by Walter C. Stevens (Hayes, Bromley, Kent: ETU, 1949).

Sheridan, Thomas. *Mindful Militants: The Amalgamated Engineering Union in Australia, 1920–1972* (Melbourne: Cambridge University Press, 1975).

Sims, George R. *How the Poor Live* and *Horrible London* (London: Chatto & Windus, 1889).

Southgate, Walter. *That's the Way It Was: A Working-Class Autobiography.* Ed. with Afterword by Terry Philpott (London: New Clarion Press, 1982).

Standage, Tom. *The Victorian Internet: The Remarkable Story of the Telegraph and the Nineteenth Century's Online Pioneers* (London: Phoenix, 1999).

Stedman Jones, Gareth. *Languages of Class: Studies in English Working-Class History, 1832–1982* (Cambridge: Cambridge University Press, 1983).

———. *Outcast London: A Study in the Relationship between Classes in Victorian Society* (Oxford: Oxford University Press, 1971).

———. "Working-Class Culture and Working-Class Politics in London, 1870–1900: Notes on the Remaking of a Working Class," *Journal of Social History* 7/4 (Summer 1974).

Still, John. *The Jungle Tide* (New Delhi: Asian Educational Services, 1999).

Stokes, John, ed. *Eleanor Marx (1855–1898): Life, Work, Contacts* (Aldershot, Hants: Ashgate, 2000).

Swinburne, Algernon Charles. *Songs before Sunrise* (London: F. S. Ellis, 1871).

Terrett, J. J. *"Municipal Socialism" in West Ham: A Reply to The Times* (London: Twentieth Century Press, ca. 1902).

The Holy Bible, King James Edition of 1611 (London: British and Foreign Bible Society, Eyre and Spottiswoode, 1837).

Thompson, E. P. *The Making of the English Working Class* (Harmondsworth: Penguin, 1991).

Thorne, Will. *My Life's Battles*. Foreword by J. R. Clynes and Introduction by John Saville (London: Lawrence and Wishart, 1989).

Tillett, Ben. *Memories and Reflections* (London: John Long, 1931).

Torr, Dona. *Tom Mann* (London: Lawrence and Wishart, n.d.).

Trotsky, Leon. *The Russian Revolution*, vol. 1. Trans. Max Eastman (London: Sphere Books, 1967).

Tsuzuki, Chushichi. *The Life of Eleanor Marx, 1855–1898: A Socialist Tragedy* (Oxford: Clarendon Press, 1967).

Tully, John. "A Victorian Ecological Disaster: Imperialism, the Telegraph, and Gutta-Percha," *Journal of World History* 20/4 (December 2009).

———. "Silvertown 1889: The East End's Great Forgotten Strike," *Labour History Review*. (forthcoming.)

———. *The Devil's Milk: A Social History of Rubber* (New York: Monthly Review Press, 2011).

United Rubber Workers of America. *25 Years of the URW: A Quarter-Century Panorama of Democratic Unionism* (Akron, OH: United Rubber, Cork, Linoleum and Plastic Workers of America, 1960).

Victoria and Albert Museum. *Penny Dreadfuls and Comics: English Periodicals from Victorian Times to the Present Day* (London: V & A Museum, 1983).

Went, Robert. *Globalization: Neoliberal Challenge, Radical Responses*. Trans. Peter Drucker (London: Pluto Press, 2000).

Windscheffel, Alex. *Popular Conservatism in Imperial London 1868–1906* (London, 2007).

Woods, Robert, and Nicola Shelton. *An Atlas of Victorian Mortality* (Liverpool: Liverpool University Press, 1997).

Woods, Robert, and Joan Woodward, eds. *Urban Disease and Mortality in Nineteenth-Century England* (London: Batsford Academic and Educational, 1984).

3. PERIODICALS

Amalgamated Engineers Monthly Journal of Trade Unionism and Brotherhood, London

Barking, East Ham and Ilford Advertiser, Barking, Essex

Belfast Newsletter, Belfast

Cobbett's Weekly Political Register, London

Commonweal, London

Daily News, London

East and West Ham Gazette, London

East End News, London

East London and Tower Hamlets Advertiser, London

Electrical Engineer, London

Electrician, London

Essex Standard, West Suffolk Gazette, and Eastern Counties' Advertiser, Colchester, Essex.

Financial Times, London

Graphic, London

Illustrated Police News, London
India-Rubber, Gutta-Percha and Electrical Trades Journal, London
Justice, London
Labour Elector, London
Labour Tribune, The Organ of the Miners, Ironworkers, National Bolt Forger &c of Great Britain, West Bromwich
Lloyd's Weekly Newspaper, London
London Gazette, London
Morning Post, London
The Nation, New York
Nineteenth-Century: A Monthly Review, London
Pall Mall Gazette, London
Penny Illustrated Paper, London
Pictorial Weekly, London
Queenslander, Brisbane
Reynold's Newpaper, London
Standard, London
Star, London
Stratford Express, London
Telegraphist: A Monthly Journal for Postal, Telegraph and Railways Clerks, London
The Times, London
West Ham Guardian, West Ham
York Herald, York
Young Ladies' Journal, London

4. INTERNET SOURCES

Abandoned Communities—Central Silvertown, http://www.abandonedcommunities.co.uk/silvertown.html.
Alderman, Geoffrey. "Collison, William (1865–1938)," *Oxford Dictionary of National Biography*, Oxford University Press, 2004, http://www. Oxforddnb. com/view/article/48216.
Bax, E. Belfort. *Reminiscences and Reflections of a Mid- and Late Victorian*, (1918). Marxists Internet Archive, http://www.marxists.org/archives/ bax/1918/autobiog/index.htm.
Beeton, Isabella. *Mrs. Beeton's Book of Household Management: Comprising Information for the Mistress, Housekeeper, Cook, Kitchen-maid, Butler, Footman, Coachman, Valet, Upper and under house-maids, Lady's-maid, Maid-of-all-work, Laundry-maid, Nurse and nurse-maid, Monthly, wet, and sick nurses, etc. etc. also, sanitary, medical, & legal memoranda; with a history of the origin, properties, and uses of all things connected with home life and comfort.* http://www.Mr.sbeeton.com/42-chapter42.html.
Bell, Megara. "The Fallen Women in Fiction and Legislation," http://www. gober.net/victorian/reports/prostit.html.
Benjamin, Walter. "On the Concept of History," VII, 1940, http://www.marxists. org/reference/archives/benjamin/1940/history.htm.
Carlyle, E. I., and M. C. Curthoys. "Price, Bartholomew (1818–1898)," *Oxford Dictionary of National Biography*, Oxford University Press, 2004, http:// www.oxforndb.com/view/article/22741.

CoinMill.com–The Currency Converter http://coinmill.com/GBX_calculator. html#GBX=6

Debs, Eugene. "An Ideal Labor Press," *The Metal Worker*, May 1904, E. V. Debs Internet Archive, www.marxists.org/archive/debs/works/1904/laborpress.htm.

Eastside Community Heritage. Hidden Histories: Stories from Silvertown, http://www.hidden-histories.org.uk/wordpress/?page_id=180.

Historical UK Inflation and Price Converter, http://safalra.com/other/historical-uk-inflation-price-conversion/.

History of Stratford, Silvertown Index. http://historyofstratford.co.uk/Silvertown/Silvertown-index.shtml.

Hood, Thomas. "The Song of the Shirt," The Poem Hunter, http://www.poemhunter.com/poem/the-song-of-the-shirt/.

James, William. "What Makes Life Significant?" Talks to Students, 1899. http://philosophy.lander.edu/intro/introbook2.1/c9204.html#FTN.AEN9239.

Jones, Mother. *The Autobiography of Mother Jones*, chap 27, http://www.angelfire.com/nj3/RonMBaseman/mojones.htm. First published 1925.

Lebergott, Stanley, "Wage Trends, 1800-1900," in The Conference on Research in Income and Wealth, *Trends in the American Economy in the Nineteenth Century* (Princeton NJ: Princeton University Press, 1960). http://www.nber.org/chapters/c2486.

Marx, Eleanor. "Women's Trade Unions in England," http://www.marxists.org/archive/draper/1976/women/5-emarx.html.

Marx, Karl. Introduction to Contribution to the Critique of Hegel's *Philosophy of Right*, Marx/Engels Internet Archive, http://www.marxists.org/archive/marx/works/1844/df-jahrbucher/law-abs.htm.

Marx, Karl. "Wages of Labour," First Manuscript, *Economic and Philosophical Manuscripts*, 1844, http//marx.eserver.org/1844-ep.manuscripts/1st. manuscript/1-labor.wages.txt.

Marx-Engels Correspondence, Marx-Engels Internet Archives,http://www.marxists.org/archive/marx/works1888/letters/89_11_20.htm.

Miller, Emily Huntington. "Hang Up the Baby's Stocking," in The Hymns and Carols of Christmas, http://www.hymnsandcarolsofchristmas.com/Poetry/hang_up_the_babys_stocking.htm.

"Modern Colchester: Town Development," *A History of the County of Essex*, vol. 9, *Borough of Colchester*, 1994, 199–208, and "Modern Colchester: Introduction," *A History of the County of Essex*, vol. 9, *Borough of Colchester*, 1994, 176–79, http://www.british-history.ac.uk/report.aspx?compid=21988.

Morrison, Andrew L. "A Very Discreet Man: James Monro and the Whitechapel Murders," http://www.casebook.org/police_officials/po-monro.html.

National Minimum Wage Rates, http://www.direct.gov.uk/en/Employment/Employees/TheNationalMinimumWage/DG_10027201.

Officer, Lawrence H., and Samuel H. Williamson. Measuring Worth, http://www.measuringworth.com/.

Our Family History, The Peerage, http://thepeerage.com/index.htm.

Owen, W. B., and Matthew Lee. "Thompson, William Marcus (1857–1907)," *Oxford Dictionary of National Biography*, Oxford University Press, 2004, http://www.oxforddnb.com.view/article/36497.

Pickles, John D. "Latham, Henry (1821–1902)," *Oxford Dictionary of National Biography*, 2004, http://www.oxforddnb.com/view/article/34417.

Powell, W. R., ed. *A History of the County of Essex* 6 (1973), http://www.british-history.ac.uk/report.aspx?compid=42740.

Relative Values of Sums of Money, Nominal Annual Earnings for Various Occupations in England and Wales, 1710–1911, http://privatewww.essex.ac.uk/-alan/family/N-money.html.

Seidman, Joel. "Sit-Down," League for Industrial Democracy, 1937, http://www.labournet.de/internationales/usa/sitdown37.pdf.

Soldon, Norbert C. "Douglas, Francis Wemyss-Charteris, Eighth Earl of Wemyss and Sixth Earl of March (1818–1914)," *Oxford Dictionary of National Biography*, http://www.oxforndb.com/view/article/36833.

Spencer, Herbert. *The Principles of Biology* (London: Williams and Norgate, 1864), http://www.archive.org/details/principlesbiolo05spengoog.

Tate & Lyle. http://www.tateandlyle.com/AboutUs/history/Pages/History.aspx.

New Testament, Corinthians 11:27, http://bible.cc/2_corinthians/11-27.htm.

Turner, Ian. "Anstey, Francis George (Frank) (1865–1940), *Australian Dictionary of Biography*, http://adb.anu.edu.au/biography/anstey-francis-george-frank-5038.

UNITE. The Union for Life, http://www.unitetheunion.org/about_us/history/history_of_aeeu.aspx.

Webb, R. K. "Brooke, Stopford Augustus (1832–1916)," *Oxford Dictionary of National Biography*, http://www.oxforddnb.com/view/article/32094.

5. Unpublished Theses

Banks-Conney, Diana Elisabeth. "Political Culture and the Labour Movement: A Comparison Between Poplar and West Ham, 1889–1914." PhD diss., University of Greenwich, September 2005.

Buck, Nicholas Hedley. "Class Structure and Local Government Activity in West Ham, 1886–1914." PhD diss., University of Kent at Canterbury, June 1980.

Foster, A. A. "The British Electrical Industry, 1875–1914: A Study of Three Essex-Based Engineering Companies Involved in Its Early Development." Master of Studies diss., University of Cambridge, 30 August 1999.

Marriott, John W. "London Over the Border: A Study of West Ham During Rapid Growth, 1840–1910." PhD diss., University of Cambridge, 1985.

Notes

1. Jack London, *The People of the Abyss* (London: Isbister, 1904), 288.
2. Bertolt Brecht, *The Threepenny Opera* (Harmondsworth: Penguin Classics, 2007), 91.
3. Melanie McGrath, *Silvertown: An East End Family Memoir* (London: Fourth Estate, 2003) 140.
4. *Penny Illustrated Paper*, Saturday, 14 December 1889.
5. John Tully, "Silvertown 1889: The East End's Great Forgotten Strike," *Labour History Review*, forthcoming.
6. John Saville, "Trade Unions and Free Labour: The Background to the Taff Vale Decision," in *Essays in Labour History: In Memory of GDH Cole 25th September 1889—14th January 1959*, ed. Asa Briggs and John Saville (London: Macmillan, 1960).
7. Calculated using Lawrence H. Officer and Samuel H. Williamson, MeasuringWorth. com, http://www.measuringworth.com/ppoweruk/result.php?use[]=CPI&use[]=N OMINALEARN&year_early=1889&pound71=&shilling71=&pence71=6&amount =0.025&year_source=1889&year_result=2010.
8. Calculated using CoinMill.com–The Currency Converter http://coinmill.com/GBX_ calculator.html#GBX=6.
9. See Stanley Lebergott, "Wage Trends, 1800-1900," in The Conference on Research in Income and Wealth, *Trends in the American Economy in the Nineteenth Century* (Princeton NJ: Princeton University Press, 1960). http://www.nber.org/chapters/ c2486
10. John Tully, *France on the Mekong: A History of the Protectorate in Cambodia* (Lanham, MD: University Press of America, 2002).
11. John Tully, *The Devil's Milk: A Social History of Rubber* (New York: Monthly Review Press, 2011).
12. William Clarence Smith, review of *The Devil's Milk* in the *International Journal of Social History* 56/3 (December 2011): 542.
13. E. Belfort Bax, *Address to the Trades Unions. The Socialist Platform No 1* (London: Socialist League, 1885), 7.
14. Cited in Eric Hobsbawm, "History and the 'Dark Satanic Mills'," *Labouring Men: Studies in the History of Labour* (London: Weidenfeld and Nicolson, 1968), 118.
15. London, *The People of the Abyss*, 39.
16. Isabella Beeton, *Mrs. Beeton's Book of Household Management: Comprising Information for the Mistress, Housekeeper, Cook, Kitchen-maid, Butler, Footman, Coachman, Valet, Upper and under house-maids, Lady's-maid, Maid-of-all-work, Laundry-maid, Nurse and nurse-maid, Monthly, wet, and sick nurses, etc. etc. also, sanitary, medical, & legal memoranda; with a history of the origin, properties, and uses of all things connected with home life and comfort,* chap. 42. http://www.Mr.sbeeton.com/42-chapter42. html. Double emphasis in the original.
17. Hobsbawm, *Labouring Men*, 106, 109.

18. Ibid., 106.
19. "Swing" or "Captain Swing" was a revolt of agricultural laborers early in early nine-teenth-century England who smashed labor-saving machinery. See Eric Hobsbawm and George Rudé, *Captain Swing* (London: Lawrence and Wishart, 1969).
20. Hobsbawm, *Labouring Men,* 118–19.
21. Ibid., 106.
22. Ibid,. 119.
23. "The Silvertown Strike," *Times,* Tuesday, 10 December 1889.
24. William Shakespeare, *Romeo and Juliet,* Act 2, scene 3, *The Complete Works of William Shakespeare* (London: Rex Library, 1973), 753.
25. H. V. Morton, *The Heart of London* (London: Methuen, 1925), 18.
26. Dr. Pagenstecher, *History of East and West Ham* (Stratford, Essex: Wilson & Whit-worth, 1908), 198.
27. "Silvertown: The Strike at Messrs. Silver's Works," *Stratford Express*, Wednesday, 2 October 1889.
28. "The Revolt of Labour. Tower Hill," *Labour Elector*, Saturday, 7 September 1889.
29. "The Strike of London Dock Labourers," *Labour Elector*, Saturday, 24 August 1889.
30. Engels to Laura Lafargue, 27 August 1889, in Frederick Engels, Paul and Laura Lafargue, *Correspondence*, vol. 2: 1887–1890 (Moscow: Foreign Languages Pub-lishing House, 1959), 304. Engels's estimate of 40–50,000 dockers is an exaggera-tion, but many thousands of supporters and other waterfront workers swelled the numbers.
31. Tom Mann, *Tom Mann's Memoirs* (London: Labour Publishing, 1923), 82. For num-bers employed on the docks, see Michael Ball and David Sutherland, *An Economic History of London, 1800–1914* (London: Routledge, 2001), 223–24.
32. John Lovell, *Stevedores and Dockers: A Study of Trade Unionism in the Port of London, 1870–1914* (London: Methuen, 1969), 33.
33. Ibid.
34. Ben Tillett, *Memories and Reflections* (London: John Long, 1931), 172–73.
35. "Fatal accident at Victoria Dock," *West Ham Guardian*, Saturday, 3 August 1889.
36. Lovell, *Stevedores and Dockers*, 88. See also Harry Gosling, *Up and Down Stream* (London: Methuen, 1927).
37. Tillett, *Memories and Reflections*, 110–11.
38. Ibid., 174.
39. *Commonweal,* 7 September 1889.
40. "The Great Strike," *East and West Ham Gazette*, Saturday, 7 December 1889.
41. The National Archives contains an interesting file of correspondence between the Chamber of Shipping, Metropolitan Police Commissioner James Monro, and the Home Office on the question of the legality of picketing. See National Archives, Public Record Office, Kew, HO 144/235/A51405. (Hereafter NA.) This matter is discussed in more detail below as it impacts directly on the Silvertown dispute.
42. *East and West Ham Gazette,* Saturday, 14 September 1889.
43. Henry Mayers Hyndman, *Further Reminiscences* (London: Macmillan, 1912), 477.
44. Cited in Charlton, *The Mass Movement and New Unionism,* 9. John Charlton. The Mass Movement and the New Unionism in Britain, 1889: "It just went like tinder" (London: Redwords, 1999).
45. "Our Triumph," *Labour Elector*, Saturday, 21 September 1889.
46. Harry Stone, letter to the editor, *India-Rubber and Gutta-Percha and Electrical Trades Journal*, London, 8 November 1889. (Hereafter *IRJ.*)
47. Little industrial work is actually unskilled. I use the term to differentiate between craft workers and those who had not completed formal apprenticeships.
48. Will Thorne, Foreword by J. R. Clynes and an Introduction by John Saville, *My Life's Battles* (London: Lawrence and Wishart, 1989), 91.
49. Yvonne Kapp, *Eleanor Marx,* vol. 2: *The Crowded Years, 1884–1898* (London: Virago, 1979), 334–56.
50. Tom Phillips, *A London Docklands Guide,* ed. Peter Marcan (London: Peter Marcan Publications, 1986), 41.

51. See Lewis Blake, *The Great Explosion: Silvertown 1917* (London: Park Hill Publications, 2001); and Graham Hill and Howard Bloch, *The Silvertown Explosion: London 1917* (Stroud, Gloucestershire: Tempus Publishing, 2003).

52. Interview with R. G., Eastside Community Heritage (ECH), Hidden Histories: Stories from Silvertown, http://www.hidden-histories.org.uk/wordpress/?page_id=180.

53. E. P. Thompson, *The Making of the English Working Class* (Harmondsworth: Penguin, 1991), 12.

54. The Silvertown Company, a subsidiary of British Tyre & Rubber (BTR), still has a factory at Burton-on-Trent. The Akron-based multinational B. F. Goodrich, with which BTR was later associated, also sold "Silvertown" tires for a while in the United States. Since 1955, the firm has been a subsidiary of British Tyre & Rubber. (*West Ham, 1886-1986*, 64.)

55. "Abandoned Communities—Central Silvertown," http://www.abandonedcommunities.co.uk/silvertown.html. During the same period, the number of electors in East and West Silvertown fell, respectively, from 1,708 to 799 and 1,385 to 600.

56. Personal correspondence with the author, Wednesday, 22 February 2012.

57. Interview with Connie Hunt, ECH, North Woolwich, 12 June 2003.

58. John Still, *The Jungle Tide* (London: W.M. Blackwood and Sons, 1930), 117.

59. Engels to Laura Lafargue, *Marx-Engels Correspondence*, 309. Emphasis in the original.

60. Tillett, *Memories and Reflections*, 116–17.

61. Tom Mann and Ben Tillett, *The "New" Trades Unions: A Reply to Mr. George Shipton* (London: Green & McAllan, 1890), 15.

62. Details of the formation of the union can be found in Giles and Lisanne Radice, *Will Thorne: Constructive Militant—A Study in New Unionism and New Politics* (London: George Allen & Unwin, 1974); and Thorne, *My Life's Battles.*

63. *West Ham, 1886–1986* (Newham: Council of the London Borough of Newham, 1986), 52.

64. Figures from *Beehive*, 25 March 1871, cited in Hobsbawm, *Labouring Men*, 275.

65. Mann and Tillett, *The "New" Trades Unions*, 13. Nevertheless, by 1888, there was an average of ten strikes per month across Britain. According to the *Labour Tribune*, published by miners' and ironworkers' unions in the Black Country, there were some 509 strikes in 1888, the vast majority of which were successful. Of the total, 332 were settled by conciliation and fifteen by arbitration. Most of these, however, occurred in unionized industries. *Labour Tribune: The Organ of the Miners, Ironworkers, National Bolt Forgers &c of Great Britain*, West Bromwich, 7 December 1889.

66. Hobsbawm, *Labouring Men*, 181.

67. George R. Sims, *How the Poor Live and Horrible London* (London: Chatto & Windus, 1889), 114.

68. William J. Fishman, *East End 1888: A Year in a London Borough among the Labouring Poor* (Nottingham: Five Leaves Publications, 2005), 55.

69. See Gareth Stedman Jones, *Outcast London: A Study in the Relationship between Classes in Victorian Society* (Oxford: Oxford University Press, 1971); and Gareth Stedman Jones, *Languages of Class: Studies in English Working-Class History, 1832–1982* (Cambridge: Cambridge University Press, 1983).

70. Alex Windscheffel, *Popular Conservatism in Imperial London 1868–1906* (Woodbridge; Boydell and Brewer, 2006).

71. Diana Elisabeth Banks-Conney, "Political Culture and the Labour Movement: A Comparison between Poplar and West Ham, 1889-1914" (PhD diss., University of Greenwich, 2005).

72. Stedman Jones, *Languages of Class*, 179.

73. London, *The People of the Abyss*, chap. 12, "Coronation Day."

74. Ibid.

75. Stedman Jones, *Languages of Class*, 179.

76. Hyndman, *Further Reminiscences*, 42.

77. Roy Porter, *London: A Social History* (London: Penguin Books, 1996), 306.

78. Ibid., 306–7.

79. Ibid., 307.
80. Charlton, *The Mass Movement and the New Unionism in Britain 1889*, 50.
81. See, for instance, Margaret Harkness, *In Darkest London* (London: Black Apollo Press, 2003); and George Gissing, *The Nether World,* ed. Stephen Gill (Oxford: Oxford University Press, 2008), originally published in 1889.
82. Giles and Lisanne Radice, *Will Thorne,* 14.
83. London, *The People of the Abyss,* 75.
84. Frederick Engels to Margaret Harkness, April 1888, Marx-Engels Correspondence.
85. George Shipton in the *Evening News and Post*, 1890, cited in Mann and Tillett, *The "New" Trades Unions*, 11.
86. On Hyndman and the SDF, see for instance Hobsbawm, *Labouring Men,* chap. 10. Mann's relationship with Hyndman is discussed in Dora Torr, *Tom Mann,* 12–13. Dona Torr, Tom Mann (London: Lawrence and Wishart, nd).
87. Arthur Field, "Eleanor Marx," *Social Democrat* 11/9 (September 1898): 265.
88. Ibid.
89. Anonymous Trade Unionist, "Organising the Great Unskilled: The Fighting History of the General Workers Union," *Pictorial Weekly* 124, no. 1603, 22 February 1930.
90. Louise Raw, Foreword by Sheila Rowbottom, *Striking a Light: The Bryant and May Matchwomen and Their Place in Labour History* (London: Continuum, 2009).
91. *British Weekly* Commissioners, *Toilers in London; or Inquiries Concerning Female Labour in the Metropolis* (London, 1889), 176.
92. Engels to Laura Lafargue, *Marx-Engels Correspondence*, 309. Emphasis in the original.
93. Karl Marx, "Introduction to Contribution to the Critique of Hegel's Philosophy of Right," Marx/Engels Internet Archive, http://www.marxists.org/archive/marx/works/1844/df-jahrbucher/law-abs.htm.
94. Kapp, *Eleanor Marx*, 336.
95. London Metropolitan Archives (hereafter LMA), "Minute Book of the India-Rubber, Gutta-Percha & Telegraph Works Co Ltd, Silvertown, July 5, 1888–April 21, 1892"; "Minutes of Special Meeting of the Board of Directors, Thursday December 12, 1889," B/BTR/IRGP/11.
96. See, for instance, Benjamin Stolberg, "Vigilantism,," *The Nation* 145/8 (14 August 1937): 166–68.
97. John Tully, "Silvertown 1889: The East End's Great Forgotten Strike," *Labour History Review* (forthcoming).
98. Saville, "Trade Unions and Free Labour.."
99. *ASE Monthly Journal,* February 1897.
100. Saville, "Trade Unions and Free Labour," 317.
101. "The Silvertown Strike," *East End News*, Tuesday, 19 November 1889.
102. See Buck, "Class Structure and Local Government Activity in West Ham," 59–66. The heavier industries in the older East End were dying out. See John Marriott, *Beyond the Tower: A History of East London* (New Haven and London: Yale University Press, 2011), 50. Nicholas Hedley Buck, "Class Structure and Local Government Activity in West Ham, 1886-1914", PhD diss., University of Kent at Canterbury, June 1980.
103. Buck, "Class Structure and Local Government Activity," 105.
104. Strictly speaking, it was the second, given that the Bryant and May's matchwomen's union later merged with the NUG&GL.
105. "The Gas Stokers at Upton Park. Want double pay for Sunday work. Women to be admitted to the Union," *Barking, East Ham and Ilford Advertiser*, Saturday, 7 September 1889.
106. London, *The People of the Abyss,* 225.
107. Calculated using Officer and Williamson, Measuring Worth tables. http://www.measuringworth.com/ukcompare/relativevalue.php.
108. "The Silvertown Strike," reprinted in the *East End News*, Tuesday, 19 November 1889.
109. "Termination of the Silvertown Strike," *Essex Standard, West Suffolk Gazette, and Eastern Counties' Advertiser,* Colchester, Saturday, 14 December 1889.

110. Algernon Charles Swinburne, *Songs Before Sunrise* (London: F. S. Ellis, 1871), 30.
111. Archer Philip Crouch, *Silvertown and Neighbourhood (including East and West Ham): A Retrospect* (London: Thomas Burleigh, 1900), 17.
112. W. R. Powell, ed., *A History of the County of Essex*, vol. 6 (1973), http:www.british-history.ac.uk/report.aspx?compid=42740.
113. Probably a corruption of "Duval's House," a pub built by a Dutchman called Duval. Crouch, *Silvertown and Neighbourhood*, 51–52.
114. Ibid., 199.
115. Powell, *A History of the County of Essex*.
116. Anon., *The Professional Excursions of an Auctioneer*, 1843, cited in Crouch, *Silvertown and Neighbourhood*, 49.
117. Ibid., 55.
118. Pagenstecher, *History of East and West Ham*, 216, cites Tacitus on the forcible employment of "native Britons" to work in clearing woods and draining marshes. Dale H. Porter writes that up to AD 1000, "Celts, Romans, and Anglo-Saxons build earthen dikes along the Thames riverbanks downriver of London for flood prevention. Romans embank the Thames for the first time, using the forced labor of Britons." See Dale H. Porter, *The Thames Embankment: Environment, Technology, and Society in Victorian London* (Akron, OH: University of Akron Press, 1998), 258.
119. Phillips, *A London Docklands Guide*, 44. North Woolwich, which was administratively part of Kent until the 1960s, later developed into an industrial center with a dockyard and the W.T. Henley Cable Works.
120. Crouch, *Silvertown and Neighbourhood*, 58.
121. Ibid., 61–62.
122. The first large industry on the marsh was C. J. Mare's shipyard.
123. Crouch, *Silvertown and Neighbourhood*, 63.
124. Tate & Lyle website, www.tateandlyle.com/AboutUs/history/Pages/History.aspx.
125. Cited in Newham History Workshop (hereafter NHW)n *A Marsh and a Gasworks: One Hundred Years of Life in West Ham* (Plaistow: Parents' Centre Publications, 1986), 8.
126. Buck, "Class Structure and Local Government Activity in West Ham," 59–60.
127. Stedman Jones, *Outcast London*, 20–24.
128. Buck, "Class Structure and Local Government Activity in West Ham," 59–60.
129. Gareth Stedman Jones, "Working-Class Culture and Working-Class Politics in London, 1870–1900; Notes on the Remaking of a Working Class," *Journal of Social History* 7/4 (Summer 1974): 464.
130. Buck, "Class Structure and Local Government Activity," 13.
131. Stedman Jones, *Outcast London*, 20.
132. John W. Marriott, "London Over the Border: A Study of West Ham during Rapid Growth, 1840–1910" (PhD diss., University of Cambridge, 1985), 29.
133. Cited in United Rubber Workers of America, *25 Years of the URW: A Quarter-Century Panorama of Democratic Unionism* (Akron, OH: United Rubber, Cork, Linoleum and Plastic Workers of America, AFL-CIO, 1960), not paginated.
134. Karl Marx and Frederick Engels, *Manifesto of the Communist Party*, in Marx and Engels, *Selected Works*, vol. I (Moscow: Progress Publishers, 1969), 111.
135. Buck, "Class Structure and Local Government," 69–71.
136. See Karl Marx, *Capital,* vol. 1, trans. Eden and Cedar Paul (London and New York: Everyman's Library, 1972), chap. 8.
137. Daniel Guérin, *Fascism and Big Business* (New York: Pathfinder Press, 1973). First published in 1939. The mass "shock troops" of fascism, he added, echoing Trotsky's analysis, were plebeian and petty bourgeois in social composition.
138. Buck, "Class Structure and Local Government," Appendix A, 399.
139. Stedman Jones, "Working-Class Culture," 464.
140. Buck, "Class Structure and Local Government," 65–66.
141. Ibid. Buck cites Leon Trotsky, *The Russian Revolution*, vol. 1, trans. Max Eastman (London: Sphere Books, 1967), 26–27. Large Petrograd factories such as the Putilov Works were hotbeds of industrial militancy and a bastion of support for the Russian Social Democratic Labor Party and later the Bolshevik faction. On page 27, Trotsky

claims that 41.4 percent of Russian industry in 1917 was super-large compared with 17.8 percent in America.
142. Banks-Conney, "Political Culture and the Labour Movement."
143. Using a process invented by the Glaswegian chemist and entrepreneur Charles Macintosh, sheets of vulcanized rubber were sandwiched between layers of cotton cloth. Vulcanization is the process patented by the American chemist Charles Goodyear in 1844 in which raw rubber is heated with sulfur to produce a substance that does not melt in hot weather or crack in cold, and lacks the unpleasant smell of the original. It is named after Vulcan, the Roman god of fire.
144. "Fashions," *Graphic*, Saturday, 8 September 1883.
145. Crouch, *Silvertown and Neighbourhood*, 63–64.
146. *West Ham, 1886–1986*, 64.
147. Calculated using Officer and Williamson, "Purchasing Power of British Pounds from 1245 to Present," http://www.measuringworth.com/ukcompare/result.php.
148. Crouch, *Silvertown and Neighbourhood*, 76.
149. LMA, B/BTR/IRGP/03, "Silver's India Rubber Works & Telegraph Cable Company Limited. Minutes of meeting of the Provisional Committee held at 77 Gresham House, March 23rd, 1864."
150. Ibid., Minutes of board meeting of 17 January 1866.
151. Ibid., Minutes of extraordinary board meeting, 10 January 1866.
152. This claim is made in Crouch, *Silvertown and Its Neighbourhood*, 75.
153. This claim is made in A. A. Foster, "The British Electrical Industry, 1875–1914: A Study of Three Essex-Based Engineering Companies Involved in Its Early Development," (Master of Studies diss., University of Cambridge, 30 August 1999), 15. This is an otherwise useful source.
154. "The Silvertown Strike," *Labour Elector*, Saturday, 5 October 1889.
155. See, for example, "Police," *Times*, Thursday, 12 December 1889.
156. *Stratford Express*, Saturday. 23 November 1889.
157. Foster, "The British Electrical Industry," 23.
158. Ibid., 17. See also, LMA, B/BTR/IRGP/13, in which the claim is supported by the minutes of the Board of Directors.
159. *London Gazette*, 18 April 1902.
160. "An interview with Mr. Gray," *Essex Standard*, Saturday, 23 November 1889.
161. Marx, *Capital*, 1:139.
162. "The India-Rubber, Gutta-Percha, and Telegraph Works Company, Limited," *Telegraphist: A Monthly Journal for Postal, Telephone, and Railway Telegraph Clerks*, 1 April 1887.
163. Foster, "The British Electrical Industry," 22.
164. Crouch, *Silvertown and Neighbourhood*, 90.
165. *Telegraphist*, 1 April 1887.
166. Crouch, *Silvertown and Neighbourhood*, 90.
167. *Telegraphist*, 1 April 1887.
168. Tom Standage, *The Victorian Internet: The Remarkable Story of the Telegraph and the Nineteenth Century's Online Pioneers* (London: Phoenix, 1999).
169. See for instance, George Johnson, ed., *The All Red Line: The Annals and Aims of the Pacific Cable Project* (Ottawa: James Hope, 1903); Christina Phelps Harris, "The Persian Gulf Submarine Telegraph of 1864," *Geographical Journal*, 135/2 (June 1969); and Daniel R. Headrick, *The Tentacles of Progress: Technology Transfer in the Age of Imperialism, 1850–1940* (Oxford: Oxford University Press, 1988),
170. Headrick, *The Tentacles of Progress*, 98.
171. H. V. Morton, *The Spell of London*, 12th ed. (London: Methuen, 1935), 132.
172. Crouch, *Silvertown and Neighbourhood*, 88.
173. *Telegraphist*, 1 April 1887.
174. Foster, "The British Electrical Industry," 15–16.
175. Crouch, *Silvertown and Neighbourhood*, 90.
176. Ibid., 11.
177. Calculated using Officer and Williamson, "Purchasing Power of British Pounds from 1245 to Present," http://www.measuringworth.com/indicator.php.

178. Ibid.
179. McGrath, *Silvertown*, 140.
180. Foster, "The British Electrical Industry," 18.
181. Ibid., 24–26.
182. Officer and Williamson, "Purchasing Power of British Pounds from 1245 to Present."
183. LMA, B/BTR/IRG/01, "Minutes of General Meetings, IRGP&W Co Ltd 1864–1918" "Minutes of ordinary general meeting, Tuesday, 28 February 1888," and "Minutes Half-Yearly Meeting of the Company, 19 July 1888."
184. Britain's domestic telegraphs, however, were nationalized in 1870 under the control of the Post Office.
185. For further reading, see John Tully, "A Victorian Ecological Disaster: Imperialism, the Telegraph, and Gutta-Percha," *Journal of World History* 20/4 (December 2009): 559–79; and Tully, *The Devil's Milk*, 123–29.
186. "The Silvertown Telegraph Works," *Standard*, Monday, 23 August 1869.
187. Ibid.
188. *Telegraphist,* 1 April 1887.
189. Foster, "The British Electrical Industry," 22–23.
190. *Telegraphist,* April 1, 1887. See also Tully, *The Devil's Milk,* chap. 8; and Tully, "A Victorian Ecological Disaster."
191. *Telegraphist,* 1 April 1887.
192. Foster, "The British Electrical Industry," 17.
193. Tully, "A Victorian Ecological Disaster," 575.
194. Crouch, *Silvertown and Neighbourhood*, 89.
195. *Telegraphist,* 1 April 1887.
196. Robert Went, *Globalization: Neoliberal Challenge, Radical Responses,* trans. Peter Drucker (London: Pluto Press, 2000), 67.
197. Tully, *The Devil's Milk*, 69–70.
198. Foster, "The British Electrical Industry," 26.
199. Calculated using http://www.measuringworth.com/ukcompare/result.php.
200. Ibid.
201. *Electrical Engineer*, 14 February 1890.
202. *Times*, 8 October 1868.
203. London, *The People of the Abyss*, 50.
204. The attribution is disputed, but it is clear that they were Rhodes's sentiments.
205. Porter, *London: A Social History*, 225.
206. Bertolt Brecht, *The Threepenny Opera* (Harmondsworth: Penguin Classics, 2007) 91.
207. Michael Ball and David Sunderland, *An Economic History of London, 1800–1914* (London: Routledge, 2001), 4.
208. *Cobbett's Weekly Political Register,* London, 5 January 1822, cited in Asa Briggs, *Victorian Cities* (Harmondsworth: Penguin, 1968), 59.
209. Cited in Briggs, *Victorian Cities*, 75.
210. Patrick Geddes, *Cities in Evolution* (London: 1949), cited in Briggs, *Victorian Cities*, 12.
211. Briggs, *Victorian Cities*, 317.
212. Cited in ibid., 317–18.
213. London, *The People of the Abyss*, 7.
214. Ibid., 228.
215. Ibid., 2.
216. Walter Benjamin, "On the Concept of History," 1940, http://www.marxists.org/reference/archives/benjamin/1940/history.htm. Emphasis added.
217. Bertolt Brecht, "Questions from a Worker Who Reads," in *Bertolt Brecht Poems 1913–1956,* ed. John Willett and Ralph Manheim with Erich Fried (New York: Methuen, 1976), 252.
218. Brecht, *The Threepenny Opera*, 61.
219. Ibid., 57.
220. Cited in Ellen Ross, ed., *Slum Travelers in London: Ladies and London Poverty, 1860–1920* (Berkeley: University of California Press, 2007), 7.

221. *British Weekly* Commissioners, *Toilers in London*, 214.
222. The metaphor was originally that of the English economist J. A. Hobson. See his *Imperialism: A Study* (Ann Arbor: University of Michigan Press, 1972). Originally published in 1902.
223. See, for instance, Tully, *The Devil's Milk*, pt. 2.
224. London, *The People of the Abyss*, 6.
225. Edward Aveling and Eleanor Marx Aveling, *The Factory Hell*, Socialist Platform No. 3 (London: Socialist League, 1885).
226. McGrath, *Silvertown*, 34.
227. Torr, *Tom Mann, 9*.
228. London, *The People of the Abyss*, 40.
229. Cited in Fishman, *East End 1888*, 11.
230. Thorne, *My Life's Battles*, 54.
231. London, *The People of the Abyss*, 254.
232. "Silvertown as It Is," London *Daily News*, Wednesday, 30 November 1881.
233. Cited in Chushiehi Tsuzuki, *The Life of Eleanor Marx, 1855–1898: A Socialist Tragedy* (Oxford: Clarendon Press, 1967), 198.
234. J. J. Terrett, *"Municipal Socialism" in West Ham: A Reply to 'The Times,' and Others* (London: Twentieth Century Press, ca. 1902), 5. St. Helens and Widnes were grim industrial towns in south Lancashire. Much of what George Orwell later wrote in *The Road to Wigan Pier* could also describe them.
235. Howarth and Wilson, *West Ham*, 58. Edward G. Howarth and Mona Wilson, *West Ham: A Study in Social and Industrial Problems* (London: J. M. Dent, 1907), 58.
236. Essex Record Office (ERO), Chelmsford, Essex, T/Z 25/407-459, "Memories of an anonymous Silvertown resident." Contained in a file of recollections from old people's centers in Essex dating from 1961.
237. Howarth and Wilson, *West Ham*, 58.
238. Pagenstecher, *History of East and West Ham*, 102.
239. Terrett, *"Municipal Socialism" in West Ham*, 5.
240. *London Gazette*, 18 April 1902.
241. "London Over the Border," *Daily News*, Wednesday, 30 November 1881.
242. Charles Dickens, *Household Words* (London: September 12, 1857); cited in Crouch, *Silvertown and Neighbourhood*, 66.
243. "Silvertown as It Is," *Daily News*, Wednesday 30 November 1881.
244. Herbert Spencer, *The Principles of Biology* (London: Williams and Norgate, 1864), http://www.archive.org/details/principlesbiolo05spengoog.
245. Marx, *Capital*, 1:274.
246. Porter, *The Thames Embankment*, 57.
247. Grace Foakes, *Four Meals for Fourpence* (London: Virago, 2011), 10.
248. Duncan Barrett and Nuala Calvi, *The Sugar Girls: Tales of Hardship, Love and Happiness in Tate & Lyle's East End* (London: Collins, 2012), 179–80.
249. NHW, *A Marsh and a Gasworks*, 31.
250. Crouch, *Silvertown and Neighbourhood*, 68.
251. "Silvertown as It Is," *Daily News*, Wednesday 30 November 1881.
252. Barrett and Calvi, *The Sugar Girls*, 191–92.
253. NHW, *A Marsh and a Gasworks*, 7.
254. Terrett, *"Municipal Socialism" in West Ham*, 5.
255. Cited in McGrath, *Silvertown*, 33.
256. London, *The People of the Abyss*, 44.
257. The fog lent its name to the thick green pea and ham soup still favored by Londoners.
258. Crouch, *Silvertown and Neighbourhood*, 71.
259. Interview with Mick and Rose Geany, ECH, Silvertown, 2 March 2000.
260. Morton, *Heart of London*, 34.
261. Howarth and Wilson, *West Ham*, 58.
262. Dickens, *Household Words*, cited in Crouch, *Silvertown and Neighbourhood*, 66.
263. Ibid., 86.
264. Barrett and Calvi, *The Sugar Girls*, 168.

265. Porter, *London: A Social History*, 232.
266. Crouch, *Silvertown and Neighbourhood*, 64.
267. Porter, *London: A Social History*, 232.
268. Interview with Ken and June Griffiths, ECH, North Woolwich, 12 December 2002.
269. Ibid.
270. LMA, B/BTR/ IRGP/01, "Minutes Book, General Meetings IRGP"; "Minutes of Extraordinary General Meeting, Held at the London Tavern, Thursday 30 June 1864."
271. "Terrible Explosion at Silvertown," *Daily News,* Wednesday, 30 November 1880.
272. "Fatal Explosion Near North Woolwich," *Penny Illustrated Paper*, Saturday, 17 April 1880.
273. "The Explosion at Silvertown," *Graphic*, Saturday, 24 April 1880.
274. "Great Fire at Silvertown," *Standard*, Monday, 8 February 1886.
275. "Great Fire at Silvertown," *Reynold's Newspaper*, Sunday, 12 June 1887.
276. "The Fatal Boiler Explosion at Silvertown," *Morning Post,* 18 August 1897.
277. Ibid. "Fire at Silvertown," Tuesday, 4 April 1899.
278. Blake, *The Great Explosion*; and Hill and Bloch, *The Silvertown Explosion*.
279. "Tragedy at Silvertown," *Lloyd's Weekly Newspaper,* Sunday, 17 July 1892; and "Tragedy at Silvertown," *Illustrated Police News*, Saturday, 23 July 1892.
280. "Tragedy at Silvertown," *Illustrated Police News*, Saturday, 23 July 1892.
281. NHW, *A Marsh and a Gasworks*, 1.
282. Ibid.
283. Ibid., 20.
284. "Memories of an anonymous Silvertown resident."
285. Ibid.
286. Crouch, *Silvertown and Neighbourhood*, 67.
287. Raw, *Striking a Light*.
288. Marriott, *Beyond the Tower*, 80.
289. James Thorold Rogers, *Six Centuries of Work and Wages: The History of English Labour* (London: Swan Sonnensschein, 1884), 538.
290. London, *The People of the Abyss*, 219.
291. Stan Dyson, Silvertown resident and writer, personal communication to the author, 22 February 2012.
292. Howarth and Wilson, *West Ham*, 58. "Coppers" in this sense were large metal basins in which the weekly wash was boiled before being laboriously rinsed and wrung out.
293. Porter, *London: A Social History*, 253. The author does not give any sources for this information.
294. London, *The People of the Abyss*, 217.
295. Howarth and Wilson, *West Ham*, 10–12.
296. Ibid.
297. *Stratford Express*, Wednesday, 9 October 1889.
298. Interview with Alfie, Eddie, Norman and Rose, ECH, Cundy's pub, Silvertown, 28 February 2000.
299. Dickens, *Household Words*, cited in Crouch, *Silvertown*, 66.
300. Crouch, *Silvertown and Neighbourhood*, 67.
301. Mrs. Pember Reeves, *Round About a Pound a Week* (London: G. Bell and Sons, 1914), 55, 61.
302. C. F. G. Masterman, ed., *The Heart of Empire* (repr. London: Harvester Press, 1973), cited in Banks-Conney, "Political Culture and the Labour Movement," 35.
303. NHW, *A Marsh and a Gasworks*, 34. Emphasis added.
304. Banks-Conney, "Political Culture and the Labour Movement," 35.
305. Interview with Alfie, ECH, Cundy's pub, Silvertown, 28 February 2000.
306. Dickens, *Household Words*, cited in Crouch, *Silvertown and Neighbourhood*, 66.
307. Crouch, *Silvertown and Neighbourhood*, 67.
308. Donald McDougall, ed., *Fifty Years a Borough, 1886–1936: The Story of West Ham* (West Ham: County Borough Council of West Ham, 1936), 100.
309. Howarth and Wilson, *West Ham*, 60.
310. Robert Woods and Nicola Shelton, *An Atlas of Victorian Mortality* (Liverpool: Liverpool University Press, 1997), 50.

311. "List of countries by infant mortality rate," http://en.wikipedia.org/wiki/List_of_countries_by_infant_mortality_rate.

312. Foakes, *Four Meals for Fourpence*, 73.

313. Woods and Shelton, *An Atlas of Victorian Mortality*, 68.

314. Ibid., 83.

315. Interview with Rose, ECH, Cundy's pub, Silvertown, 28 February 2000.

316. Quoted in "Silvertown: The Strike at Messrs. Silver's Works," *Stratford Express*, Saturday, 5 October 1889.

317. Bill Luckin, "Evaluating the Sanitary Revolution: Typhus and Typhoid in London, 1851–1900," in *Urban Disease and Mortality in Nineteenth-Century England,* ed. Robert Woods and Joan Woodward (London: Batsford Academic and Educational, 1984), 116.

318. Interview with A.B., ECH, "Hidden Histories: Stories from Silvertown," http://www.hidden-histories.org.uk/wordpress/?page_id=180.

319. McDougall, *Fifty Years a Borough*, 101.

320. NHW, *A Marsh and a Gasworks*, 30.

321. LMA, B/BTR/1/IRGP/11, "Minutes of Silver's Board of Directors Meeting," 10 January 1889.

322. Cited in Fishman, *East End 1888,* 237.

323. Elizabeth A. Cundy was married to Simeon Cundy, nine years her senior. The pub appears to have been built in 1871, with Francis James Pierson as the first landlord. See "History of Stratford, Silvertown Index," http://historyofstratford.co.uk/Silvertown/Silvertown-index.shtml. The pub closed its doors in 2008 after an altercation with the local council over substandard residential rooms.

324. Thorne, *My Life's Battles*, 44.

325. *Stratford Express,* Saturday, 7 December 1889.

326. Pember Reeves, *Round About a Pound a Week,* 9-10, 76.

327. Derek Matthews, "1889 and All That: New Views on the New Unionism," *International Review of Social History* 36 (1991): 32.

328. Interview with Connie Hunt, ECH, North Woolwich, 12 June 2003.

329. Mr. Podsnap was a character in Charles Dickens's novel *Our Mutual Friend,* a religious hypocrite who excused the suffering of the poor by misquoting the biblical injunction that "the poor are always with us."

330. Sims, *Horrible London*, 119.

331. *Stratford Express,* 15 July 1905, cited in Banks-Conney, "Political Culture and the Labour Movement," 65.

332. Phillips, *A London Docklands Guide*, 44.

333. Cited in Fishman, *East End 1888,* 155.

334. Brecht, *The Threepenny Opera*, 57.

335. Tillett, *Memories and Reflections*, 92.

336. Quoted in the *Stratford Express,* Saturday, 7 December 1889.

337. "Memories of an anonymous Silvertown resident."

338. Foakes, *Four Meals for Fourpence*, 127.

339. Stories from Silvertown.

340. Interview with Connie Hunt, ECH, North Woolwich, 12 June 2003.

341. Foakes, *Four Meals for Fourpence*, 277.

342. ECH, Stories from Silvertown.

343. *British Weekly* Commissioners, *Toilers in London*, 1889, 176.

344. Thomas Hood, "The Song of the Shirt," Poem Hunter website, http://www.poemhunter.com/poem/the-song-of-the-shirt/.

345. Proverbs 24:20, King James Edition of 1611 (London: British and Foreign Bible Society, Eyre and Spottiswoode, 1837), 693.

346. Engels to Guesde, 20 November 1889, Marx-Engels Correspondence.

347. Saville, "Trade Unions and Free Labour," 322–23.

348. LMA, B/BTR/IRGP/11, "Board Minutes of the India Rubber, Gutta Percha and Telegraph Works Co. Ltd, Silvertown, July 5 1888–April 21 1892"; "Board of Directors Minutes, 11 & 25 April and 9 & 16 May 1889."

349. Ibid., 12 September 1889.
350. Harry Stone, letter to the editor, *IRJ*, 8 November 1889.
351. Ibid.
352. "The Silvertown Strike," *Labour Elector* No. 40, Saturday, 5 October 1889.
353. "Silvertown Strike at Silver's Factory," *Stratford Express*, Saturday, 28 September 1889.
354. Thorne, *My Life's Battles*, 91.
355. LMA, Silver's Board of Directors minutes, Thursday 19 September 1889.
356. "Silvertown: The Strike at Messrs Silver's Works," *Stratford Express*, 2 October 1889.
357. "Our Family History," Peerage website, http://thepeerage.com/index.htm.
358. Saville, "Trade Unions and Free Labour," 335.
359. See Edward Bristow, "The Liberty and Property Defence League and Individualism," *Historical Journal* 18/4 (1975): 761–89.
360. Kapp, *Eleanor Marx*, 345.
361. London, *The People of the Abyss*, 145.
362. "The Silvertown Strike," *Labour Elector*, Saturday, 5 October 1889.
363. Information from the *Electrical Engineer*, vol. 5, new series, 14 February 1890; LMA, B/BTR/IRGP/03, "Silver's India Rubber Works & Telegraph Cable Company, Limited, Minutes of meeting of the provisional committee held at 77 Gresham House, 23 March 1864"; LMA, B/BTR/IRGP/11, "Board minutes of the India Rubber, Gutta Percha and Telegraph Works Co Ltd, Silvertown, 5 July 1888-21 April 1892."
364. "The Silvertown Strike," *Labour Elector*, Saturday, 5 October 1889. Some details in this paragraph are from ThePeerage.com website.
365. Some information is from "The Strike at Silvertown," *IRJ 6/3*, 3 October 1889; and LMA, B/BTR IRGP/01, "IRGP&TW Co Ltd, Minutes General Meetings. 1864–1918"; "Minutes of ordinary general meeting, 14 February 1890."
366. Ibid., Minutes.
367. LMA, B/BTR/IRGP/11, "Board Minutes of the India Rubber, Gutta Percha and Telegraph Works Co Ltd, Silvertown, 5 July 1888—21 April 1892"; "Minutes of the meeting of the Board of Directors, Thursday 1 November 1888."
368. "The Finances of the Silvertown Company," *Labour Elector*, Saturday, 12 October 1889.
369. Ibid., "The Shareholders," No. 40, Saturday 5 October 1889.
370. John D. Pickles, "Latham, Henry (1821–1902)," *Oxford Dictionary of National Biography*, http://www.oxforddnb.com/view/article/34417.
371. Foster, "The British Electrical Industry," 26.
372. Calculated using http://www.measuringworth.com/ukcompare/result.php.
373. *Electrical Engineer* 5/14, February 1890.
374. "Collapse of the Silvertown Strike," *Commonweal*, 14 December 1889.
375. "The India Rubber Works, Silvertown," *Stratford Express,* Wednesday, 18 September 1889.
376. Ibid., *Stratford Express*, Saturday, 21 September 1889.
377. LMA, B/BTR/IRGP/11, "Minutes of Meeting of Board of Directors, 19 September 1889."
378. "The India Rubber Works," *Stratford Express*, Saturday, 21 September 1889.
379. "Strikes," *Times*, Friday, 20 September 1889.
380. "Silvertown: Strike at Silver's Factory," *Stratford Express*, Saturday, 28 September 1889.
381. *Electrical Engineer,* 5/14, February 1890.
382. "End of the London Strike," *East and West Ham Gazette*, Saturday, 21 September 1889.
383. Karl Marx, "Wages of Labour," First Manuscript, *Economic and Philosophical Manuscripts*, 1844, http//marx.eserver.org/1844-ep.manuscripts/1ˢᵗ.manuscript/1-labor.wages.txt.
384. Reported in the *Times*, Monday, 14 October 1889.
385. Victoria and Albert Museum, *Penny Dreadfuls and Comics: English Periodicals from Victorian Times to the Present Day* (London: V & A Museum, 1983), 6.

386. Engels to Laura Lafargue, 17 October 1889, in Engels, Paul and Laura Lafargue, *Correspondence*, vol. 2.
387. E. Belfort Bax, *Reminiscences and Reflections of a Mid- and Late Victorian* (London: 1918), chap. 5, Marxists Internet Archive,http://www.marxists.org/archive/bax/1918autobiog/index.htm.
388. Engels, *Correspondence*, vol. 2. Editor's note to Paul Lafargue to Engels, 4 August 1889.
389. "The Strike at Silvertown," *IRJ*, 6/3, 3 October 1889.
390. "Silvertown: The Strike at Messrs Silver's Works," *Stratford Express,* Wednesday, 2 October 1889.
391. "The Silvertown Strike," *East End News*, Tuesday, 19 November 1889.
392. Wm. J. Tyler, letter to the editor, *East End News,* Tuesday, 22 October 1889. He repeated his claims in a letter to the *Labour Elector* published on 12 October 1889 and in numerous other newspapers.
393. W. J. Davis, *The British Trades Union Congress: History and Recollections* (London: TUC Parliamentary Committee, 1910), 29. Repr. as F. M. Leventhal, ed., *The World of Labour: English Workers, 1850–1890* (New York and London: Garland Publishers, 1984).
394. For example, London Metropolitan University, TUC Library, Minute Book vol. 6. 1889 (Jan 3)–1891 (April 2); Minutes of Executive Council Meeting London Trades Council (LTC); Minutes of Council Meeting, 16 May 1889. The bounty was a government subsidy paid to producers of beet sugar to enable them to compete with cane sugar from the West Indies—a puzzle, given that the ex-slave-owning planters were themselves British!
395. Ibid., 18 April 1889.
396. *Times,* 2 December 1889.
397. Minutes of LTC Council Meeting, 5 December 1889.
398. *Times,* 2 December 1889.
399. "Silvertown: The Strike at Messrs Silver's Works," *Stratford Express*, Wednesday, 2 October 1889.
400. Ibid., Saturday, 7 December 1889.
401. See George Lansbury, *Smash Up the Workhouse* (London: National Labour Press, ca. 1909); and London, *The People of the Abyss*. Originating in 1381, the system lingered on, under different names, until its final abolition in 1948.
402. Wm. J. Tyler, letter to the editor, *East End News*, 22 October 1889.
403. *Times,* 2 December 1889.
404. "The Silvertown Strike," *IRJ* 6/5, 9 December 1889.
405. "Silvertown: The Strike at Messrs Silver's Works," *Stratford Express*, Wednesday, 2 October 1889.
406. *Stratford Express*, 7 December 1889.
407. *British Weekly* Commissioners, *Toilers in London*, 1889, 174.
408. Quoted in the *Times*, 12 October 1889.
409. National Minimum Wage Rates, at http://www.direct.gov.uk/en/Employment/Employees/TheNationalMinimumWage/DG_10027201.
410. Relative Values of Sums of Money, Nominal Annual Earnings for Various Occupations in England and Wales, 1710–1911, http://privatewww.essex.ac.uk/~alan/family/N-money.html.
411. Estimates based on figures in Ross, *Slum Travelers*, xiv.
412. Relative Values of Sums of Money, Nominal Annual Earnings for Various Occupations in England and Wales, 1710–1911.
413. See Historical UK Inflation and Price Converter at http://safalra.com/other/historical-uk-inflation-price-conversion/.
414. "Life on a Guinea a Week," *Nineteenth-Century: A Monthly Review* (London: Sampson, Low, Marston, 1888), 464.
415. Ibid.
416. Foakes, *Four Meals for Fourpence*, 64.
417. Ibid., 57.

418. "The Silvertown Strike," *Times*, 10 December 1889.
419. ECH, Stories From Silvertown.
420. Interview with Rose, ECH, Cundy's pub, Silvertown, 28 February 2000.
421. Marx, *Capital*, 1;232.
422. Cecil Frances Alexander, *Hymns for Little Children*, 5th ed. (London: Joseph Masters, 1852).
423. "Silvertown Strike," *Justice*, 26 October 1889.
424. "The Silvertown Strike," reprinted in *East End News*, 19 November 1889.
425. Mother Jones, *The Autobiography of Mother Jones*, chap. 27. http://www.angelfire.com/nj3/RonMBaseman/mojones.htm. First published 1925.
426. J. P. McKay, *The Moral and Physical Conditions of the Working Classes*, 1832, cited in Marx, *Capital*, 1:451.
427. Wm. J. Tyler, letter to the editor, *East End News*, Tuesday, 22 October 1889.
428. "The Silvertown Strike," *IRJ* 6/5, 9 December 1889.
429. "Silvertown: The Strike at Messrs Silver's Works," *Stratford Express,* Wednesday, 2 October 1889.
430. Ibid.
431. "The Silvertown Strike," *Labour Elector* 2/4 , Saturday 5 October 1889.
432. "Silvertown: The Strike at Messrs Silver's Works," *Stratford Express,* 2 October 1889.
433. "The Silvertown Strike," *Labour Elector,* 5 October 1889.
434. Marx, *Capital*, 1:630.
435. The Silvertown Strike," *IRJ* 6/3, 3 October 1889.
436. Marx, *Capital*, 1:269-270.
437. "Silvertown: The Strike at Messrs Silver's Works," *Stratford Express,* 2 October 1889.
438. Wm. J. Tyler, letter to the editor, *East End News*, Tuesday, 8 October 1889.
439. Harry Stone, letter to the editor, *IRJ* 6/4, 8 November 1889.
440. *Times*, 2 December 1889.
441. *Stratford Express*, 16 October 1889.
442. *Stratford Express*, 7 December 1889.
443. Ibid.
444. "Silvertown: The Strike at Messrs Silver's Works," *Stratford Express,* Saturday, 5 October 1889.
445. Woods and Shelton, *An Atlas of Victorian Mortality*, 27.
446. *Times*, Monday, 14 October 1889.
447. W. Stephen Sanders, *Early Socialist Days* (London: Hogarth Press, 1927), 12.
448. London, *The People of the Abyss*, chap. 10.
449. Marx, *Capital*, 1:698.
450. Cited in Charlton, *The Mass Movement and New Unionism in Britain 1889*, 78.
451. "The Silvertown Telegraph Works," *Financial Times*, 15 February 1890. The article is a paraphrase of remarks made by Samuel Silver to a shareholders' meeting after the end of the strike.
452. Wm. J. Tyler, letter to the editor, *East End News*, 8 October 1889.
453. See the *Stratford Express*, Wednesday 20 November 1889. Kapp describes Ling as a semiskilled worker; Kapp, *Eleanor Marx*, 344.
454. *Stratford Express*, Saturday, 12 October 1889.
455. University of Warwick, Modern Records Centre (hereafter UW MRC), MSS.192/GL/4, "First Yearly Report and Balance Sheet of the National Union of Gasworkers and General Labourers of Great Britain and Ireland (NUG&GL), 1889."
456. Ibid., "Second Yearly Report and Balance Sheet of the NUG&GL, 1891."
457. Ibid., "Quarterly Balance Sheet of the NUG&GL January 1 to March 31 1898."
458. Ling does not seem to have been chairman of the Strike Committee. A report in the *Standard* of 30 September 1889 informs us that "Mr. Long" was a speaker at a rally in Hyde Park the day before and that he was Secretary of the Silvertown branch of the NUG&GL.
459. UW MRC, MSS.192/GL/4, "General Secretary's Balance Sheet for the Quarter ending June 30th 1906."
460. A Frederick George Ling, age not recorded, died in London in 1906. Register of deaths, July–August–September 1906. Ling is a fairly common English surname.

461. Gray died on 16 December 1901. *London Gazette*, 18 April 1902.
462. British Library, St. Pancras, British Labour History. Ephemera, 1880–1900, MFR 2454, Item 15, Edward Aveling, "The Eight-Hours Working Day."
463. *Stratford Express*, 13 September 1890.
464. See, for instance, "The Silvertown Strike. A Colchester Man Maltreated," *Essex Standard*, Saturday, 14 December 1889.
465. "The Silvertown Strike," *Times*, 10 December 1889.
466. "Silvertown: The Strike at Messrs Silver's Works," *Stratford Express*, 2 October 1889.
467. UW MRC, MSS 259/ASE/1/1/64, Amalgamated Society of Engineers (ASE) Executive Council (EC), "Minutes of meeting of Friday night, 4 October 1889."
468. LMA B/BTR/IRGP/11, "Board of Directors minutes, Thursday, 26 September 1889."
469. "Silvertown: The Strike at Messrs Silver's Works," *Stratford Express*, Wednesday, 2 October 1889.
470. Ibid.
471. Ibid.
472. "Silvertown: What Does the ASE Say?" *Labour Elector* No 48, Saturday, 30 November 1889.
473. LMA. B/BTR/IRGP/11, "Minutes of Silver's Board meeting, Thursday 5 December 1889."
474. "Mr. Gray of Silvertown," *Labour Elector* No 53, Saturday, 4 January 1890.
475. *Stratford Express*, Wednesday, 2 October 1889.
476. Ibid.
477. Ibid.
478. Calculated using http://www.measuringworth.com/ukcompare/result.php.
479. "The Tailors' Strike," *Standard*, Monday, 30 September 1889.
480. William J. Fishman, *East End Jewish Radicals, 1875–1914* (London: Duckworth, 1975), 169, 322.
481. Sanders, *Early Socialist Days,* 52.
482. For details of Will Thorne's life and work, see Giles and Lisanne Radice, *Will Thorne: Constructive Militant*; Thorne, *My Life's Battles*; and François Bédarida, *Will Thorne: La voie anglaise du socialisme* (Paris: Fayard, 1987).
483. Engels to Laura Lafargue, 17 October 1889, in Frederick Engels, Paul and Laura Lafargue, *Correspondence*, vol. 1, 1868–1886 (Moscow: Foreign Languages Publishing House, 1959), 331.
484. Hyndman, *Further Reminiscences*, 51. Burns's subsequent political career is sketched out in the Epilogue to this book.
485. Engels to Laura Lafargue, 27 August 1889, Engels, Lafargue and Lafargue, *Correspondence*, 1: 304.
486. Sanders, *Early Socialist Days*, 24.
487. Ibid.
488. Thorne, *My Life's Battles*, 92.
489. Ibid., 94–95.
490. Matthews, "1889 and All That," 32.
491. "Silvertown: The Strike at Messrs Silver's Works," *Stratford Express*, Wednesday, 2 October 1889.
492. "The Silvertown Strike," *Labour Elector* No. 40, Saturday, 5 October 1889.
493. "Silvertown: The Strike at Messrs Silver's Works," *Stratford Express*, 2 October 1889.
494. "The Silvertown Strike," *Labour Elector* No.no 40, Saturday, 5 October 1889.
495. Thorne, *My Life's Battles*, 96.
496. "Silvertown. The Strike at Messrs Silver's Works," *Stratford Express*, Wednesday, 2 October 1889.
497. Ibid.
498. "Silvertown: The Strike at Messrs Silver's Works," *Stratford Express*, Saturday, 5 October 1889.
499. LMA, B/BTR/IRGP/11, "Minutes of Silver's Board meeting of Thursday, 10 October 1889."

500. *Stratford Express*, Wednesday, 9 October 1889.
501. Ibid.
502. Ibid.
503. For instance, Ross, *Slum Travelers*, 5.
504. Engels to Laura Lafargue, 17 October 1889, Engels, Paul and Laura Lafargue, *Correspondence*, vol. 2: 1887–1890, 330.
505. Laura Lafargue to Engels, Thursday, 14 November 1889, ibid., 338.
506. "Silvertown," *Penny Illustrated Paper*, Saturday, 14 December 1889.
507. Tillett, *Memories and Reflections*, 135.
508. Mann, *Memoirs*, 92.
509. Field, "Eleanor Marx," 259.
510. Hyndman, *Further Reminiscences*, 147.
511. Olga Meier, commentary and notes, *The Daughters of Karl Marx: Family Correspondence, 1866–1898,* trans. and adapted by Faith Evans with an introduction by Sheila Rowbotham (Harmondsworth: Penguin, 1984), xxvii.
512. Ibid.
513. Edward Aveling and Eleanor Marx-Aveling, *The Woman Question* (London: Swan, Sonnenschein, Lowery, 1887), 6. It is likely that Marx was the book's primary author.
514. The sobriquet is mentioned in Bax, *Reminiscences and Reflections of a Mid- and Late Victorian*. It is repeated by a number of later authors including Ronald Florence, *Marx's Daughters: Eleanor Marx, Rosa Luxemburg, Angelica Balabanoff* (New York: Dial Press, 1975), 58, 199.
515. *Stratford Express*, 9 October 1889.
516. Buck, "Class Structure and Local Government Activity in West Ham," 105.
517. John Stokes, Introduction, in *Eleanor Marx (1855–1898): Life, Work, Contacts,* ed. John Stokes (Aldershot, Hants: Ashgate, 2000), 7.
518. Eleanor Marx, "Women's Trade Unions in England," http://www.marxists.org/archive/draper/1976/women/5-emarx.html.
519. Ibid.
520. Eleanor Marx, letter to the editor, *Pall Mall Gazette*, 13 November 1887, cited in Stokes, *Eleanor Marx*, 5.
521. Aveling and Marx, *The Woman Question*, 16.
522. Tsuzuki, *The Life of Eleanor Marx*, 2.
523. Henrik Ibsen, *An Enemy of the People: Play in Five Acts,* ed. William Archer, trans. Eleanor Marx Aveling (London: Walter Scott, 1901); Henrik Ibsen, *The Lady from the Sea,* trans Eleanor Marx Aveling (Stilwell, KS: Digireads.com Publishing, 2008).
524. Stokes, *Eleanor Marx*, 4.
525. Lyn Pykett, "A Daughter of Today: The Socialist-Feminist Intellectual and Woman of Letters," in Stokes, *Eleanor Marx*, 7.
526. Cited in ibid., 16.
527. Marion Comyn, "My Recollections of Karl Marx," in *The Nineteenth Century and After* (1922), 91, cited in Pykett, "A Daughter of Today," 16.
528. Sanders, *Early Socialist Days*, 84–85.
529. Tsuzuki, *The Life of Eleanor Marx*, 2.
530. Ibid., 199.
531. Tsuzuki, *The Life of Eleanor Marx*, 321.
532. E. P. Thompson, "English Daughter," review of Yvonne Kapp's *Eleanor Marx: The Crowded Years*, in *New Society*, 3 March 1977, 457.
533. Interview with R.G., ECH, Stories From Silvertown.
534. LMA, B/BTR/IRGP/11, "Silver's Board minutes, Thursday, 10 October 1889."
535. UW, MSS 259/ASE/1/1/64, "ASE EC minutes, Wednesday, 16 October 1889."
536. *Stratford Express*, Saturday, 12 October 1889.
537. "Wages Questions," *Times*, Saturday, 12 October 1889.
538. "The Silvertown Strike," *Justice*, Saturday, 12 October 1889.
539. *Stratford Express*, Wednesday, 16 October 1889.
540. Mann, *Memoirs*, 87.
541. Tillett, *Memories and Reflections*, 18.

542. Ibid., 69.
543. Ibid., 91–92.
544. Stokes, *Eleanor Marx*, 7.
545. *Stratford Express*, Wednesday, 16 October 1889.
546. Ibid.
547. Hyndman, *Further Reminiscences*.
548. William Greenlade, "Revisiting Edward Aveling," in *Eleanor Marx (1855–1898): Life, Work, Contacts*, ed. John Stokes (Aldershot, Hants: Ashgate, 2000), 41. Havelock Ellis, "Eleanor Marx," parts 1 and 1, *Adelphi* (London: September 1935); and Hyndman, *Further Reminiscences*, also deal with his character at some length.
549. Greenlade, "Is This Friendship? Eleanor Marx, Margaret Harkness and the Idea of Socialist Community," in Stokes, *Eleanor Marx*, 133.
550. Greenlade, "Revisiting Edward Aveling," 42, 47.
551. Bax, *Reminiscences and Reflections*.
552. "Wages Questions," *Times*, Monday, 14 October 1889. The Patriotic Club's Clerkenwell Green premises are now occupied by the Marx Memorial Library.
553. *Justice*, Saturday, 21 September 1889.
554. "School Children on strike," *East and West Ham Gazette*, Saturday, 12 October 1889.
555. "Strike of School Children at East Ham," *Barking, East Ham and Ilford Advertiser*, Saturday, 12 October 1889.
556. Ibid., Saturday, 2 November 1889.
557. Kapp, *Eleanor Marx*, 348.
558. LMA, B/BTR/IRGP/11, "Minutes of Silver's Board meeting, 17 October 1889."
559. *Commonweal*, 19 October 1889.
560. *Stratford Express*, Wednesday, 23 October 1889.
561. Ibid.
562. Ibid.
563. "Help and Advice for Silver's Strikers," *Labour Elector* No. 43, Saturday, 26 October 1889.
564. "Bravo, Barking!" *Justice*, Saturday, 19 October 1889.
565. "Help and Advice for Silver's Strikers," *Labour Elector*.
566. *Stratford Express*, Saturday, 26 October 1889.
567. LMA, B/BTR/IRGP/11, "Minutes of Silver's Board meeting, 24 October 1889."
568. Kapp, *Eleanor Marx*, 350.
569. LMA, B/BTR/IRGP/13, Minutes of Silver's Board meeting, 19 November 1896.
570. LMA, B/BTR/IRGP/11, Minutes of Silver's Board meeting, 24 October 1889.
571. *Stratford Express*, 26 October 1889.
572. London Trades Council, Minute Book vol. 6, 1889 (Jan 3)–1891 (April 2), "Minutes of delegate meeting of 24 October 1889."
573. Ibid., minutes of Council meeting of 18 April 1889.
574. Ibid., minutes of Council meeting of 12 September 1889.
575. Ibid., minutes of Council meeting, 3 October 1889.
576. Tillett, *Memories and Reflections*, 93.
577. LTC, minutes of delegate meeting, 7 November 1889
578. Cooper and Parnell were delegates to the International Working Men's Association conference held in Paris in 1889 that set up the Second International.
579. Mann, *Memoirs*, 12.
580. Ibid., 41.
581. Torr, *Tom Mann*, 13.
582. Tillett, *Memories and Reflections*, 114–15.
583. Ibid.; Mann, *Memoirs*, 200. See also Ian Turner, "Anstey, Francis George (Frank), (1865–1940)," *Australian Dictionary of Biography*, http://adb.anu.edu.au/biography/anstey-francis-george-frank-5038.
584. "The Silvertown Strike," *Justice*, Saturday, 26 October 1889.
585. *Stratford Express,* Wednesday, 30 October 1889.
586. William Shakespeare, *The Tragedy of Othello the Moor of Venice*, Act 1, scene 3 (New York: Signet Classics, 1963), 58.

587. *Stratford Express,* Wednesday, 30 October 1889.
588. Victoria and Albert Museum, *Penny Dreadfuls and Comics: English Periodicals from Victorian Times to the Present Day* (London: V & A Museum, 1983), 73, and Denis Gifford, *Victorian Comics* (London: George Allen & Unwin, 1976), 9, 27.
589. *Stratford Express,* Wednesday, 30 October 1889.
590. LMA, B/BTR/IRGP/11, "Minutes of special Silver's Board meeting, Tuesday, 29 October 1889."
591. Ibid., Minutes of Board meeting, Thursday, 31 October 1889.
592. Ibid., Minutes of Board meeting, Saturday, 9 November 1889.
593. *Commonweal,* Saturday, 2 November 1889.
594. *Stratford Express,* Saturday, 9 November.
595. Ibid.
596. Cited in Hobsbawm, *Labouring Men,* 275.
597. In Britain, the term "engineer" often refers to skilled tradesmen such as fitters, tool-makers, and turners; called machinists in the United States. In this context it does not mean "professional" engineers, white-collar and supervisory staff who do not work "on the tools." Both types of engineers shared a common origin in the early years of the Industrial Revolution when the distinction between hand and brain work was blurred.
598. The turners were skilled engineers who operated lathes and other metal-shaping machinery to make or repair machine parts. The job is often combined with fitting work, hence the classification of fitter and turner, but this was not the case at Silver's. The smiths were skilled forge workers. Their actions indicate that at least some ASE men had a more inclusive class consciousness than their fellows. This fact has a bearing on the union's later trajectory toward the New Union model.
599. Amalgamated Society of Engineers, Rules (Part 1), as revised at the fourteenth delegate meeting, held at Manchester, 1915.
600. The union's full name was the Amalgamated Society of Engineers, Machinists, Millwrights, Smiths and Pattern-Makers. The Rules specified that workers in the following trades were eligible for membership: smiths, fitters, turners, pattern makers, millwrights, planers, borers, slotters, mechanical draftsmen, brass finishers, coppersmiths, machine joiners, and ship smiths. Seagoing engineers were also eligible for membership. See the *Rules of the Amalgamated Society of Engineers,* revised at Nottingham, May 25, 1885 (Melbourne: Australasian-American Trading Company, 1890).
601. Mann and Tillett, *The "New" Trades Unions,* 10.
602. UW, MRC MSS 259/ASE/1/1/65, "Minutes of ASE EC, 7 November 1889." The union was also to a degree multinational, with members in the United States, Canada, and South Africa, and branches in Australia and New Zealand. In 1920, it merged with nine other unions to form the Amalgamated Engineering Union, and subsequently went through numerous amalgamations to emerge as today's UNITE. See UNITE, The Union for Life, http://www.unitetheunion.org/about_us/history/history_of_aeeu.aspx.
603. Torr, *Tom Mann,* 8. The 1851 income would today be worth between £1.89 million (using the retail price index) and £53.6 million (as a share of GDP). The income for 1884 would today be worth between £12.7 million (using the retail price index) and £183 million (as a share of GDP). Calculated using http://www.measuringworth.com/ukcompare/.
604. ASE, *Rules,* 1915. In 1915, members in dispute could claim up to 10 shillings a week strike pay, depending on how much they paid in dues. Ten shillings is today worth between £31 and £144, depending on whether we use the retail price index or average earnings. Calculated using http://www.measuringworth.com/ppoweruk/ .
605. Helen Merrell Lynd, with an introduction by Gerald M. Pomper, *England in the Eighteen-Eighties: Toward a Social Basis for Freedom* (London: Oxford University Press), 260.
606. ASE, *Revised Rules,* 1885, 57.
607. Lynd, *England in the Eighteen-Eighties,* 261.
608. ASE, *Revised Rules,* 1885, 7.

609. Torr, *Tom Mann*, 4.
610. Cited in Gordon Scheffer, *Light and Liberty: Sixty Years of the Electrical Trades Union* (Hayes, Bromley, Kent: ETU, c1949), 4.
611. George Stephenson did not undergo a formal apprenticeship. He started work as a colliery engineman and banksman before being promoted to enginewright. He went on to become one of the most celebrated engineers of all time. One wonders if the ASE leaders ever pondered this. The Akron-born inventor Stan Ovshinsky, a toolmaker by trade, is an excellent contemporary example of the self-taught engineer-inventor. He was also a socialist.
612. R. Angus Buchanan, "Gentlemen Engineers: The Making of a Profession," *Victorian Studies* 26/4 (Summer 1983): 427–29.
613. Porter, *The Thames Embankment*, 174.
614. Mann, *Memoirs*, 16–18.
615. Hobsbawm, *Labouring Men*, 290.
616. Torr, *Tom Mann*, 4.
617. ASE, *Rules (Part 1)*, 1915. Rule 20.
618. UW, MRC MSS 259/ASE/1/1/63, ASE EC minutes, Wednesday 2 October 1889.
619. Women were only admitted to the Amalgamated Engineering Union in Australia in 1943. See Marian Aveling and Joy Damousi, *Stepping Out of History: Documents of Women at Work in Australia* (North Sydney: Allen & Unwin, 1991), 145–46.
620. Mann and Tillett, *The "New" Trades Unions*, 4.
621. Eric Hobsbawm, ed., Introduction, *Labour's Turning Point, 1880–1900: Extracts from Contemporary Sources*, 2nd ed. (Brighton: Harvester Press, 1974), 4.
622. Hobsbawm, *Labouring Men*, 291–92.
623. J. Lynch, cited in Hobsbawm, *Labour's Turning Point*, 4. In some instances, tradesmen's helpers were on day wages while the craftsmen they worked alongside were on piecework and thus had a pecuniary interest in screwing the maximum production from their laborers. It should be stressed that the ASE (unlike the Boilermakers) strongly opposed piecework, and it was an offence against the union's rules to seek where it was not in place. See ASE Revised Rules, 1885, 105.
624. Walter Wyckoff, cited in William James, "What Makes Life Significant?" Talks to Students, 1899, http://philosophy.lander.edu/intro/introbook2.1/c9204.html#FTN. AEN9239.
625. UW, MRC MSS 259/ASE/1/1/65m ASE EC minutes, Friday, 15 November 1889. See also ETU, *Souvenir of Fifty Years of the Electrical Trades Union, 1889-1939* (Manchester: ETU, 1939), 5. The engineers' and electricians' unions finally amalgamated in 1992, almost a century later.
626. Walter Southgate, ed., *That's the Way It Was: A Working-Class Autobiography* (London: New Clarion Press, 1982), 59. Afterword by Terry Philpot.
627. Mann and Tillett, *The "New" Trades Unions*, 4.
628. UW, MRC MSS 259/ASE/1/1/65, ASE EC minutes, 2 October and 4 October 1889.
629. Mann and Tillett, *The "New" Trades Unions*, 4.
630. Robert Knight candidly informed a parliamentary inquiry that his boilermakers' union could not afford an influx of new members as unemployed members were eligible for unemployment benefit and the union could not pay. Lynd, *England in the Eighteen-Eighties*, 260.
631. Hobsbawm, *Labouring Men*, 290.
632. Toolsetters are skilled engineering tradesmen employed to set up semiautomatic metal-shaping machines that are then worked by semiskilled operatives or process workers (or done automatically today). In 1889, the ASE EC gave their approval for the employment of toolsetters at Silver's. UW, MRC MSS 259/ASE/1/1/65, Minutes of ASE Executive Council, 7 November 1889–6 February 1890; Minutes of EC meeting of 26 November 1889.
633. The impact of the new technology on Silver's engineers, and their response to it in 1897, is discussed in the Epilogue of this book.
634. Ibid.
635. Mann and Tillett, *The "New" Trades Unions*, 13.

636. Hobsbawm, *Labouring Men*, 179–81.

637. Ibid.

638. Ibid., "General Labour Unions," 187–89.

639. *Times*, 2 December 1889.

640. *Stratford Express*, 2 October 1889.

641. *Stratford Express*, 5 October 1889.

642. UW, MRC MSS 259/ASE/1/1/64, Minutes of ASE's EC meeting, Friday night, 4 October 1889. Italics, punctuation and grammar as in the original.

643. *Labour Elector*, 9 November 1889.

644. UW, MSS 259/ASE/1/1/64, ASE EC minutes, 4 October 1889.

645. Ibid.

646. Ibid., ASE EC minutes, 15 October 1889.

647. Ibid., ASE EC minutes, 8 October 1889.

648. Ibid. ASE EC minutes, 11 October 1889.

649. Ibid. ASE EC minutes, 14 October 1889.

650. Ibid. ASE EC minutes, 16 October 1889.

651. *Star*, 13 October 1889.

652. UW, MSS 259/ASE/1/1/64, ASE EC minutes, 15 October 1889.

653. "Silvertown Blacklegs," *Labour Elector* No. 42, Saturday, 19 October 1889.

654. ASE EC minutes, 18 October 1889.

655. "Silvertown Strike," *Labour Elector* No. 43, 26 October 1889.

656. *Stratford Express*, 9 November 1889.

657. UW, MRC MSS 259/ASE/1/1/65, ASE EC minutes, 18 November 1889.

658. Ibid., ASE EC minutes, 19 November 1889.

659. Ibid., EC minutes, 20 November 1889.

660. "The Gas Stokers at Upton Park," *Barking, East Ham and Ilford Advertiser*, Saturday, 19 October 1889.

661. ASE EC minutes, 25 November 1889.

662. Ibid., EC Minutes, 26 November 1889.

663. Ibid., EC minutes, 27 November 1889.

664. Ibid., EC minutes, 29 November 1889.

665. W. B. Owen and Matthew Lee, "Thompson, William Marcus (1857–1907)," *Oxford Dictionary of National Biography*, http://www.oxforddnb.com.view/article/36497.

666. UW, MRC MSS 259/ASE/1/1/65, ASE EC minutes, 4 December 1889.

667. *Times*, Monday, 25 November 1889; and LMA, B/BTR/IRGP/11, Silver's Board minutes, 28 November 1889.

668. *Labour Elector* No. 48, Saturday, 30 November 1889.

669. "The Silvertown Strike: Summonses for Intimidation and Assault," *West Ham Guardian*, Saturday, 23 November 1889.

670. *Labour Elector* No. 48, Saturday, 30 November 1889. Emphasis added.

671. Ibid. No. 49, Saturday, 7 December 1889.

672. Ibid., 9 November 1889.

673. Letter from Robert Austin, ASE General Secretary, to the *Star*, 5 October 1889.

674. "Silvertown: Things Look More Hopeful," *Labour Elector*, Saturday, 7 December 1889.

675. "London Trades Council," *Labour Elector* No. 50, 14 December 1889.

676. Ibid.

677. "Collapse of the Silvertown Strike," *Commonweal*, 14 December 1889.

678. "Silvertown," *Labour Elector* No. 50, Saturday, 14 December 1889.

679. Frederick Engels to H. Schluter, trans. Dona Torr, 11 January 1890, *Marx and Engels Correspondence*. http://www.marxists.org/archive/marx/works/1890/letters/90_01_11.htm. Engels's claim that it was against the ASE's rules for fitters to work without laborers is not substantiated. There is nothing about this in the ASE's Revised Rules of 1885.

680. The ASE did change as a result of the efforts of George Barnes, Tom Mann, and other socialists. I must add that its successor, the AEU—or its Australian offshoot—was my first union and I remember it with respect and affection, not the least for living up to its motto of "Educate, Agitate, Organize."

681. Brecht, *Threepenny Opera*, 63.
682. Cited in Joan Ballhatchet, "The Police and the London Dock Strike of 1889," *History Workshop Journal* 32/1 (1991): 54.
683. Engels to Laura Lafargue, 27 August 1889, in Engels, Paul and Laura Lafargue, *Correspondence*, 2:303–4.
684. Cited in Saville, "Unions and Free Labour," 322.
685. *Queenslander*, Brisbane, 21 September 1889.
686. Saville, "Unions and Free Labour," 322–23.
687. Ballhatchet, "The Police and the London Dock Strike of 1889," 54.
688. Andrew L. Morrison, "A Very Discreet Man: James Monro and the Whitechapel Murders," http://www.casebook.org/police_officials/po-monro.html.
689. "The Silvertown Telegraph Works," *Financial Times*, 15 February 1890.
690. Letter from James Monro to the Home Office, 6 December 1889, NA, PRO, Kew, Home Office files, HO 144/235/A51405.
691. LMA, B/BTR/IRGP/11, Minutes of Silver's Board meeting, 31 October 1889.
692. James Monro to C.M. Norwood, 17 September 1889, NA HO 144/235/A51405.
693. James Monro to the Home Office, 17 September 1889, ibid. Emphasis in original.
694. Information on the Wontner family can be found at The Peerage website, http://thepeerage.com/p15372.htm.
695. NA, HO 144/235/A51405, letter and enclosure from Wontner & Sons, St. Paul's Chambers, Ludgate Hill, to the Chief Clerk of the Metropolitan Police, 12 September 1889.
696. James Monro to the Home Office, December 6 1889, ibid.
697. LMA, B/BTR/IRGP/11, Minutes of Silver's Board meeting, 14 November 1889. This meeting was held a fortnight after the previous one for reasons not explained. Monro's letter had arrived some time beforehand. It has not been preserved.
698. *Stratford Express*, Saturday, 9 November 1889.
699. Ibid. See also Kapp, *Eleanor Marx*, 351.
700. LMA, B/BTR/IRGP/11, Minutes of Silver's Board meeting, Thursday, 21 November 1889.
701. Ibid.
702. The fine was worth £431 in 2010 terms using the retail price index as an indicator. Calculated using http://www.measuringworth.com/ppoweruk/.
703. LMA, B/BTR/IRGP/11, Minutes of Silver's Board meeting, 14 November 1889.
704. "Intimidation at Silvertown: A striker knocks down an old lady of 63 and brutally kicks her," *East End News*, Friday, 22 November 1889.
705. Ibid.
706. "The Silvertown Strike," *Lloyd's Weekly Newspaper*, Sunday, 10 November 1889.
707. Ibid.
708. Ibid.; see also *Commonweal*, 16 November 1889.
709. "Silvertown Strike," *Labour Elector*, 16 November 1889.
710. Ibid.
711. "The Silvertown Strike," *Lloyd's Weekly Newspaper*, Sunday, 17 November 1889.
712. Bertolt Brecht, "When Evil-Doing Comes Like Falling Rain," *Poems, 1913–1956*, 247.
713. Corinthians 11:27, http://bible.cc/2_corinthians/11-27.htm.
714. *Stratford Express*, Saturday, 9 November 1889.
715. "Wages Questions," *The Times*, Wednesday 6 November 1889.
716. *Stratford Express*, Saturday 9 November 1889.
717. Kapp, *Eleanor Marx*, 351.
718. Hilary Evans, *The Oldest Profession: Illustrated History of Prostitution* (Newton Abbot: David and Charles, 1979), 104–5.
719. Ibid. According to the Commissioner of Police, there were 933 brothels and 848 other "disreputable houses" in London in the 1840s.
720. Megara Bell, "The Fallen Women in Fiction and Legislation," http://www.gober.net/victorian/reports/prostit.html.
721. Thorne, *My Life's Battles*, 139.
722. See Louise Raw, *Striking a Light* for a discussion of middle-class prejudices about women factory workers.

723. *Stratford Express*, Saturday, 16 November 1889.
724. Beeton, *Mrs. Beeton's Book of Household Management*.
725. Ibid.
726. *Stratford Express*, 7 December 1889.
727. Fishman, *East End 1888*, 48.
728. *Commonweal*, 9 November 1889.
729. "The Silvertown Strike," *IRJ* 6/4, 8 November 1889.
730. Ibid.
731. LMA, B/BTR/IRGP/11, Minutes of Silver's Board meeting, 14 November 1889. Webster was aligned with the radical wing of the Liberal Party and had some sympathy for the New Unions. See David Howell, *British Workers and the Independent Labour Party, 1888–1906* (Manchester: Manchester University Press, 1983), 259.
732. *Justice*, Saturday, 23 November 1889.
733. *Stratford Express,* Wednesday, 20 November 1889.
734. "The Silvertown Strike," *East End News*, Thursday, 19 November 1889.
735. UW MRC, MSS 259/ASE/1/1/65, Minutes of ASE EC meeting, 19 November 1889. See also the *Stratford Express*, 20 November 1889.
736. UW MRC, MSS 259/ASE/1/1/65, Minutes of ASE EC meeting, Wednesday, 20 November 1889.
737. "The Colchester Labourers and the Silvertown Strike," *Essex Standard,* Saturday, 23 November 1889.
738. "Modern Colchester: Town Development," *A History of the County of Essex*, vol. 9: *The Borough of Colchester*, 1994, 199–208; and "Modern Colchester: Introduction," 176–79, http://www.british-history.ac.uk/report.aspx?compid=21988.
739. *Labour Elector* No. 48, 30 November 1889.
740. "The Colchester Labourers," *Essex Standard*, Saturday, 23 November 1889.
741. *Labour Elector*, 30 November 1889.
742. "The Colchester Labourers," *Essex Standard*, Saturday, 23 November 1889.
743. "The Silvertown Strike," *Essex Standard*, Thursday, 30 November 1889.
744. *Labour Elector*, 30 November 1889.
745. Robert Tressell's classic working-class novel was published in 1914, after his death in 1911. It is available at Project Gutenberg, http://www.gutenberg.org/ebooks/3608.
746. "The Colchester Labourers," *Essex Standard*, 23 November 1889.
747. "Modern Colchester," *A History of the County of Essex*.
748. *Stratford Express*, Wednesday, 20 November 1889.
749. Ibid.
750. "The Silvertown Strike: Summonses for Intimidation and Assault," *West Ham Guardian*, Saturday, 23 November 1889.
751. "The Silvertown Strike," *East and West Ham Gazette*, 23 November 1889.
752. LMA, B/BTR/IRGP/11, Minutes of Silver's Board meeting, Thursday, 21 November 1889.
753. "Intimidation at Silvertown," *East End News*, Friday, 22 November 1889.
754. LMA B/BTR/IRGP/11, Minutes of Silver's Board meeting, Thursday, 28 November 1889.
755. "The Silvertown Strike," *West Ham Guardian*, Saturday, 23 November, and Saturday, 30 November 1889.
756. "Wages Questions," *Times*, Friday, 29 November 1889.
757. *East and West Ham Gazette*, Saturday, 21 December 1889.
758. "The Silvertown Strike: Summonses for Intimidation and Assault," *West Ham Guardian*, 23 November 1889.
759. Albert Camus, preface to Georges Bataille, ed., *L'Espagne Libre* (Paris: Calmann-Lévy, 1946). Camus's eloquent words are a lament for the vanquished Spanish Republic, but they are applicable to any "good fight" crushed by brute force.
760. *Stratford Express,* Wednesday, 27 November 1889.
761. "Wages Questions," *Times*, Friday, 29 November 1889.
762. Ibid..
763. London Trades Council Minutes of Special Council Meeting, 27 November 1889.

764. "London Trades Council," *Labour Elector* No. 48, Saturday, 30 November 1889.
765. UW MRC, ASE EC Minutes, Wednesday, 27 November 1889.
766. *Times*, Monday, 2 December 1889.
767. "Work and Wages," *York Herald*, Saturday, 30 November 1889.
768. Kapp, *Eleanor Marx*, 354–55.
769. LMA, B/BTR/IRGP/11, Minutes of Board meeting, Thursday 28 November 1889.
770. Ibid., Friday, 29 November 1889.
771. *Times*, Monday, 2 December 1889.
772. *Stratford Express*, Saturday, 30 November 1889.
773. William J. Tyler, letter to the editor, *Times*, Saturday, 30 November 1889.
774. *Stratford Express*, Saturday, 7 December 1889. Also *IRJ* 6/5, 9 December 1889.
775. *Oxford Dictionary of National Biography*, http://pubneteris/mymavis.php.
776. "Mr. Stopford Brooke," *Penny Illustrated Paper*, Saturday, 7 December 1889.
777. R. K. Webb, "Brooke, Stopford Augustus (1832–1916)," *Oxford Dictionary of National Biography*, http://www.oxforddnb.com/view/article/32094.
778. Kapp, *Eleanor Marx*, 356.
779. *Stratford Express*, Saturday, 7 December 1889.
780. LMA, B/BTR/IRGP/11, Minutes of Silver's Board meeting, Thursday, 5 December 1889.
781. LTC, Minutes of (Third) Adjourned Delegate meeting, Thursday, 5 December 1889.
782. LTC, Minutes of Adjourned (Fourth) Delegate meeting, Thursday, 19 December 1889.
783. *Stratford Express*, Saturday, 7 December 1889.
784. Kapp, *Eleanor Marx*, 356.
785. "The Silvertown Strike," *Times*, Tuesday, 10 December 1889.
786. *Labour Elector*, 14 December 1889.
787. LTC, Minutes of Adjourned (Fourth) Delegate meeting, Thursday, 19 December 1889.
788. "The Silvertown Strike," *Times*, 10 December 1889.
789. LTC, Minutes of Adjourned (Fourth) Delegate meeting, Thursday, 19 December 1889.
790. *IRJ* 6/6, 8 January 1890.
791. LMA, B/BTR/IRGP/01, IRGP & TW Co Ltd. Minutes, General Meetings, 1864–1918; Minutes of ordinary general meeting, Tuesday, 28 February 1890.
792. E. I. Carlyle and M. C. Curthoys, "Price, Bartholomew (1818–1898)," *Oxford Dictionary of National Biography*, http://www.oxforddnb.com/view/article/22741.
793. Ibid.
794. LMA, B/BTR IRGP/11, Minutes of Silver's Board meeting, 12 December 1889.
795. Editorial, *IRJ* 6/5, 9 December 1889.
796. LMA, B/BTR/IRGP/11, Minutes of Silver's Board meeting, Thursday, 12 December 1889.
797. "Police," *Times*, Thursday, 12 December 1889.
798. "The Silvertown Strike: A Colchester Man Maltreated," *Essex Standard*, Saturday, 14 December 1889.
799. Calculated using http://www.measuringworth.com/ukcompare/relativevalue.php.
800. LMA, B/BTR/IRGP/11, Minutes of Silver's Board meeting, Thursday, 12 December 1889.
801. *IRJ* 6/6, 8 January 1890.
802. London, *The People of the Abyss*, 161–63. Michael Davitt was an Irish socialist and the organizer of the Land League, which fought against evictions of Irish peasants. The term "boycott" stems from this agitation.
803. "Poor Silvertown," *Justice*, Saturday, 14 December 1889.
804. *East London and Tower Hamlets Advertiser*, Saturday, 14 December 1889.
805. "The Silvertown Strike," *IRJ*, 9 December 1889.
806. LMA, B/BTR IRGP/11, Minutes of Silver's Board meeting, 5 Dec. 1889.
807. 'Mr. Stopford Brooke and the Silvertown Strike," *Pall Mall Gazette*, 11 December 1889.

808. "Church News," *Graphic*, Saturday, 14 December 1889.
809. *IRJ* 6/6, 8 January 1890.
810. Ibid.
811. "The Salvation Army," *Times*, Friday, 27 December 1889.
812. "Silvertown," *Labour Elector*, 14 December 1889.
813. *East and West Ham Gazette*, Saturday, 21 December 1889.
814. Cited in Schaffer, *Light and Liberty*, 4.
815. "Silvertown," *Labour Elector* No. 50, Saturday, 14 December 1889.
816. Ibid.
817. In 1913, thousands of rubber workers spontaneously walked off the job in Akron, Ohio. The city's giant factories were non-union, so the workers turned to the radical Industrial Workers of the World (IWW) for help. As at Silvertown, the employers starved the strikers back to work. Afterward, it was revealed that the new IWW local had been infiltrated by spies and provocateurs. See Tully, *The Devil's Milk*, 149–58.
818. LMA, B/BTR/IRGP/11, Minutes of Silver's Board meeting, Thursday, 5 December 1889; and "Mr. Gray of Silvertown," *Labour Elector*, Saturday, 4 January 1890.
819. Pember Reeves, *Around About a Pound a Week*, 78.
820. Fishman, *East End 1888*, 325.
821. *Stratford Express*, Saturday, 28 December 1889.
822. Supplement to the *Young Ladies' Journal*, London, Christmas Day 1889.
823. Pember Reeves, *Round About a Pound a Week*, 64.
824. London, *The People of the Abyss*, 19.
825. Beeton, *Mrs. Beeton's Book of Household Management*, 1005.
826. Cited in ibid.
827. Foakes, *Four Meals for Fourpence*, 199.
828. Emily Huntington Miller, "Hang Up the Baby's Stocking," in The Hymns and Carols of Christmas, http://www.hymnsandcarolsofchristmas.com/Poetry/hang_up_the_babys_stocking.htm.
829. Pember Reeves, *Round About a Pound a Week*, 193.
830. "Silvertown," *Penny Illustrated Paper*, Saturday, 14 December 1889.
831. Saville, "Trade Unions and Free Labour."
832. "Mrs. Aveling and the Strike Leaders at Silvertown," *Penny Illustrated Paper*, Saturday, 14 December 1889.
833. Hobsbawm, *Labouring Men*, 106–18.
834. *Commonweal*, 23 November 1889.
835. "Poor Silvertown," *Justice*, Saturday, 14 December 1889.
836. Frederick Engels to Jules Guesde in Paris, 20 November 1889, Marx-Engels Correspondence, Marx-Engels Internet Archives, http://www.marxists.org/archive/marx/works1888/letters/89_11_20.htm.
837. "Poor Silvertown," *Justice*, 14 December 1889.
838. Thorne, *My Life's Battles*, 91.
839. In 1891, frustrated by the blunders of the dockers' leaders, Frederick Engels lamented that the dockers had won "solely as a result of the £30,000 contributed blindly from Australia; but they think they did it themselves." Frederick Engels to Friedrich Adolph Sorge, 9–11 August 1891, in Marx-Engels Correspondence, http://www.marxists.org/archive/marx/works/1891/letters/91_08_11.htm.
840. Thorne, *My Life's Battles*, 76–77.
841. Hobsbawm, *Labour's Turning Point*, 111.
842. Edward Aveling, "The Eight-Hours Working Day," pamphlet, British Labour History Ephemera, 1880–1900, MFR 2454, Reel 1, Item 15, British Library.
843. Schaffer, *Light and Liberty*, 11.
844. UW MRC, MSS.192/GL/4, "First Half-Yearly Report and Balance Sheet of the National Union of Gasworkers and General Labourers of Great Britain and Ireland and Reports of Conferences held at the Cannon Street Hotel, November 4th and 11th, 1889."
845. The union had closed the books to new members, and was "breeding its own scabs," noted Engels, who was scathing about the union's refusal to countenance a "cartel" with the NUG&GL. Many workers, he pointed out, worked in the gasworks in the

winter and on the docks in summer. The NUG&GL's suggestion that one union ticket should cover both types of work was rejected. See Frederick Engels to Friedrich Adolph Sorge, 9–11 August 1891, in Karl Marx and Friedrich Engels, *Marx and Engels on the Trade Unions* (Moscow: Progress Publishers, 1971).

846. Second Yearly Report and Balance Sheet of the NUG&GL, March 1891.

847. Ibid. Fourth Yearly Report and Balance Sheet, NUG&GL, 1893.

848. Ibid. First Half-Yearly Report and Balance Sheet, NUG&GL, 1889.

849. Ibid., Fifth Yearly Report and Balance Sheet, NUG&GL, 1894.

850. Ibid. Sixth Yearly Report and Balance Sheet, NUG&GL, 1895.

851. Ibid. Quarterly Balance Sheets of the NUG&GL for 1898.

852. Ibid. Quarterly Balance Sheets for the final quarter of 1905 and the second quarter of 1906.

853. Cited in ETU, foreword by Walter C. Stevens, *The Story of the ETU: The Official History of the Electrical Trades Union* (Hayes, Bromley, Kent: ETU, c. 1953), 43. The library of the London School of Economics and Political Science holds a copy of the federation's constitution, at HD9/D645.

854. Norbert C. Soldon, "Douglas, Francis Wemyss-Charteris-, eighth earl of Wemyss and sixth earl of March (1818–1914)," *Oxford Dictionary of National Biography*, http://www.oxforddndb.com/view/article/36833.

855. *Amalgamated Engineers' Monthly Journal of Trade Unionism and Brotherhood* (hereafter *ASE Monthly Journal*), 1/4, April 1897.

856. Ibid., General Office Report.

857. Quoted in Hobsbawm, *Labour's Turning Point*, 155.

858. For a discussion of Dyer's bid to "Americanize" the British engineering industry, see Wayne Lewchuk, *American Technology and the British Vehicle Industry: A Century of Production in Britain* (Cambridge: Cambridge University Press, 1987), 69–73.

859. Karl Marx, "Effect of Competition on the Capitalist Class, the Middle Class and the Working Class," *Wage Labour and Capital*, http://www.marxists.org/archive/marx/works/1847/wage-labour/ch09.htm.

860. Ibid.

861. Hobsbawm, *Labouring Men*, 301.

862. Ibid., 106.

863. Tom Mann, "Rally," *ASE Monthly Journal*, January 1897.

864. Hobsbawm, *Labour's Turning Point*, 155.

865. Mann, "Rally."

866. Tom Mann, "The Machine Question," *ASE Monthly Journal* 1/6, June 1897.

867. J. T. Brownlie, "Federation," *ASE Monthly Journal* 1/6, June 1897.

868. General Office Report, *ASE Monthly Journal*, November 1897.

869. *ASE Monthly Journal*, July 1897.

870. I.R.E., "The Engineers' Strike-Work or Cadging," *IRJ* 15/1, Friday, 7 January 1898.

871. Foster, "The British Electrical Industry," 61.

872. LMA, B/BTR/IRGP/13, Minutes of Silver's Board meeting, 3 February 1898.

873. *East London Advertiser*, Saturday, 12 June 1897.

874. "The Engineering Crisis: A Universal Lock-Out Imminent," *Belfast Newsletter*, Wednesday, 7 July 1897.

875. *ASE Monthly Journal*, August and September 1897.

876. "The Engineering Strike," *Electrician* 39/1012, 8 October 1897.

877. "Company Report," *Electrician*, 18 February 1898. If any attempt was made to seek the support of French workers, it is not recorded in union minutes.

878. Mann, "Rally."

879. Reissued as Herbert Spencer et al., *A Plea for Liberty: An Argument against Socialism and Socialistic Legislation; Consisting of an Introduction by Herbert Spencer and Essays by Various Writers,* ed. Thomas Mackay (Indianapolis: Liberty Fund, 1981). The original publisher was the Liberty and Property Defence League.

880. Ibid., 320–21.

881. The New Unionists do not appear to have thought of the sit-down strike, which would have been an effective countermeasure against scabbing and continued pro-

duction during strikes. Although invented independently by workers in a number of countries, the first British example seems to have been a series of "stay-downs" on the South Wales coalfields in 1935–36. See Joel Seidman, "Sit-Down," New York: League for Industrial Democracy, 1937, http://www.labournet.de/internationales/usa/sitdown37.pdf.

882. Saville, "Trade Unions and Free Labour," 335.

883. Cecil, a.k.a, Lord Salisbury, also admitted to knowing NFLA boss Collison.

884. Stedman Jones, *Outcast London*, 148.

885. Ibid.

886. "The Engineering Dispute," *Times*, Thursday, 15 July 1897.

887. Ibid.

888. Bristow, "The Liberty and Property Defence League and Individualism," 761.

889. The league's prominent members are also named in "Another month of the trial of strength has gone by," *ASE Monthly Journal*, September 1897.

890. For a concise biography of Wemyss, see Soldon, "Douglas, Francis Wemyss-Charteris."

891. Geoffrey Alderman, "The National Free Labour Association: A Case-Study of Organised Strike-Breaking in the Late Nineteenth and Early Twentieth Centuries," *International Review of Social History* 21/3 (December 1976): 314.

892. Hobsbawm, *Labour's Turning Point*, 159.

893. NFLA, *The National Free Labour Association: Its Foundation, History, and Work* (London: NFLA, 1898), 88.

894. Alderman, "The National Free Labour Association," 317.

895. Geoffrey Alderman, "Collison, William (1865–1938)," *Oxford Dictionary of National Biography*, http://www. Oxforddnb.com/view/article/48216.

896. NFLA, *The National Free Labour Association*, 88.

897. Alderman, "The National Free Labour Association," 314.

898. Ibid.

899. Mr. Geoghegan, Collison's lawyer, quoted in "The Free Labour Association," *Reynold's Newspaper*, Sunday, 15 August 1897.

900. NFLA, *The National Free Labour Association*, 66.

901. Saville, "Trade Unions and Free Labour," 337.

902. NFLA, *The National Free Labour Association*, 88.

903. Alderman, "The National Free Labour Association," 315.

904. Nominal Earnings for Various Occupations.

905. Alderman, "The National Free Labour Association," 315.

906. "Police," *Times*, Tuesday, 10 August 1897.

907. Ibid. Censored in the original article.

908. Alderman, "The National Free Labour Association," 326.

909. Ibid., 332.

910. John Whittaker Ellis, *The Irish Land Question Considered Historically and Economically* (Kingston-on-Thames: W. Drewett, 1886).

911. And still isn't, as was highlighted during the 2011 Occupy movement at St. Paul's Cathedral. On the current Council structure, see George Monbiot, "The medieval, unaccountable Corporation of London is ripe for protest," *The Guardian*, 31 October 2011.

912. *ASE Monthly Journal*, September 1897.

913. *ASE Monthly Journal*, November 1897.

914. *Electrician*, Friday, 7 January 1898.

915. *Electrician*, Friday, 14 January 1898.

916. ETU, *The Story of the ETU*, 43.

917. *Electrician*, 21 January, 28 January, and 4 February 1898.

918. *Electrician*, Friday, 24 December 1897.

919. "The Engineers' Strike-Work," *IRJ*, 7 January 1889.

920. Ibid. and "Chairman's Report at the I-R-G-P and T Wks Company Ltd 34th Ordinary General Meeting," Friday, 25 February 1898. S.W. Silver resigned as Chairman at the 18 June 1896 Board meeting of the firm and Matthew Gray took over. His son,

R.K. Gray, took over in turn as Managing Director. B/BTR/IRGP/13, Minutes of Silver's Board meeting of 18 June 1896.

921. *ASE Monthly Journal,* November 1897.
922. Hobsbawm, *Labouring Men,* 179–81.
923. Lewchuk, *American Technology and the British Vehicle Industry,* 72.
924. Calculated using http://www.measuringworth.com/ukcompare/relativevalue.php.
925. UW MRC, MSS.192/GL/4, "NUG&GL Quarterly Report and Balance Sheet, 25 September 1915–25th December 1915."
926. These matters are ably summarized in Saville, "Trade Unions and Free Labour."
927. *Stratford Express,* 13 September 1890.
928. UW MRC, MSS.192/GL/4, "Sixth Yearly Report and Balance Sheet, NUG&GL, 1895."
929. W. Raymond Powell, *Keir Hardie in West Ham: "A Constituency with a Past,"* Socialist History Occasional Papers Series 19 (London: Socialist History Society, 2004), 3.
930. Buck, "Class Structure and Local Government Activity," 155.
931. Powell, *Keir Hardie in West Ham,* 3. See also J. J. Terrett, *"Municipal Socialism in West Ham: A Reply to 'The Times,' and Others* (London: Twentieth Century Press, c. 1902.)
932. Banks-Conney, "Political Culture and the Labour Movement," 58.
933. Borough of West Ham, *Book of West Ham* (London: Official Publications Bureau, 1923), 73, 39.
934. Cited in Terrett, *Municipal Socialism in West Ham,* 2, 6.
935. Bristow, "The Liberty and Property Defence League," 784.
936. Terrett, *Municipal Socialism in West Ham,* 2, 6.
937. Stedman Jones, *Outcast London,* 348.
938. Eugene V. Debs, "An Ideal Labor Press," *The Metal Worker,* May 1904, E.V. Debs Internet Archive, http://www.marxists.org/archive/debs/works/1904/laborpress.htm.

Index